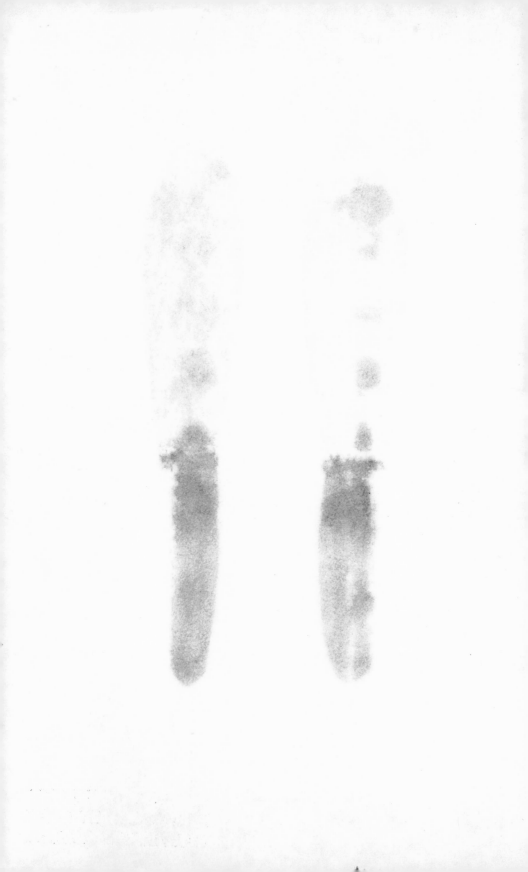

Women
On Love

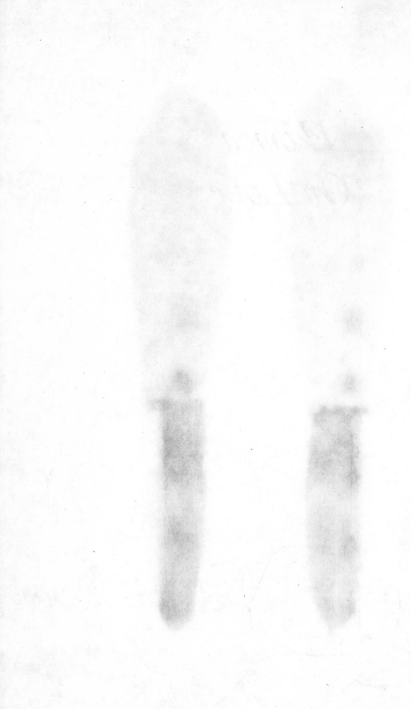

Women On Love

Eight Centuries of Feminine Writing

Evelyne Sullerot

Translated by Helen R. Lane

DOUBLEDAY & COMPANY, INC.
GARDEN CITY, NEW YORK
1979

Library of Congress Cataloging in Publication Data

Sullerot, Evelyne.
Women on love.

Translation of Histoire et mythologie de l'amour.
Includes bibliographical references.
1. French literature—Women authors—Translations
into English. 2. English literature—Translations from
French. 3. Love—Literary collections. 4. Women—
literary collections. 5. French literature—Women
authors—History and criticism. I. Title.
PQ1113.S9   840'.9'9287

ISBN: 0-385-11247-5
Library of Congress Catalog Card Number 76-51985

Contents

roque than Classical. The myths of love in fairy tales by women: from the Pig Prince to Prince Charming. Women, the organizers of the court that must be paid them, making forthright use of modesty as a weapon to earn "glory." But libertine women also lead men a merry chase, without modesty. The hatred of marriage and the fear of it continue, as does the quenching of desire through its frank satisfaction; all this allows the woman to attain the heights of the absolute.

"I love you as though I were only fifteen and the world were in the Golden Age," or the century of sensibility, even though it believes itself to be the century of reason. Young girls first make their appearance. Slowly, women rehabilitate marriage. They invent a new sentiment: tenderness. Toward the end of the century feminine romantic passion appears, the total gift of oneself, till death.

"Like life, involuntary/inevitable as death," or romantic feminine love. How in ten years the change from a very permissive society of a repressive one takes place without protest on the part of women. How libertines rediscover religion and invent spiritual discipline through passion, the salvation of the soul through profane love. But this is accomplished by sacrificing the body: Women use modesty for their own ends—and are sick from it. Marriage triumphs, but it is the century of mistresses who are saints of love, and of the first women to be revolutionary rebels.

"In the limitless desert of love, sexual pleasure has an ardent but very small place, so incandescent that at first one sees nothing else." The twentieth century opens with an explosion of pantheistic sensualism: It marks the beginning of the liberation of the feminine body. And an explosion of lesbianism: Does it represent a revolt against men or a "gearing down" of narcissism? The psychology of the relationship between the man and the woman grows more delicate. And then the great adventure of the century: living together, the couple as a life experience. And of course the liberation of the woman, the mistress now of her fecundity. And the woman's genitals, which, imitating men, she now speaks of for the first time. And what of tomorrow?

Illustrations

to the man who is well loved,
to the man who is loved too much,
to the man who is loved badly

The Sighs of the Female Saint
and the Cries of the Fairy
Gérard de Nerval

· I ·

INTRODUCTION

Eight Centuries of Feminine Love

In French literature, the passionate cries of women in love have come from men: the real names of Phèdre, Bérénice, Madame de Mortsauf, Madame de Rênal, Emma Bovary, are Racine, Balzac, Stendhal, or Flaubert.

As for myths, aren't almost every one of them masculine?: Pygmalion bringing his creature Galatea to life through the power of love; Orpheus losing Eurydice, searching for her, losing her again; Lancelot prevented from reaching the Holy Grail because of his love for Guinevere; Tristan laying down his sword between himself and his Isolde, who is beside him yet unattainable; Faust, become all-powerful, outwitting Marguerite; and finally, Don Juan and all his successors, even more numerous than his conquests.

There is Psyche, of course, bending over Cupid as he sleeps, and Artemis contemplating Endymion as he slumbers—two disturbing images of the fascination of masculine beauty in repose, beauty that is an object, there for the taking. And the lamp trembles in Psyche's hand.

But these count for very little when compared to the myriad Christian myths that follow a strange itinerary marked out in the form of a cross: In most cases the man is making his way toward God, and suddenly the woman crosses the path of this self-denying pilgrimage. Sometimes she will aid him in his journey toward salvation; at other times she will turn him aside from his goal, distract him from it, tear him away from it. In either case it scarcely matters. The one important thing, the real drama, takes place between the man and God, between the man and his destiny as the image of God, or between the man and his idea of what man is, if he is a freethinker. The woman makes her appearance only after the story has already begun; she is the pretext for new twists in the plot, she is a trial for the knight, a trap for the saint, a temptation for the good man, a tender revelation for the wicked one. She is desired, loved, feared, pursued, lost, or abandoned. But she is always part of the man's story. She is mystery, salvation, or perdition for the man. All her roles can be summed up in these three. But ever and always, her role is simply a response to the man's principal one.

Every love story remains a personal one, even when it is a search for the myths of love, and the story of this book is no exception. It begins in a quite unusual way, at a Protestant charity bazaar.

In my staid little provincial town, the Catholics held church fairs that were called *kermesses* (a word that fascinated me, for it rhymed with the mysterious word *messes*, masses), and the handful of us in the town who were "heretics" held a "charity sale" each year, which we spent long months getting ready for, sewing, embroidering, making toys, useless objects, and delicious cakes for which the good souls who attended the sale, with imperturbable good humor, bought up every available lottery ticket. That year—I must have been about ten years old—once I had sold all my share of raffle tickets I had joined my grandmother, who was presiding over the "bookstall." She moved over a little to make room for me on a bench beside her, behind her cashbox with a few meager coins in it, and knowing how voracious my appetite for books was, she let me look through an illustrated volume whose title, as I remember, was *Tales of the Middle Ages*. Sitting there beside me, she went on smiling at her prospective customers and exchanging friendly words with them as she sold off the edifying volumes and the terrifying stories of the Camisards des Cévennes[1] which constituted the stock of her bookstore-for-an-evening. Opening this book of popular stories, I looked at the table of contents and was immediately attracted by a name far more beautiful than any of the many that I had tried to make up myself: Griselda. Whether it turned out to be the name of an enchanted cat, a princess, or a city that no longer existed, it was so musical that I wanted to read that tale and no other, and plunged into my reading.

Since that day, I have never reread *Griselda*. This is what I shall remember of it, for the rest of my life: A very rich and powerful king

[1] Protestant forebears of the seventeenth century who gathered together, wearing their white mountaineers' blouses, in the fastnesses of the Cévennes to hear the sermons of preacher-reformers despite persecution by the soldiers of Louis XIV. (*Translator's note.*)

falls in love with a very poor and very beautiful girl, named Griselda, and eventually marries her, making her his queen. On their wedding day, a vision of innocent beauty in her snow-white wedding finery, Griselda vows to her lord and master at the altar that she will love and honor him, never fail him, and forever obey him. But once the splendid wedding feast is over, the king immediately takes Griselda's beautiful jewels and handsome gowns away from her and hands her a sack-cloth dress, which she dons forthwith, repeating her vows of fidelity and obedience to him. Little by little he forbids her access to the stately halls and apartments of the palace and confines her in a sort of damp, dark dungeon. He pretends to depart on a long journey to a distant land, and a royal steward disloyal to the king pays her court; faithful to her lord and master, she stubbornly resists his advances. The king then returns, and she has a son by him, whom he takes away from her. She then bears him a daughter, whom the king likewise spirits away. At each trial to which she is subjected, she avows her love for him once again, and repeats her promise to honor and obey him. Years pass. I was already cringing with horror, there on the wooden bench amid the affable din being created by the friendly parishioners and excited Boy Scouts and Cub Scouts round about the game booths and stalls. One day the king announces to Griselda that he finds her old and ugly, that he wishes to take as his new wife a young and beautiful princess whom his steward has gone to fetch in her kingdom, and that the ceremonial procession will be arriving at any moment. He wants Griselda, the queen, to come to meet it wearing her sack-cloth garment and present the keys of the palace to the new queen. Acceding to the king's demands, Griselda comes forward, bearing on a cushion the keys for this daughter of a king who is taking her king from her. And then, before the assembled crowd, the king orders her to raise her head, and falling to his knees, calls her the most faithful and best of spouses possible, and introduces to her the young prince and the radiant princess at the head of the procession that is approaching, revealing to her that the two of them are her own son and daughter. He has set every possible trap for her, caused her to undergo the sorest possible trials, and still her love has triumphed over all. Hence he swears that from that day forward she will be the most beloved, the most honored of all the women in the world and orders his entire court, beginning with his son and daughter, to kneel before Griselda and her loving patience as he himself has done.

I had managed to read the end of the story through the blur of tears that filled my eyes only because I wanted to know the reason for all this horror. But the moment I had read the last word, I fainted and fell to the floor underneath the bookstall. Everyone panicked, not knowing what in the world had happened. I don't remember any of the rest, except that my father, who was a doctor, attributed this fainting spell to my "critical" age, which had already caused me to have sudden unexpected nosebleeds, his odd term for which was "vicarious hemorrhages." My mother was the only one I told about the tale of Griselda, once I was home in bed that night. I kept asking her the frantic question: why, why? Was that what love was? If so, I would never have the courage to love, even though I wanted so much to love, to learn how to love. . . . She understood immediately that it was useless to tell me that it was all just a fairy tale, useless to remind me that I had simply read a story that someone had made up.

She cleverly kept me from dwelling on my feelings of utter distress by pointing out to me that the person who was to be pitied most was the king. "The king? But he keeps torturing her!" I objected. "Because he's afraid," she answered. "He's the weaker of the two, you see, he's afraid he's not loved for himself alone, because she was very poor and he was very rich and very powerful. He's afraid she loves him only for the splendid robes, the palace, the wonderful future that the children whom she bears him will have; he trembles with fear that he's not loved. So he thinks up all those things. He's a pitiful sort, you know. But there are lots and lots of men like that, who seem to be strong, dreadful monsters, but they're afraid and they hurt others because they're afraid. What's more, that story was surely invented and written by a man of that kind for other men of that kind. To reassure themselves, men like that tell each other stories in which they're always the strongest, in which they're loved, respected, obeyed. They make up stories like that for themselves and for each other, out of fear of not being loved."

Many years later, I told all that to a man I loved. He listened gravely to every word, then sat there for a long time, saying nothing, impressed by this intimate conversation between a mother and her daughter about men, and therefore about him. "You had a very unusual mother," he said to me. And since nothing could have been truer, and nothing could have given me more pleasure to hear, I began to talk about my mother. But lost in his own thoughts, letting a handful of sand from the beach run through his fingers, he finally said: "Perhaps the king wasn't so much afraid of not being loved as he was afraid of not being in love any more. . . ." Like my mother long before, I too resisted the temptation to reply that it was only a made-up story and let him go on: "Is there anything more agonizing than the fear of satiety, of the end of desire? By tormenting her, abandoning her, humiliating her, making her look ugly, and isolating her, he was playing a dangerous and terrible game. But he could always imagine what she would be like when he rewarded her, at the end of this long test. He lived in fear that she would waver and give in, and in the horribly long-deferred hope for the day when the trial would be over: For him she was an obsession. So he could not stop loving her, he was forearming himself against the ashen taste of indifference." During the long pause that ensued, it was for once with profound rejoicing that I counted up in my heart of hearts the interminable list of all the obstacles that separated the two of us, forcing us (despite ourselves, or so we thought) to wait endlessly, to put each other continually to the test, to continue our interminable quest.

In answer to my mother's explanations, that long-ago day when I had fainted dead away, I had finally asked a question: "But haven't *women* written any stories?" My mother first told me about a lady as wicked as this king, or nearly as wicked, who had kept promising a knight who loved her that she would marry him if . . . If he recovered the ring that she had nonchalantly thrown into a deep lake and brought it to her. And the poor knight, risking drowning, dived down once, twice, ten times, deathly pale and out of breath.

Then she went to get me the volume of fairy tales by Madame d'Aulnoy, and opened it to the first page of "The Bluebird." "This is a story written by a woman," she told me. I reread it, in a different light. The poor prince: changed into a bird who was left dripping blood from the sharp knives placed on the window sill of his beloved Florine, shut up in a dungeon, by her jealous, wicked half sister! But what I noted that day—and have never forgotten—was the comforting tenderness of the very long love dialogue that Madame d'Aulnoy had conjured up in her imagination. Once Florine is imprisoned, the prince transforms himself into a bird and *for seven long years* comes every night to talk of love with the young woman he adores. "And I finally chose to be a Bluebird for seven long years rather than betray the fealty that I vowed to you." Florine experienced a pleasure "so intense at hearing the words of her gracious lover that she no longer remembered the sorrows of her imprisonment. . . . And what cause for lament would she have had? She had the satisfaction of conversing all night long with the one she loved. So many sweet words have never before been exchanged."

I was not aware of it, but that day I discovered a feminine myth of love, a proud and enduring one. I shall call it the "Myth of the Bluebird." It is the myth of the lover who never tires of *talking* with us and of listening to us. What a great distance there is between the faithful and attentive Bluebird, perching on Florine's shoulder night after night to exchange "so many sweet words," and the bird that fornicates with Leda, that swan that furiously flaps its wings between the woman's legs, only to fly away immediately thereafter, doubtless to transform himself into a bull for Europa! The latter is a typical myth for men, whereas the Bluebird is a myth by a woman for women, who take such pleasure in the inspired exchanges that serve as a prelude to desire, and are so fearful of the impenetrable silences of their satiated lovers. Alba de Céspedes's heroine in *Elles* finally kills her taciturn husband by shooting him in the back, that back that is a deaf-and-dumb wall that he presents to her after making love. "She's a hysteric," all the men who bristle at this book say. Naturally. She is suffering from the Bluebird complex. This is a serious existential complex, as serious as the Oedipus complex that we keep hearing of *ad nauseam.* (Moreover, Oedipus plays only a passive role therein, for it is Jocasta who—moved by this young man who has saved the city—offers him her body and her throne. And as compared to the yards of embroidery on the subject of Oedipus and his famous complex, we have heard very little in the last three quarters of a century on the subject of *her* torment when she learns that he is her own son.

That was how my quest for feminine myths of love began. Later I added to it the myth of Beauty and the beast, another tale written by a woman: a repulsive, hairy beast, an animal with a tender heart but an absolutely horrifying outward appearance. Yet a kiss from a young woman is all that is needed to turn him into a prince. . . .

Men tell us often enough that by possessing a girl they make a woman of her. Every woman is vaguely aware that the intervention of a man is necessary to rend the taut veil of virginity, an experience that is the opposite of birth, yet nonetheless the birth of the woman. Men have played this game so often and taken such advantage of it over the centuries that they have contrived to complete the metamorphosis by adding to it a social baptism: When they marry, they "give" to the woman their name and (even in this day and age!) their worldly status to share. "I will give you the finest gowns in the world, you will travel only in a coach and be carried in a litter, and you will be called Milady," the sorcerer says to the princess.[2] You will be the wife of the barber, of the apothecary, of the soldier, of the farmer of Long Prairie, of the magistrate, or of Jacques the peasant who has nothing he can call his own. You will be what your spouse makes you, even if you "bring" him a dowry or property. You will bear his name, whether you like it or not. Thanks to him, your birth as a woman will take place. You will owe your fortune or misfortune to this man, you will be made a woman physically and socially by him and by him alone. "Who is that? Oh, that's Mr. X's wife. . . ."

This crucial role played by the man in the metamorphosis of the woman avenges him a little for his frustration at not being able to bring children into the world. He will therefore invent endless compensatory myths: Prometheus will steal fire from heaven to bring the creature that he has fashioned from clay to life, and so on. But often he will confuse his power over the young woman and his frustration at being

[2] Madame d'Aulnoy.

unable to bear children by multiplying the myths concerning the way in which women are born: Aphrodite, that most womanly of all women, will be said to have been born of Chronos' seething sperm as it fell into the sea; Athena to have sprung from the forehead of Zeus; Eve fashioned from Adam's rib. . . .

As the answer to this burdensome dependence, at once a fact of nature and a pure and simple fabrication, women will invent a birth of man that is their doing, through the magic of love. We women alone can make a gentleman out of a lout. We women alone can cure the Beast of his bestiality and reveal his superior humanity. Everywhere in the tales written by women one finds this covert but ever-present myth, serving as consolation to seventeenth-century "Précieuses" and nineteenth-century Romantics alike. The Pig-Prince[3] will lose his "porcine envelope" only when he truly loves a true princess. With a kiss, we women tirelessly transform bears, swine, big bad wolves, into men worthy in our eyes of the name of men.

Our menagerie of love as seen "before and after" speaks volumes. Men are fearful beasts that we tame and save from themselves. The illusion of women-as-subjects finding in love a new power, the illusion that they are fairies. In the tales that they have invented, women also imprison charming princesses in envelopes of animal flesh, but when they do so, these princesses are female cats,[4] frogs, or white does[5] in grave danger of being captured or killed. The one purpose of their animality is to serve as proof of their vulnerability. The love of the prince is in fact often merely an additional danger, for he hunts them and wishes to kill them or to possess them. A fairy must intervene.

The love of the princess or simply her pity, on the other hand, suffices to make a real man of a brutish monster who terrifies her. She is responsible for the second birth of this man, through the magic of the sentiment that she inspires in him. She transforms him and cures him merely by touching him.[6]

[3] Madame d'Aulnoy.
[4] "The White Cat."
[5] "The Doe in the Forest."
[6] Professional research that I have undertaken has been responsible for the fact that I have happened to peruse a great number of novels published in installments and "gothics" written by women: The heroine inevitably metamorphoses the most hardhearted, the most "brutish," the most Caliban-like of male characters that she chances to encounter, and it is this character whom she will marry once she has transformed him. These British, American, or French narratives are contemporary ones and invariably meet with great success with women readers who are bored to death with mystery stories. They are sometimes well-written fiction. They are always greeted with sarcasm on the part of men who read them, for they find that the power of the myth of Beauty and the Beast diminishes them, and hence they refuse to recognize its validity, lumping all such works together under the pejorative label of "sentimental" or "romantic" fiction. In point of fact it is not so much a question of a taste for the saccharine and sickly-sweet as of the comforting representation of feminine power on the part of women writers.

But how to gather together these myths of love, at once powerful and nameless, as intimately experienced by women? "Who, then, are you, Eve?" Alfred de Vigny asked, thus giving voice to the mystery of the woman for the man. But where to find the expression of the question asked by the woman, for whom the man is a mystery?

At this point I went back to a book that as a young woman my mother had read and reread many times before her early death and was very fond of: Throughout *Love in the Western World* by the Swiss writer Denis de Rougemont, I rediscovered the subjects that I had heard crop up again and again as I listened to the "grown-ups'" conversation between my mother and her friends. Passion, the reverse side of the coin of love, the opposite of life, an ascetic search that leads nowhere. . . . Debates of the soul versus the body, the mystic adventures of the lover. . . . An apologia for marriage, "that institution that keeps passion within limits not through morality but through love." . . . A paradoxical definition of Europe because of the importance that it attributes to the forces of passion. . . . I would have allowed myself, once again, to be overcome by this wealth of ideas, this fervor, had I not realized on page after page that this entire book spoke solely of masculine love. Yet the author was completely unaware that this was the case, as I discovered in 1970, when I happened to be invited to a conference[7] where Denis de Rougemont was to speak on the subject of social participation. He was unfortunately unable to attend the conference, but his most remarkable contribution was read to the gathering. It was based on the example of direct democracy provided in his opinion by Switzerland, but it never occurred to him to mention the fact that in this Arcadia of Swiss democracy that he was describing, only men had the vote at the time. And I began adding, mezzo voce, the adjective "masculine" every time the reader of this contribution uttered the word "democracy." In like manner, the title of his fine and well-known book ought clearly to have been not *Love in the Western World*, but *Masculine Love and the Western World*. A perfect unconscious blindness, a totally inadvertent omission. Throughout the pages of *Love in the Western World* there is outlined only the history of the love of men for woman and for God, in spite of or because of woman.

And the love of love? For De Rougemont, it is Chrétien de Troyes who expresses it, Tristan who experiences it. "And after him Isolde."[8] Woman enters the picture only in the form of a plural "they"—the two lovers viewed as a couple. And the Celts? They appear on the scene later, and one might hope that the woman would be the determining

[7] *Europe An 2000*, Stockholm, September 1970.
[8] French text, p. 31.

factor then, as was the case in their culture according to Celtic myth.[9] But no: The Celtic woman is described such as she appears "in the eyes of the Druids." "Eros took on the form of Woman, a symbol of the hereafter that makes *us* scorn earthly joys."[10] Us, that is to say men. The "Woman is the aim of man."[11] The psychic revolution of the twelfth quote Goethe: "The Eternal Feminine draws us onward," and Novalis: "Woman is the aim on man."[11] The psychic revolution of the twelfth century? It is that upheaval that led to "celebrating the Lady of our thoughts," to "the cult of the idealized Woman." And the author at one point gives the game away: "But what does woman have to do with all of this?" he asks, and answers his own question. She remains the *object* of a cult . . . she is the road to salvation.[12]

It is pointless to continue to leaf through the book. Tirso de Molina and Don Juan, Rousseau and the New Héloïse, Novalis, Wagner, pursue their quest, their discovery, their unfortunate experiences with women throughout each chapter. And Book VII, an attempt to draw certain conclusions from everything that has gone before, follows the same line of argument. "Irrational does not in any way mean sentimental. To choose a woman for one's spouse is not to say . . ." (etc.).[13] "It would be more apt to state, in the words of Benedetto Croce, that marriage 'is the grave of wild love,' and more commonly, of sentimentalism. Wild, natural love is manifested in the form of rape . . ." (etc., etc.). The avowed aim of this extraordinary discourse from a strictly masculine point of view is to stress the fact that it is necessary to acquire a conception of "the reality of a woman's person," and that since men have not yet arrived at that point they do not yet know how to love.

But when read by a woman, this long and beautifully written history cannot help but sound odd from beginning to end. Have we women no other history of our mystery of love than the one that men have traced for us in the course of their pathetic attempts to define it and their methods that have for so long been patently wrong? Have we been waiting, and are we waiting still, for *them* to discover the reality of our person in order to exist as women in love?

No, of course not. For every woman the evidence is implicit. We women, too, have had our history of love. We women have also lived our debate between the body and the soul. We women have also met the man on the road to our spiritual perfection. We women have also

[9] See Jean Markal, *Les Celtes et la civilisation celtique, mythe et histoire* (Paris: Payot, 1969).
[10] My italics. E.S.
[11] French text, p. 51.
[12] French text, p. 99.
[13] French text, p. 257.

expressed our love of love, and our defiance of love. We women have also experienced and cried out our horror of marriage as the "grave of love." And we women have also sung of our hope for marriage as the "grave of wild love," for we, too, have our forms of wild love, which for us does not mean rape. We women, too, have aspired to be saints out of love as we have aspired to be fairies in and through love.

Have we now written this history, as men have written theirs? Every woman in love who has made up a song, written a love letter, thought up a poem, composed a novel, or invented tales has participated in this collective task. But unfortunately there remains very little of all that has been said, sung, written by women in the course of the centuries.

This long discourse in bits and pieces and never brought together to form a whole had to be rediscovered, as Isis searched for the scattered members of her spouse. It had to be reconstituted without being overly concerned about literary values, but rather, with the aim of bringing these cries, these laments, these sighs, and these songs together so as to bring to light the basic themes and their variations.

I pursued this research for four years, every time I had a free moment in a life that is far too busy.

I knew, alas, how limited the field of my research necessarily was. With the rarest of exceptions, only those women who were educated highborn women, and then later women of the upper middle class— had written of love down through so many centuries. It will be said that the same is true of literature written by men. But this is nonetheless much less the general rule in the latter case. Bertrand de Ventadour, a simple servant, was able to become famous through his talent alone, Molière was the son of an upholsterer, and so on. One can object that so little is known of Marie de France that her origins remain obscure and that Louise Labé was the wife of a humble ropemaker. This is quite true, but yet another obstacle makes writings by women rare for a long period in the past: Young women who are not yet married can be said not even to exist, or scarcely so; once married, they hesitate to publish their celebrations of love. Here too many exceptions to this statement will be found in the pages of this anthology. Even in the periods of greatest austerity, married women published their works, either under pen names or anonymously (Madame de La Fayette is the best-known example). And the spinsters who wrote were not dealt with so harshly, far from it: Mademoiselle de Gournay was given considerable help and encouragement (even though as a militant feminist she wrote not of love, but of things that were even more displeasing to men). Madeleine de Scudéry, another spinster, reached the pinnacle of fame, and Julie de Lespinasse, a poor, illegitimate, unmarried woman, was most highly regarded in eighteenth-century intellectual circles.

But the evidence nonetheless remains: This anthology is a collection of writings by educated women or at least by literate women—whereas the vast numbers of women who have shared this long history could neither read nor write, and left nothing that would allow us to analyze their modes of loving. I was unable in any case to collect a body of works that would be genuinely representative and hence worthy of methodical analysis, and was well aware that it would be impossible to draw very general conclusions from these many particular cases.

And yet, even though they were not typical of women as a whole and represented only a small and privileged minority, there were still too many of them and they had written too much for me to be able to find room for all of them in this anthology. It was necessary first of all to restrict myself to those women who had written in French—and there were already too many of them!—and leave love literature in English, Spanish, Italian, German, Japanese, etc., for another work, or encourage foreign researchers to undertake such a study.

With regard to French women, or women writing in French, my first concern was to assure myself that they were indeed women, and not feminine pseudonyms behind which a man was hiding—particularly in the case of very old writings. One error of this sort would have ruined the entire project. Hence, despite the pleading of certain friends, I omitted the *Letters of a Portuguese Nun,* for eminent specialists have put forward more than adequate proof that they were written by a Paris editor, Guilleragues. In this anthology as it stands, there are two cases where I have certain little nagging doubts. Lucile Desmoulins copied out in her own hand in her red notebook poems of which she was the author, and also had her men friends copy out their poems for her in it. But might she not have also copied writings not her own that she particularly liked, without noting the names of their authors? She was too representative, however, of the desire of ardent and independent young women of the eighteenth century to enter into a love marriage, and then later during the Revolution, to enjoy conjugal love, to be omitted. Sometimes my doubts are based on nothing more than a personal feeling. Verdun Saulnier, the scholar who unmasked Guilleragues as the author of the *Portuguese Letters,* confirms that "Jeanne Flore" was the pen name of Jeanne Gaillarde, the intimate friend of the poet Clément Marot. There was thus ample justification for including her. Yet something keeps whispering to me that her writings are not those of a woman. Her style is too frankly risqué: the pre-eminence accorded sexual needs and above all the lively and bitingly mocking denunciation of the moral and physical ruin brought about by abstinence strike me as characteristically masculine, particularly in an age in which this type of preaching in favor of sexual activity as necessary and as a remedy for all ills was typical of all men yearning to conquer the fortress of virtue and overcome the resistance of women who were aware that they would be taking great risks and hence held back. I am not saying that women have not celebrated sexual pleasures: far from it. But not in that particular way. Certain women, however, may feel very close to her, and I could not trust my intuitions alone. If I were not to compromise the most basic standards of scholarship, she would have to be included, even with that slightly discordant note in her voice, since the known evidence indicates that this author was indeed a woman.

Even after applying these rules, the harvest of works was too abundant for all of them to be included. Although I believe it to be a broad one, my choice is nonetheless an entirely personal one—if only because it was impossible for me (doubtless a deplorable defect of mine) to bring myself to enlist the help of others in carrying out this project. The fact that this anthology represents only my own solitary research (despite countless conversations with so many. friends and scholars whom I here thank most warmly) explains, though it does not excuse, certain lacunae that may well be obvious to some readers. But the overall picture that was taking shape fascinated me too much—especially at the stage when it was still a chaotic jumble, an unfinished puzzle with all sorts of pieces missing—for me to resign myself to allowing anyone else to read texts for me, since any one of them might put me on the track of a new theme, an answer to a question, a confirmation of a theory. For this chaos had become an intimate part of me, and it would have been very difficult to describe it to someone who had not shared the whole adventure from the very beginning, perused the two thousand or so texts that I read for this anthology, and tried again and again to frame explanations, to discover the historical continuities that this inspiring chorus of voices constantly hinted at.

From the very start, I set three rules for myself, or rather three guidelines to help me choose the texts that were to be included:

1. To give first priority to texts that were beautiful, regardless of whether that beauty had been created by a famous writer, a forgotten one, or an unknown one. The great love song of humanity ought to be enriched by these voices. Some of the most beautiful cries of love have been forthcoming from women. A number of the most clear-sighted critiques of love were penned by women. Many women mastered the art of writing well, some of them incomparably well. Even those who write too much, drowning what were absolute successes in a sea of mere words. In their case, and to an even greater degree in the case of those with lesser gifts, I sometimes took upon myself the perhaps dubious task of cutting, extracting a verse, two verses, three lines of an elegy that was too long or a letter that was prolix. I believe that I have thus rendered a service to the chorus of women's voices as a whole, and even to these women authors themselves, by drawing attention to what is

very pure and extremely beautiful, even if certain readers will sigh:
"Oh, the next part is so pretty . . ." and can quote it by heart.

I would have liked to have what was chosen for its beauty, for its eloquent style, appear in this book in capital letters or in color. But each
reader will choose his or her own laureates in the realm of aesthetics.

In order that this choice on the reader's part may be freer and less
conditioned by his or her literary education, the extracts are never followed by the name of their author, but rather only by a number that
refers to the biographical and bibliographical index at the end of the
volume. In this way it will not only not be possible to read only those
authors who are already well known, but all these women will have an
equal chance of being chosen as the reader's favorites. What is said and
the manner in which it is said will take precedence over the reader's
cultural prejudices. And since those friends of mine who are university
professors of literature assure me that almost half of these women
writers are unknown to them, this game of "anonymous authors" will
lead, I hope, to new critical perspectives.

2. Even if they are somewhat awkwardly expressed, the genuineness
of feelings, the sincerity of the writer, seemed to me to be a valid criter-
ion for inclusion. This sincerity is usually self-evident. All my friends
were touched by the same texts that I myself had found moving. In
making my choice, however, the study of the biographies of their authors was often a help. How to forget, moreover, all those encounters in
the course of my research in dusty libraries with women in love who
had lost none of the charm or pathos that had marked their lives!
These verifications almost always led me to discover that their biographies bore out the sincerity of their writings; thus the adorable Countess of Sabran waiting thirteen long years for her Chevalier de Boufflers
(who proved, to my vast relief on reading her letters to him, to be
worthy of her love for him); the touching Aïssé, fighting for the salvation of her soul as death approached, unable, despite her profound faith
and her fear of hell, to find her lover hateful after so many years, even
though theirs was an illicit relationship, unable to part from him as she
sought her particular sort of saintliness, at a time and in a milieu where
frivolous affairs were the general rule; the extraordinary Julie de
Lespinasse, writing her last letter to Monsieur de Guibert just a few
hours before her death, after having barred him from her door in order
that he might not see how grotesque she looked after the stroke that
she had had; the faithful, gentle Madame de Berny, still madly in love
with Honoré de Balzac even though she was well past fifty, writing yet
another letter to him on the eve of her death and having her wheel
chair rolled over to the window to be able to catch a glimpse of him the
moment he arrived, and dying there as she watched for her lover, who
never came. And Juliette Drouet, the very brightest star in the firma-

ment of famous women in love, faithful for fifty long years: *sanctissima*.

3. And finally, an unavoidable and much less pleasant duty: It was also necessary to choose texts that were representative of an era, whether or not they were well written, whether or not they were sincere. Being even more constrained than men to conform, or at least to appear to conform, to the manners and morals of their time, women transparently express what we may be sure were the rules of proper behavior and the fashion in a given period. They likewise provide ample proof of the style of writing that was fashionable at the moment, especially in view of the fact that they were usually more smitten with the ambition to compose elegant little trifles than to write masterpieces, this being a precise reflection of the relative emphasis placed on these two sorts of writing in their literary education. Even if they are not geniuses at either writing or loving, these conformists are significant and it was necessary to include certain of their texts. There were countless numbers of them. For one Julie de Lespinasse, for one Marceline Desbordes-Valmore, how many dozens of female versifiers there were who composed deadly-dull pastoral poems or elegies! How many Mélanie Waldors, Anaïs Ségalases, Amable Tastus, Louise Colets there were who felt it their vocation to write what they believed to be romantic verse! If I had erased every trace of these pedestrian or pedantic exercises, the history of the expression of love by French women would have been badly distorted. Of the veritable mountain of such typical texts, I have kept only a very small percentage. But at least a few samples had to be included, even though some of them are inane and frivolous and others downright ridiculous. All of them are witnesses of their time, however. Their authors were almost always highly respected by their contemporaries. One readily sees that these ladies, not content to lace in their waists or bosoms, also tightly restrained their true selves (their feelings, their sexuality, their imagination) in order to squeeze themselves into the corset of fashion and the proprieties. One can either laugh or weep at these slaves to convention—I leave that choice to the reader. Optimist that I am, I find it a sort of miracle that in each period—despite these bluestockings—atypical women, strong personalities, mutants, or infinitely touching creatures, threw aside all this cumbersome paraphernalia and spoke for all eternity. Were their lovers even aware that they were doing so?

Among my discoveries: counterimages of the typical woman in love as defined by men, in each period. In the Middle Ages, counterbalancing the ideal Lady, a dominating flesh-and-blood woman: "And yet how often I lost my head / In bed or fully clothed! How I should like one night to hold / My knight in my arms!"[14] "If out of love he wishes to

[14] Béatrix de Die.

love me / And assure me of his body's handsomeness / I shall do every-thing for his pleasure."[15] "Providing only that you first promise to do everything I wish."[16] During the Renaissance the woman is not licen-tious, but passionate, tense, romantic before the age of Romanticism, prefiguring the English metaphysical poets. "One sees every living thing die / When the subtle soul leaves the body / I am the body, you the better part: / Where are you then, O my beloved soul?"[17] "I do not wish your death, I desire mine / But my death is your death and my life is yours / Hence I wish to die, and yet do not so wish."[18] In the seven-teenth century a Baroque woman, not a Classic one, who makes up mad tales that follow none of the rules and have no traditional unity, and practices love as though it were magic, for "the kingdom of love is full of thorns."[19] And a woman who is a libertine as well, turning her back on heroic Christian martyrdom for love of God and heroic deeds to avenge the family's honor. "False love, false duty. If love is a vice, / It is a vice more beautiful than all the virtues."[20] In the eight-eenth century, the century of dissolute and licentious women, grand ro-mantic passion: "My friend, I love you as one ought to love: to excess, in madness, ecstasy, and despair."[21] "To love, to suffer, heaven, hell: that is what I should like to feel, that is the climate that I should like to live in, and not this temperate state in which slaves and all the au-tomata with which we are surrounded live."[22] And in the nineteenth century of Alfred de Vigny's "sick child twelve times impure," every sort of woman, even independent, dominating ones, and flouters of con-vention and revolutionaries who are for "the test of flesh by flesh"[23] outside of marriage and as a matter of principle.

Another discovery: tendencies that oscillate between two extremes within the over-all continuity of history. In the twelfth and thirteenth centuries woman defines herself as the supreme prophetess. She is man's road to spiritual perfection, she intends to force him to journey upward toward her, along a path that she herself lays out for him. This path will be beset by trials imposed by her and made radiant with re-wards that she will grant him as she sees fit. It is she who imposes order, in every sense of the word: setting up rules and recom-mendations, marking out the paths that lead to her, causing a sem-blance of order to reign in the chaos of desires, aspirations, interests,

[15] Marie de France.
[16] Béatrix de Die.
[17] Louise Labé.
[18] Queen Margot.
[19] Henriette de Coligny.
[20] Madame de Villedieu.
[21] Julie de Lespinasse.
[22] Julie de Lespinasse.
[23] Claire Demar.

feelings. Ruling over her vassal as his sovereign, issuing orders in the most authoritarian sense of the term ("I shall be the queen and you a servant!"); and conferring, finally, the dignity of knighthood on the one who is worthy of that title, ordaining her lovers as a monk is ordained in order that they may enter the kingdom of love and obey the rules of this game in which she wholeheartedly believes.

For women believed that they were queens in the era of courtly love. To confirm the truth of this, one need only carefully analyze the language that they use: There is not a single passive turn of phrase, not the slightest trace of the concept of woman as an object. They are subjects, they "give" the kiss of love, they "have the right" to enjoy the body of the man. They are the first to say "I love you," thus signifying that they have made their choice.

This naturally does not exclude the fact that there were many of these women who suffered the pain of being abandoned for another, and bitterly lamented their lot. But the reigning atmosphere of the time was nonetheless clearly that of the profound change in manners and morals of a twelfth century that was at once individualistic and thirsty for the absolute. Women played this role of ruler over the life of the heart, of Maecenases and Egerias of cultural life, of judges of the courts of love, so skillfully that it really is of little moment that this movement was imposed upon them by men!

The dark and dreary days of the fourteenth century and the excesses of the "end of an era" in the fifteenth diluted this faith of women in themselves, and men in turn took command in the sixteenth century, taking women outside the bonds of matrimony as though they were choice game, and taking them by force in the marriage bed. Any and every tactic is legitimate: "honeyed words," court orders, sequestration, and as goes without saying, brute force. If certain determinedly chaste Dianas escape, the majority succumb to the temptation that is the precise counterpart of domination: becoming the man's possession, not yet as a form of mysticism, though already an attitude based on the sheer pleasure it brings: "With you I have everything—without you nothing."[24] "If serving merits recompense / And recompense is the aim of desire / I should like to serve more than one thinks / So that my pleasure never ends."[25] The woman herself describes herself as a servant of love. The knight who is the lady's obedient servant is now only a memory. For the woman who has given herself totally to her master, passion even justifies the forgetting of the hierarchies based on birth and property—a most serious matter in those days. "For even though the man who possesses my heart is not my equal in nobility or in wealth of landed estates and riches, he is sublime to me and I am lowly and in-

[24] Louise Labé.
[25] Pernette du Guillet.

significant."[26] "Not that I wish to take away the freedom / Of the man who is born to be master over me."[27] Such is the new order of things. Love is the sensual pleasure of crying out, "I am yours," and thus doubling the pleasure of being chosen through being possessed.

But to belong to these fickle and violent warriors, to serve men smitten by beauty that soon fades, leads, despite the new elegant turns of phrase; to the "painful accesses of anguish occasioned by love."[28]

And from the beginning of the seventeenth century, as a reaction against this already-Romantic servitude that men do not yet properly appreciate, the "Précieuses" reverse the tendency and as women again claim the role of rulers of the art of loving, acting as judges and awarding the proper recompenses. The woman learns once again to say: "It is my wish." "It is my wish that he tell me all his secrets, that he share all my sadnesses, that my conversation and the sight of me constitute his entire happiness."[29]

Whether libertines or prudes, they invent and impose a new vocabulary. The expression "sighing lover" has no feminine form in French (just as the word "weepers" has no masculine form). Once again persuaded of their divine nature or seeking to persuade their lovers ("lovers," that is, before the act of love has been consummated) that such is their nature, they reveal to them the psychological subtleties of the path of love. They are not yet aware of the fact that the weapon that they have resorted to in order to ward off men's assaults on them and prolong the pleasure of being pursued by them—modesty, a concept that they have just invented and polished until it gleams with a mirror-finish—will little by little make them die of boredom in the cold and lifeless shadow that it casts. Smothering in the trap that they themselves have set, shivering in the chill of their own easily offended honor, freezing to death in the grip of the modesty that is their own creation, their only escape is spicy language and risqué behavior. That is precious little. Certain of them do wonders with such meager resources in the eighteenth century, which has a horror of being bored. Others eventually yearn to put an end to the war between the sexes, however pleasurable it might be, and invent tenderness, that effusion from the heart that can live only in an atmosphere of equality and even complicity. The couple at this point is no longer that shared conflagration that ends in the dubious victory of one of the partners and the certain death of love, but instead a long and quiet conversation, a balance of interests of all sorts, above all psychological ones.

But most important, reversing the reigning tendency yet again,

[26] Hélisenne de Crenne.
[27] Pernette du Guillet.
[28] Title of a novel by Hélisenne de Crenne, 1538.
[29] Madeleine de Scudéry.

women, even before men do so, will reinvent passion—in all the senses of that word: suffering, enduring, waiting, belonging to the loved one. In the nineteenth century men will follow their lead. But Romanticism clearly starts much earlier for women, and their romanticism takes the form of the surrender of themselves, slavery freely chosen, personal salvation sought in the gift of oneself to the man. Only when they have surrendered wholly will they be worthy of the holy orders of love, only then will they be saints of love in the manner of that saint of saints, Juliette Drouet: "I love you with more than all my strength, I love you with my soul. I love you with the love of the life beyond that I make an intimate part of this life. I adore you."

The mystical dimension has been rediscovered, though the roles of the man and the woman have been reversed. "Is it not true that I suffer and that the man is a cruel creature? Never so accuse him. I adore him, remember." And yet Marceline Desbordes-Valmore knew that "what one gives to love is forever lost. . . ." Love now involves frightful pleasures of a spiritual pilgrimage that leads nowhere, of an annihilation of self in an Other who continually escapes one's grasp. Risking their bodies—or rather their souls—by giving themselves entirely in order to save themselves through this total surrender, attempting for better or for worse (and mostly the latter) to embody this mystic quest both within marriage and outside of it, women little by little grow disgusted at their own torrents of tears.

The reaction was a strong one, and took the form of a revolt. Beginning with the last years of the nineteenth century and above all in the first part of the twentieth, certain of them declare themselves the outright enemies of this much-celebrated lord and master for whom they have ended up embroidering so many pairs of house slippers.

These women love themselves and each other, in a closed circuit. This was how feminine Romanticism ended: in an explosion of lesbian literature. The explanations that psychoanalysis might provide in each individual case would not suffice to justify the sociological dimension that the phenomenon assumed. But inasmuch as despite all appearances only a minority (albeit a minority that writes a great deal) finds pleasure in Sapphic loves, other women slowly recognize in their writings a reflection of their own sensual pleasures. Through the intermediary, first of all, of a sort of pagan love of nature: growing things, the sun, animals, the sea, ocean waves, snow, rain, fruits and vegetables —everything that is alive is good, so long as it can be used to express the pleasure of existing and of loving.

Then slowly and gradually, the woman will again celebrate the body —her own first of all, and then, hesitantly, that of the man, and finally (much later, so much later that one may well wonder to what degree it is a personal discovery and to what degree it is a derivative phenomenon and a banal imitation of a fashion that she herself has not launched) : the genitals.

Her own, moreover, far more often than the man's. What is permanently missing in the long love song sung by many voices in eight centuries is in fact the phallus. The subject merits further discussion.

The woman in love appears to be far more preoccupied with her own body than with that of the man. Save in rare instances, she is not given to contemplation of her love object. If she hymns the masculine body (and she does so only at intervals of several centuries), it is in order to attempt to define the phases of a seduction to which she has succumbed rather than to praise the beauty that has aroused her desire. Louise Labé indeed cries, "So many torches to set a female on fire!" after having enumerated the charms of her lover, but though the poem begins "O beautiful brown eyes!" it continues with a mention of the plaintive lute and "nights in vain awaited." On reading the writings by women presented in this volume (and even on reading the complete texts from which these extracts have been taken), anyone endeavoring to imagine what the man who is loved, and often adored, by these women looks like will find that this is impossible. The woman anticipates his arrival, she waits for him, she suffers, she despairs, but he remains a total blank: without contours, without a face, without a body. Eight thousand letters from Juliette Drouet to Victor Hugo have come down to us. They enable us to share a long drama, a happiness that was most unusual, an exceptional love for an exceptional man. But on reading them it is impossible to find a single reference to the color of this genius's hair, not to mention any sort of description of his features, his bearing, the lineaments of his body.

In the fourteenth century, Christine de Pisan is the only woman to offer us a detailed description of her beloved. "The splendor of his proud breast / Still moves me. And I sweat with pain / Remembering. Many times have I been received / In sweetest love there. The beauty / Of his robust, imposing, stout, virile chest / Surpassed everything." But if the young poetess recites to herself this blazon of the male body, it is because her beloved, the gentle husband for whom she has shed so many tears, is dead and buried.

We must wait until the nineteenth century and George Sand to find in a letter a precise lament by a woman who has a precise vision before her as her eyes brim over with tears: "My little warm supple body, you will no longer lie atop mine. . . . Farewell my blond hair; farewell my white shoulders; farewell everything that was mine!" This young Musset will not be confused with Michel de Bourges, with Pagello, with any other man who comes into her life. He exists in the flesh in her nostalgic memories, and in them he is naked, the lover with the "white shoulders."

Doubtless it is only in intimate personal letters that these love por-traits are to be found (thus proving that re-creating the beauty of the beloved was never a "female literary genre"). It should also perhaps be added that very young women are clearly less sensitive to a man's beauty than are mature women whose sight and touch and sense of smell have been developed for the pleasure of another, the love partner —perhaps because they are less infatuated with themselves.

We must wait even longer, until quite a few of the years of the twen-tieth century have gone by, to find a reference to the male genitals. But not in the form of a hymn of adoration: The latter-day worship of Dionysus has not yet gone that far! In the form, rather, of simple and straightforward allusions: "The axis of the world lies in your flesh."[30] "To die of your flesh in me."[31] "I listen inside me to the man strain-ing."[32]

That is all. That is very little for women who, if we are to believe the ethnologists and the mythologists, in other times and places have wor-shiped the phallus. The penis that is omnipresent in psychoanalytic lit-erature is reduced in works of literature in the traditional sense to what men themselves say of it and sing of it. Kate Millett[33] has rightly pointed out the overweening narcissism that marks the man's pleasure in describing his own penis and its feats (above all in Anglo-Saxon liter-ature, which is much more "phallocratic" than French literature). We might also note that from earliest childhood he can *see* this sex organ of his as well as feel it a part of his body, that he is aware of every aspect of it, every day. But he also describes—with fear, attraction or repulsion, longing, delight, or fascination—the sex organ of the desired woman that love reveals to him.

The woman, on the other hand, does not see her own genitals (un-less she closes her eyes or turns her head to one side?), although she sees the man's phallus so clearly that she must deliberately *want* not to see it in order not to see it. For the woman making love with a man means the discovery one day not so much of pleasure, which she has often experienced all by herself, in her own way, but of the sex organ of the other—and is shocked or delighted by it. Yet despite this, the woman does not speak of this spectacle that is offered her.

If this phallus is timidly evoked (but is it really a question of timidity?), it is as the instrument of her own pleasure, as we have seen above. It is in her, it "strains" inside her, it is the presence of the man within her. She never celebrates it as a wondrous thing, as a love object. There admittedly exist erotic feminine texts glorifying the phallus. We would not have hesitated to quote from them, but almost invariably they are of doubtful authenticity. The writings of the eighteenth cen-

30 Marie Pauguet.
31 Claudine de Burine.
32 Mireille Sorgue.
33 *Sexual Politics* (London: Hart-Davis, 1971).

tury, for example, which are signed with what are supposedly women's names or are purportedly memoirs of women are merely off-color trash by penny-a-liners artlessly playing at being young ladies.[34]

This silence regarding the phallus offered by the man should give us pause. Having had the wool pulled over their eyes, it has taken women almost three quarters of a century to shake off the dogma of their "penis envy," a supposedly universal phenomenon among females, which psychoanalysts had instilled in them. Nowadays the latter's ship is listing a bit, and this orthodoxy has been hard hit, having been first rejected and then ridiculed by women. Nonetheless there were a great many of them who were (and still are) terrified by it, convinced of it, persuaded of the truth of it. And the phallus, much more than the penis, has become an abstraction, the symbol of every sort of domination, every kind of power, to the point that for the latest-style feminists today every woman who is a "phallophile" is automatically a supporter of "phallocracy," a slave, a traitor to the cause. And by that very fact women demonstrate that they are still as much in thrall to psychoanalysis as Simone de Beauvoir and her generation were.

Though Kate Millett has denounced Freud in no uncertain terms, she too should have had second thoughts. It is dangerous to accuse one sex alone of complacency and of a drive to dominate when one has not searched out in the works of literature by the other sex the corresponding forms of self-satisfaction and the wish to dominate.

For the woman, having freed herself of prudery in the twentieth century, speaks of her vulva, of her mouth that she does not know but is constantly aware of: "Oh! may my mouths be wrenched apart and each one be cured!" Mireille Sorgue cries. And Monique Wittig chants grandiloquently: "The women warriors / say that it has been written that vulvas are traps, vises, pincers. . . . They say that vulvas have been compared to apricots to pomegranates to figs to roses to carnations to peonies to daisies."

The fact that women can now be poets singing of themselves, in a duet with the men who celebrate them, is rather comforting. The fact that they can speak of their weapons, their gifts, their dizzying will to power over this fearful being whose mysterious desire puts him at their mercy is merely to give men their due, so to speak: "Love, that is the eternal subject! To allow oneself to be loved by a man who has so few advantages compared to you that he considers you to be a goddess descended from heaven—that would have a certain charm. Someone would recognize his humble estate."[35] "That lust for domination that

---

[34] It is astonishing to find them not only mentioned but presented as historical evidence in books by serious scholars. See, for instance, F. Caprio's *L'Homosexualité féminine*, in which *Les Mémoires de Mademoiselle Sapho* are taken to be genuine memoirs by a woman, when they are known to be a spurious work by Mathieu Pidansat de Mairobert.
[35] Marie Bashkirtseff.

characterizes the woman," as George Sand put it. This is their way of getting back at that dreary bore, D. H. Lawrence, who would have them kneel before his purple penis (his very words). The fact that they have a passion for the man who is hurt or ill, an invalid who clings to them for support ("How I loved guiding your slow, feeble footsteps / To feel your arm linked in mine")[36] is a consolation for the tiresome braggadocio of suburban Dionysuses and the inveterate fascism of leftists busy resuscitating the Marquis de Sade. So each sex wants to dominate the other? Hurrah for the war between the sexes then! Noble sentiments make inane eroticism, just as, in the words of André Gide, they make bad works of literature. Let us recognize, once and for all, that the mutual fears of the two sexes are profoundly justified and that they lead, moreover, to the most tender sort of love much more surely than dull exercises in intellectual disarmament, even when these latter are accompanied by the meticulously sterilized, aseptic sweet nothings recommended by Masters and Johnson.

But the shattered symmetry must be emphasized: The woman whose physical beauty is celebrated by the man only rarely celebrates his body and never this offered phallus of which he is so proud and so jealous —which she mentions only as something taken, something she has made her own, something that has given her pleasure.

Three physical traits of the woman's beloved are, however, often mentioned, even though they may not be described: his eyes, his hands, his voice. That is to say: what looks at her, the woman; what touches her, the woman; what speaks to her, the woman. "And so, my eyes, you have so much pleasure / You are so dizzied by his gaze."[37] "Ah, I shall praise your hand, which first opened an unsuspected body to me. My night was pierced with light. I made my way within myself."[38] "It was then that his beloved voice / Awakened my entire being. . . ."[39]

But after that, alas, I have almost nothing left to say about what the woman says about the man, that creature whom she loves well, loves too much, loves badly. He is compared to nature's every element, he is the source of joy and happiness, and of fear and unhappiness. He is indispensable. He is the giver of life. But women do not appear to feel the need to describe him: It is as though they found no joy, not even that of the written word, in contemplating him and remembering this act of contemplation. The lamp that trembles in the hand of Psyche who spies on Eros as he slumbers and desires him—is this yet another masculine myth? Yet isn't this sleeping beloved beautiful, and doesn't the vision of him linger, clearly focused and unforgettable, in the depths of the eyes of each woman in love? What is the reason for this prudishness on the part of women? Is it the fear of reducing the active partner

---

[36] Pauline de Flaugergues.
[37] Louise Labé.
[38] Mireille Sorgue.
[39] Marceline Desbordes-Valmore.

to the status of a mere object offered to their gaze? But is this feminine figure kneeling in prayer, in adoration, incapable of giving this landscape of living flesh the mystical dimensions that are rightfully a part of it? You men who are loved badly by women—is it really necessary that it be only your homosexual lovers who describe your beauty? To dare to speak of you, to learn how to speak of you—is this a liberation of women that is yet to come? Would men wish for, would they tolerate, this possession of themselves if it were not totally silent, if it were put into words that were not simply sighs, if it gave to us images as perceived by those women who would not close their eyes? If this is ever to be, is today not the time?

Yet women speak endlessly about their own bodies. If we are unable to determine whether the lover has dark eyes, a hairy chest, a graceful neck, we almost always hear of some physical feature of the woman who loves him, since it is she herself who mentions it. Her golden tresses, her delicate skin, her supple waist, her thighs, her breasts—she does not leave us in the dark as regards the share of beauty that is hers. "I love my body—do you ask why? / Because in my eyes 'tis fine and comely."[40] An eloquent roundabout way of celebrating themselves, and in striking contrast to their silence as regards men, in the poetry of lesbians the object of their love, a woman is worshipfully described by the partner suffering the pangs of desire: "And I pant after the bait / Of the lithe torso, with quivering breasts / Where grace and beauty mate / And a pair of eyes green as the West."[41]

That beauty is feminine appears to be an article of faith for women. "Is there not more beauty inherent in / This flesh from which, without a model, woman's body was fashioned?" Marie de Romieu writes with assurance, without complexes, and a hundred others will repeat after her this paean to female beauty. It would be most naïve to see in this a perversity, a latent abnormality, for abnormal women would then constitute such a majority that by their number alone they would oblige us to redefine the norm.

It would also be an oversimplification to sum up this phenomenon by labeling it narcissism, without further analyzing. That this awareness of self, this self-complacency, this pleasure in contemplating oneself, soon leads to anxieties with regard to oneself is obvious. But it nonetheless makes its appearance in complex and often contradictory forms.

In the first place, physically speaking, women take pleasure in their common membership in the community of women: "Woman: subtle flesh offered to virility / Gently curving amphora in whose depths joy slumbers."[42]

[40] Marguerite de Navarre.
[41] Renée Vivienne.
[42] Lucie Delarue-Mardrus.

They speak in the plural even though they love a man in the singular, delighting in and weeping at being women.

And what is more, love for the majority of them is an *affirmation of self by way of the magic of desiring the man.* Feeling themselves loved, at first they feel doubly alive. "Oh! all thanks to you for having made me a woman! Feeling oneself alive from head to foot!"[43] Each of them feels that she is unique, someone who has been singled out, a mystery penetrated, revealed to herself in a manner of speaking. But she nonetheless always has a ready answer to the question: "Why is it that he desires *me?*" She has already studied herself sufficiently to realize that his eyes have fallen on her in particular, thus assuring her that she really exists: "Tell them how beautiful they seem / My hair as dark as a prune / My feet glistening with a mirror's gleam / And my eyes the color of the moon."[44] One can scarcely imagine a man describing himself in this fashion to the woman who loves him. . . . Unlike her, he is not prepared for this consecration of himself that being the chosen love partner represents. The man's gaze upon her affirms her existence, shapes it, rescues her from anonymity, from the limbo of a phantom existence. *This existential joy of being a Self because she is desired* takes the form of an explosion of happy, ingenuous, healthy narcissism, a sort of Song of Songs to this confirmation of herself: Everything that I was quite aware that I possessed finally really *exists* for me—my eyes, my hair, my breast, my belly, my legs. I am, I no longer doubt it. I can love myself, because he loves me. "There remains a likeness of our intimacy in the joy of opening my arms and the pride I take in my breasts."[45]

In the years of waiting, before love comes along, this pervasive narcissism is a heavy burden for so-called innocent young girls to bear: ". . . I made love to myself so well . . . / So tightly did I press my face / Against the breast of my soft soul / That no lover's encircling arms / Could have given me so passionate an embrace."[46] *Or else this self-infatuation becomes a feverish loneliness* bordering on a sickness: "My body is proof of that. . . . When I think of what I'll look like when I'm twenty, I clack my tongue approvingly. . . . I compare myself to all the statues and find no back as gracefully curved and no hips as ample as mine."[47]

The circuit is then closed and we may now speak of narcissism in the true sense of the word. The love of self then leads to a feeling of repulsion for the man and to the attempt to "gear down," to diffuse the narcissistic drive through the "mirror-effect" that sapphism represents.

[43] Madame de Berny (who was nearly forty years old and had borne nine children when she wrote these words).
[44] Anna de Noailles.
[45] Mireille Sorgue.
[46] Cécile Sauvage.
[47] Marie Bashkirtseff.

The woman who loves another woman in order to continue to love herself as a woman is only too well aware that she can conquer and keep this beloved only by offering the latter the coziest possible cocoon for *her* narcissism at its most violent. She surrounds her with mirrors. She knows how fragile anything that becomes a cult is. "Loving yourself alone, you pity that woman who / Enslaves herself to facile loves; for you, eyes filled with pride / Serve only your beauty, there in the dark."[48]

But the others, *all other women*, who love themselves because they are loved by a man, in so doing *love the man by loving themselves*. "I was you / I listened, I imitated what I love; / Long after parting, my speech kept the accents of yours / And your voice in my voice still excited my senses."[49]

Even more important, it might be said that they love themselves because they are the man's territory, his seashore, his house, his acknowledged kingdom. "I love you, my body that was his desire / His field of reaped pleasure, his garden of ecstasy / I love you, my flesh that made for his flesh / A burning tabernacle of passion fulfilled," Marie Nizet exclaims—in the nineteenth century! And how many others would willingly take up this hymn to a womb visited, to a mouth sipped to the soul, to this proof of the man's existence that they have become, the bearers of secret, hidden marks, sacred in their own eyes because they are his! Make me beautiful for you, and I will love myself through you and as a consequence for you. The mirror in which the woman looks at herself is now there only to rediscover the visitor by contemplating the one visited, to give even more of herself: *This narcissism is a sacred offering of self.* This is very close to the "sexual altruism" of the woman of which Ange-Louis Hesnard speaks.[50] But for her own self, at least in the short run, this "oblatory narcissism" is the most dangerous sort, for them all joy, all existence, all awareness of self, comes from another. I am beautiful and love myself because I am beautiful only for him. This represents a self-sanctification through the other and for the other. But when the gaze of the man no longer falls upon this miracle that is attributed to him and destined for him, the result is not merely despair but a veritable identity crisis. "For it is an absolute disaster, that leaves us utterly bereft, to feel oneself suddenly a total stranger to oneself . . . because a man has left the room where he was talking with us, in a different mood that has come over him all at once, or without leaving us his address."[51]

This "absolute disaster" that "leaves us bereft" is the source of the majority of writings by women on the subject of love. Laments and

---

[48] Nathalie Clifford Barney.
[49] Marceline Desbordes-Valmore.
[50] Ange-Louis Hesnard, *La Sexologie* (Paris: Petite Bibliothèque, 1962).
[51] Anna de Noailles.

sighs, the shock of being abandoned—but much more than that, too. It is here that we find the most marked difference between women's and men's expression of passionate love. The woman who is abandoned comes face to face with Death, for she herself feels dead. Eros and Thanatos are twins, and death is present in a thousand ways in love. But there is an essential dissimilarity between the way in which the dark underside of the pleasure of loving—death—is experienced by the two sexes. The man writing of love celebrates the beauty of the woman to whom he feels bound by desire, irresistibly attracted by his impulses. And often in the very midst of this spell that he is under, he is obsessed by death—not so much his own death as that of this woman's body which at the moment is so desirable and so smooth, so precious and invulnerable. "Woman's body, tender, soft / So smooth, so precious, and so lithe / Must you expect such ills to be your lot? / Yes! or go to heav'n while yet alive," Villon writes. And Baudelaire sees it as carrion. The dance of death lies just beneath the woman's radiant flesh. It appears inevitable at the very instant that life is being celebrated—not to mention the sadistic impulses to kill this person whom you love, and who therefore holds you fast. The death and murder of the other.

In feminine writings it is a different story. The death of the other is rarely if ever an obsession, and even the writings by women whose beloved fiancés are at the front in 1914–18 are unable to believe that they risk dying. Even when the beloved dies, it is a terrible tragedy, but not an existential one, despite the heart-rending sadness the woman feels. "Since he is dead now and far away / And his blood no longer speaks like leaves rustling / In answer to the rustling of my own / Or to its humming like a swarm of bees. . . . Take him! I abandon all claim to him!"[52]

As for the impulse to cause the death of the other, there is absolutely no sign of it that I have discovered. The hatred that is love's twin in passion may reveal itself in the case of the woman in the form of a desire to humiliate the other, or to flee forever from him or to reject him totally—but never in the form of a hidden desire to kill him, to annihilate him.

Nonetheless, for the *woman* death is there, in the very midst of her life that no longer has any meaning, once she is no longer loved. Or rather: It matters little that life goes on, since she, the beloved who has been abandoned, is no longer alive, no longer sees what lies before her eyes, *no longer exists.* "What! it is summer still / What! the meadows are in flower? / There are people in this world?"[53] One ought at this point to quote all of Marceline Desbordes-Valmore, above all her two celebrated lines which sum up the whole of love: "Like life, involuntary / Inevitable as death."

[52] Léna Leclercq.
[53] Marceline Desbordes-Valmore.

The woman who no longer basks in the light of the loving gaze of the man whom she has allowed to possess her whole life is but a pale specter. "Look at the dead woman you are when you are no longer loved," Anna de Noailles writes with a shudder, and in another poem pleads with her beloved: "I fear I shall live no more / The moment you cease to love me."

And even Christine de Pisan, that tender and gentle-hearted widow who had found such joy in marriage, penned this *cri de coeur*, which she entitled "Lay of the Lady": "O love cruel and savage / Surely the one who pays you homage / Puts himself in durance vile / And can full well expect / Grief and mourning as his lot thereby . . . / For your power is too strong / Rude and perverse / And so adverse / That every heart it pierces / Enters the port / Of mourning. . . ."

Become a stranger to herself, depersonalized, the woman beseeches death itself to deliver her: "Ah, my friend, how my soul aches, I have no words left, only cries. . . . Alas, as I told you, in my excess of sorrows, I know not whether it is you or death that I implore. It is through you or through it that I must be granted surcease from my pain, or cured forever. There is nothing in all of nature that can help me now."[54]

"There is nothing in all of nature that can help me now": The only one who can is the man into whose keeping all the keys, all the meaning of life, have been given over. He may have thought that they were a love gift. He had administered a sacrament, and the nun who had dedicated her life to him finds she is nothing at all when the god who once justified her existence, her every footstep, her round of days, abandons her. It is not only the "Whatever shall I do now?" of popular songs, but the far more profound question: "Who am I now?" and even "Do I still exist?" For as Julie de Lespinasse, dying of love, writes ironically: "This *I* of which Fénelon speaks is merely another idle fancy: I am quite persuaded that I am not *me*. I am *you*; and to be you costs me no sacrifice whatsoever."

Perhaps so. But to become herself again, the metamorphosis is so monstrous, seems so impossible to the woman abandoned, that she prefers to return to nothingness rather than go back into the chrysalis from whose confines she has so joyously burst forth, that self which she no longer even remembers.

"You have taken everything from me / The extraordinary. The simple / The complex and the commonplace. . . . This blotting-out of the world upon awakening. . . ."[55]

Where will she go, now that she exists only as a sort of vague blur after having seen so close at hand not death itself but rather *her own* death? The strongest of them, as they grow old, will make their way,

[54] Julie de Lespinasse.
[55] Claudine de Burine.

day by day, toward peace and wisdom, which consists of seeing the world upon awakening without the fear of being abandoned.

"Man, my friend, . . . you are watching the emergence of your sister, your pal: a woman who is making her way free of the age of being a woman. . . . Let us stay together: you have no reason now to leave me forever."[56]

This gradually acquired wisdom leading to a peace pact with the man, whom there is now no reason to fear, unexpectedly makes the woman realize that the splendor of the world does not depend on him, that her own self, at once a commonplace and a complex thing, is there within her reach. She no longer needs this mediator, the beloved, a magician despite himself, ruling over the world and holding as chattel her person, which she has sometimes forced upon him as a gift: "And scorn steals inside me to attempt to destroy you. / For you are nothing save the mystery of revealing all to me."[57]

The monstrous misunderstanding of passion that obliterates persons and things: The man was loved not so much for himself as because he was a magic window opening onto the world. When he is no longer there, the woman is plunged into total darkness. She no longer knows herself and recognizes nothing in the world about her.

However, after countless hours spent reading what has been written by so many women who were passionately in love and knowing their life stories, a few remarks would appear to be called for in order to correct this heart-rending impression that one cannot help but have of them.

In the first place, this extraordinary vulnerability of the female was for centuries largely due to their confinement to the realm of sentiment (and to the running of a household and the fulfilling of social obligations) that was the very definition of her estate in aristocratic and middle-class circles. There are, naturally, some exceptions to this statement, depending on the period and the milieu. It is quite evident that Eleanor of Aquitaine's love-life was not her one and only preoccupation, and the same is obviously true of the Princesse des Ursins or Julie de Lespinasse. Direct contact with the world as well as a life of the mind was possible for a few women—perhaps more of them than one would think. But it has become a cliché to see in this vulnerability one of the effects of the patriarchal system, which turns out, moreover, to be against the interests of the very males who instituted it: There is no weightier set of chains, no more paralyzing trap, than a woman "who has given all of herself," "who has totally surrendered" to a man. If it is an original and beautiful thought to write, as Novalis did, that "woman is the goal of man" (Louis Aragon, whose vision of things

[56] Colette.
[57] Andrée Vernay.

was both more far-reaching and more perceptive, will later write that she is "the future of man"), it is trite and trivial to write, "Man is the aim of woman," for that is precisely what a number of men have always prosaically believed. Does not the book of Genesis, a tale from the man's point of view if ever there was one, tell us, in that curse that is called down on the head of the woman alone: "Thy desire shall be to thy husband, and he shall rule over thee" (and "In sorrow thou shalt bring forth children")? This is how a number of men conceive of the woman's way of experiencing love: as a creature who is dominated, driven by desire, eager to surrender herself totally. What would be a genuine revelation, perhaps, would be to show men such as this that even those women who play this game whose rules have been dictated by males are not really their willing servants, nor are they the willing servants of the couple. They escape their would-be masters by the very excess of the dependence forced upon them, seeing the world only through them, breathing all of nature in through them, using them to exist, feeding upon them, paralyzing them, devouring them.

The borderline separating the sociological and the psychological is extremely difficult to establish in this particular case, however. Is this "sacrificial narcissism" of the woman that serves as the basis of her dangerous dependence due to social conditioning or to a psychological inclination? Even though totally "integrated" into the best circles of her time, her head full of the notions of the scholars and philosophers she was in the habit of seeing every day, Julie de Lespinasse, who remained a virgin until the age of thirty-seven, will afford in the last three years of her life the most typical example possible of the pathological alienation due to love—an ever-present danger for a woman.

One would be tempted to say: a danger even for those women with the strongest personalities, the most vivid imaginations. But here a second qualifying remark is called for: These women who have lost possession of themselves, these beings reduced to nothingness in their own eyes, may come into flower once again, as beautifully as the first time, a few years later, should they fall in love a second time. What a curious legend female monogamy becomes in the minds of men! It is quite true that in her amorous despair Héloïse shuts herself up in a convent and, as she herself confesses unequivocally, henceforth knows no other love than that of Abélard, not even that of God. Julie de Lespinasse and Aïssé die at the age of forty. Madame Roland is guillotined. But many other women experience a great love, a death, and then another love. A typological description of women who have experienced great passion would undoubtedly reserve a special place for these strong personalities possessed of rich imaginations and acute minds who devote to their passion not only their capacity for profound feeling but these virtues as well. Moreover, this is what drives them to tell of their hell and their death in writing. But like Phoenix, they are reborn of their own ashes when another man opens the world before them once again, living once again in the one way in which it is possible for them to live: reaching out toward love.

Hence there is one fact that is blindingly clear in these writings by women over eight centuries: the love of love. "To conjugate we love: I love you / In every tense and mood: The present that's already dead / The future, as it pants for breath / The past, imprisoned in its doublet."[58] To love for love's sake is a mode of existence, a way of truly existing, a state. Despite its torments, this state seems to the vast majority to be superior to all others: "I love only for the pleasure of loving."[59] "I know nothing, save how to love."[60] "I wish to love forever, or else cease to be."[61] The man disappears as the woman discovers an intensity of life that, paradoxically, is accompanied by a loss of awareness of her individuality.

"Take me away / Where I may be you / love / Thy sandal will I tie / And it will still be night / Yet the day's first light / Will find me gone,"[62] having reached that state that makes each glimmer of light a revelation, each flower a sign, each conversation a magic tracery of secret correspondences, which also makes my eyes shine, my flesh glow. A woman in love develops all her faculties. She believes that she is "him." She not only cares for her body and her appearance with that joy and sureness of taste of one who is fulfilling a sort of sacred duty ("The one who loves fulfills a duty," as Marguerite de Navarre wrote as early as the sixteenth century) but also engages in intense intellectual activity in order to understand her lover, to see things through his eyes, to follow his thought, to make the right impression on his friends, his family, his former mistress, his associates. She reads what interests *him*, what it would never have occurred to her to read before. She practices the strictest sort of self-discipline: She watches her behavior, her language, the sort of witticisms she indulges in. She does not allow herself a single carefree moment. She keeps as tight a rein on herself as possible, giving her utmost as men do in a race, a match, an examination, a battle for which they have trained for years. Love is not only a competition with other women but, much more important, a competition with oneself. The male seducer soon wearies of pushing himself to the limit in this fashion, of devoting all of his attention to another, of watching his language, of never letting his eyes stray. What he needs is to win a victory, then relax or rest on his laurels or simply give the whole thing up as not

---

[58] Jeanine Moulin.
[59] Adrienne Lecouvreur.
[60] Henriette de Coligny.
[61] Marguerite de Navarre.
[62] Léna Leclercq.

worth the bother. Woman in love with love never tires of this mad gallop, this unending effort. "Having fallen from the heights of a great love, I have also fallen from the heights of myself; I am once again following the low road of life. I am nothing more than an ordinary woman now."[63]

And for a woman with a noble soul it is frightful to be an ordinary woman. "Oh how unhappy I am, I am no longer loved! I am no longer in love! I am become devoid of all feeling, a sterile and accursed being!"[64] Sterile, unfruitful, a failure, and for that very reason accursed as well. This ambition to love in order to surpass oneself can lead to the heights of the purest sort of mysticism, but also to outpourings that are painfully ridiculous. The woman who writes to her beloved, a soldier in the trenches in 1915: "I don't think that you have to march through mud but if you ever did it would make me feel bad to know that you'd gotten yourself dirty. But if you said to me: 'Wipe off the spots with your hair,' I would immediately let down my golden tresses and kneeling docilely at your feet, I would do your bidding,"[65] most assuredly loves herself as a combination Virgin Mary and Mary Magdalene, and ecstatically contemplates herself in all her grandeur as a woman in love with love—but she does not love the man to whom she writes these words.

Whether sublime or ridiculous, this journey to the heights or to the farthest reaches of herself leads the woman to give voice to such self-abasing vows or such self-humbling promises that she appears to be masochistic. "Although the name of spouse might seem both more sacred and more forceful, I would rather have had for myself that of mistress, or even that of concubine or woman of pleasure, with the thought that the more I humble myself for you, the more claims I shall have to your good graces, and the less I shall tarnish the glorious luster of your genius."[66] Beyond the reasons given here for this self-abasement, which are clearly meant to tug at her lover's heartstrings and to flatter him, this admirable *cri du coeur* uttered some eight centuries ago, like so many others that have echoed it down through the years, expresses a fervent spirit of sacrifice that goes far beyond the immediate goal that is being sought. "You are my life, my joy, my soul, my religion, I adore you, I should like to kiss your feet, I should like to die for you, in your service, at your whim."[67] "As he tortured me I said: I confess I am wrong. / My doubt of myself had made a slave of me."[68]

Far from being typical of resigned or passive natures, these masoch-

---

[63] Constance de Salm.
[64] George Sand.
[65] Henriette Charasson.
[66] Héloïse.
[67] Juliette Druot.
[68] Marguerite Desbordes-Valmore.

istic cries are the mark of women in love who possess particularly strong personalities, those who go beyond what fate originally had in store for them. As women confined to a very few patterns deemed appropriate for their sex, these women have too limited a sphere of action. Burning with passion and bursting with energy thanks to a superabundance of untapped resources, they cannot help but strike out for themselves, heading straight down paths that can only lead to their own self-destruction, to that famous "I die because I do not die" Saint Theresa of Avila.

For many of them who do not have the strength to violate the world's laws, religion is there, affording them a means of expressing this unfocused excess of energy. One can even go so far as to say that religion long encouraged them to do precisely that, thus giving rise to a vast outpouring of writings on religious themes, in which Christ and the lover become more or less interchangeable figures, in a highly suspect sort of sublimation. "My beloved little Master / I am wholly yours / Can greater bliss be asked for / Than loving your whiplashes?"[69]

But moments of total awareness also await these devotees of love for love's sake, extracting from them the most terrible of confessions, an avowal at once of their strength and of their vulnerability: "It is not you I love. I love to love as I love you. I am not counting on anything from you, my beloved. I expect nothing of you save my love for you."[70]

But this "nothing" is everything—in literature at least. For the reader should be warned against the danger of drawing overhasty conclusions and applying the above remarks to all women and their love experiences: All of the foregoing is a reflection on writings by women, and the remainder of this volume is devoted to a selection of writings on love, the authors of which were or are women, who may quite possibly not be at all representative of women who do *not* write. Not all of the women I have cited in these and the following pages wrote for publication. Not all of them were seeking that putting into words that may be the writer's ultimate aim as well as his or her means of expression. But many of these texts are the work of professional writers, and in their case many open questions arise with regard to their basic need to write—the question, first of all, of whether one does not write better and more spontaneously about what compensates for or broadens one's life and one's personality than about one's actual experiences. One writes in order to exist, one writes in order to know, one writes in order to become visible, and one even writes in order to live *something different.*

Writing then becomes a projected existence. But others write in order to free themselves by freely confessing all, thus proving them-

[69] Madame de Guyon.
[70] Anna de Noailles.

selves more sincere in their writings than in their day-to-day lives. There are all sorts of writers and would-be writers, and women who write are no different: Their act of writing may serve the compensatory or liberating functions we have spoken of, and many other functions as well.

But a number of the texts cited here have been excerpted from personal letters or diaries never intended for publication. If they have been rescued from oblivion, it is often because they were addressed to a famous man. One cannot call them literary texts, whatever the quality of the writing. And yet they are an *expression*, and not merely an *experience*. A woman in love who writes to her beloved is pursuing a goal: to touch his heart and to please him. Her letter may be naïve and totally sincere, or it may be full of tactical half-truths that form part of an over-all strategy that remains unknown to us.

It may well be that this second sort of text is more representative than the first. No one will ever know the true relationship between these words, these verses, these phrases, and the real innermost feelings of the creatures who wrote them. And yet how eloquent such texts are, all by themselves!

As I end this presentation that is my regretful farewell to all these women who have loved and whom I would like so much to be loved; after these attempts to describe their uniqueness—their femininity, in a word—which has received so little attention as compared not only to men's sensibilities but also to the sensibility that men attribute to them; after these few awkward introductory pages on women and on love, I should also like to remind the reader that in the face of love, as in love, the differences between the sexes are few by comparison with the similarities once the threshold of dissimilarities has been crossed.

The man is different, a stranger even—this man whom we want only to be one with us in order to know precisely what it is that we lack in order to be "one" and possess the world and live in it; and at the same time give him what it is that *he* lacks in order to be "one" and possess the world and live in it as a stranger; this all-powerful man whose desire we exacerbate in order to study it, this man who after making love resembles the child that he must one day have been and that we learn little by little to give birth to. A stranger—this man without whom our lives are nothing but time spent waiting for him to appear, and for our own selves to appear as well. He is a stranger—this man who sometimes imagines that he can exist without us. He is forever a stranger—this man who followed the printed circuit of his desire that we are able only to trigger off, without ever really traveling the same path, as we plunge blindly into our own reality. And if we did not have this bold fear of the *other*, of the unlike, and this joyous impulse to teach the other who we are precisely because he cannot ever know us completely and hence must be made aware of that fact, if we did not have this fear that fascinates us and this illusion that enlightens us—we would have no way of loving him or of making him love us.

But the moment that one loves this other parallel being, from the moment that one follows the eternal asymptotic curve of desire and this headlong plunge toward unity—how similar the crystallizations, the blindnesses, the flaws, the uncertainties, the sweetnesses, the pains, the search, and the loneliness are! And likewise the words in which to express them. . . .

Even though a man reader may well close this book and say to himself that he has learned nothing about woman's mystery since he himself has also felt, experienced, and stammered the very same thing when he has been in love, he will nonetheless have learned a great deal: that waiting and hoping for love, the joy and the despair of loving, are not unique characteristics of either sex. They are, rather, like the word *love* in French, which is masculine in the singular, feminine in the plural—and could just as easily be the opposite.

The headlong rush to meet each other, the meeting whose secrets stand revealed, the meeting that never takes place—love is everything, even what is beyond its powers, even what made a woman once write to a man: "You have expected of me things as impossible as those I expected of you."[71]

[71] Madame de La Fayette.

You shall be Queen, and I a servant.
                              Marie de France

Four Centuries of Courtly Love

There are certain ambiguities that are revealing: the word *sens*, for instance, in French, a language celebrated for its clarity. The word *sens* may be used as a synonym for *meaning* (as in "*Ces paroles n'ont pas de sens pour moi*"— These words have no *meaning* to me) and for *direction* (as in "*Vous n'allez pas dans le bon sens*"—You are not going in the right *direction*). But sometimes there are delightful overtones of both these connotations in the use of the word. The question "*L'histoire a-t-elle un sens?*" really implies two intriguing questions: Does history have a *meaning*, and Is it going in any definite *direction*? The question implies that history is merely a series of senseless events unless one can discern which way it is more or less headed; in other words, it has no *meaning* unless it has a *direction*, from prehistory to our own day, a continuity in the process of freeing ourselves from nature, technical progress, human liberation, the realization of all our potentialities. Or, on the other hand, a series of events all tending toward the mad dance of the sorcerer's apprentices, catastrophe on a planetary scale, the apocalypse. . . .

The question of the meaning of love has at all times been marked by this frantic desire to discover a meaning in history by following some leading thread through the labyrinth of the centuries which will permit any lover, man or woman, to locate himself or herself, to measure the progress or the decline that has taken place in his or her lifetime in relation to a longer reach of time that will have seen many small shifts that in the end add up to an evolution.

In the same way, women who are aware of their existence as women seek to trace their history, and within this history, to find a meaning as defined by the gradual evolution that the sex to which they belong has experienced.

My women students, almost all of whom are indignant at the society in which they live, for the most altruistic reasons, are nonetheless universally persuaded that women have never loved more or better than they do today, that finally, after a long and painful history, woman is emerging from the darkness, that nothing will ever be the same as before, and that as a consequence love as experienced by women begins only with their generation. Everything that has come before them is supposedly only a long and dark history slowly leading to the freeing of woman, love, eroticism, pleasure from the shadowy matrix in which they lay embedded. These pessimists suffering from a severe case of *mal du siècle* turn out to be basically great—and naïve—optimists.

There is no doubt that each generation feels itself to be the end result of the past, the one that sums up all that has gone before and profits from it, the one for which history has fought, the one which should reap the benefits, for it is the one that *knows* at last. Doubtless when as a young girl I received my first kiss, that was how I felt. I remember in fact that on that day I thought of all the young girls who, for a kiss, had had their lives shattered, had found themselves condemned, imprisoned, tortured, or even put to death. . . .

Nonetheless, by attempting to trace any history, including that of love as expressed by women, we risk losing the Ariadne thread through the labyrinth: its *sens*, in both connotations of the word. For this thread seems to be a badly tangled skein. We pull on a loose end, begin to wind the thread into a ball, and come across a knot. We break the thread off and begin again with another loose end. We line up the little balls thus obtained, side by side, more and more humbly, and realize that we have learned precious little about the grand design of history that we had set out to discover and describe. We can still theorize, of course; that is to say, we can number and arrange these little balls in some order that satisfies our minds and will appear to be logical, we can classify them after the fact in accordance with some ingenious ideology or other, or stretch them over a canvas that will be called a structure— by hiding the knots and throwing away the little scraps and bits and everything that we are unable to find a handy place for. But doubts will remain, and I for my part am most unwilling to conceal them, if only out of respect for those materials accumulated for which I found little or no use, out of respect for my readers, who having been thus forewarned, ought to be able to demolish my constructs as they read and proceed to build their own, and out of a deep distaste, finally, for any sort of rigid, constricted schema.

But I must nonetheless begin this history, starting with the first texts written on our soil, those dating from the so-called medieval period. That is a somber adjective, which has overtones of the so-called Dark Ages, when the far more accurate term would be simply the Middle Ages. Let us plunge nonetheless into the shadows of these so-called Dark Ages, for we shall thus at least have the surprise of discovering in them, as cool and fresh as spring water, frank-spoken, delightful, delicate texts with a savory tang of freedom, at least in tone.

For it is beyond question that an extraordinary revolution in manners and morals takes place in the twelfth century: The woman becomes the queen, or rather the idol, of love, and this cult will last through the thirteenth century and many years that follow. What caused this revolution? The influence of the Catharist heresy, some will reply; and others, the Catholic Church. But Islam would appear to be a much more likely source. This should give us pause to ponder the *sens* of history. Today we complacently describe the Arabs as standing in the way of woman's freedom and of her freedom to love, of the idea of the couple as coequal partners, as the last surviving practitioners of a barbarous love patriarchy. But we must bow before the evidence: In the past the Arabs taught us respect for the woman, tender adoration of her, the heart's sensibilities. There came to us via Spain, where the Arabs played a major role in the creation of a culture noted for its delicacy and refinement, poems from which the Provençal troubadours adopted entire verses, scarcely changing a word, as well as the thought of Avicenna, who maintained that the worth of a man could be measured by his respect for women.

However, though we are more or less familiar with the fact that the woman was courted, praised, wooed, celebrated, by the troubadours of the era, whether of noble birth or commoners, we know far less about what women themselves wrote at the time. And once one has collected these texts by women (and translated their Provençal into modern French), another difficulty arises: What are we to make of them? Evaluations of women's writings on love are subject to two very common biases: an indulgence that borders on infatuation, on the one hand, and on the other a thoroughgoing skepticism, causing all texts attributed to women to be viewed as apocryphal, and in fact the handiwork of men.

Such doubts arise most frequently, of course, with writings from the Middle Ages, for these texts which antedate printing have come down to us through copyists and the memory of the troubadours, and hence were far more likely to give rise to imitations whose inauthenticity is very difficult to establish. Literary critics and discerning readers have thus held a variety of opinions as to the genuineness and the merits of these writings by women in this twelfth century that saw the rise of the cult of the woman.

A "first wave" of critics waxed enthusiastic over these writings by women. François Raynouard found in the poems of Claire d'Anduze "a livelier, more passionate abandon than in the love-avowals of the troubadours." The admirers of Héloïse were legion, and commented endlessly on how much they preferred her tender, tremulous missives to the cold, ponderous, empty rhetoric in Abélard's letters, which had such a false ring to them. Other critics were passionately interested in the courts of love held by ladies, courts that handed down judgments (in Latin) and thus created a love casuistry; it was woman who laid down the laws of love, and these critics hence viewed these courts as a most remarkable institution.

This sympathy, this infatuation on the part of male critics for women writers of the Middle Ages, was followed by a thoroughgoing skepticism on the part of other male critics with regard to them. The trend today is toward a re-examination of the question of the role of women in the twelfth century and the authenticity of the texts attributed to them. This skepticism is sometimes no more than the expression of the sense of caution of the professional social scientist, but sometimes it is also a form of deliberate malice. Many works by men have been largely inspired by a woman, but that has never cast discredit on these works; they are not thereby automatically suspected of being frauds. It would appear, for instance, that it was Marie de Champagne who suggested the story line of his *Lancelot* to Chrétien de Troyes, and the importance of feminine patronage of writers in the twelfth century (Eleanor of Aquitaine, Marie de Champagne, her daughter Queen Mathilde, the wife of Henry the Lion) would seem to be fair evidence that women had a strong influence on the writings of male authors of the time. Yet this in no way detracts from the merits of these works, whereas if a critic so much as suspects that Rambaud d'Orange corrected the poems of his mistress, Béatrix de Die, they immediately lose all interest in the eyes of this school. And what can be said of the grotesque hypothesis that all of Héloïse's letters were in fact penned by Abélard, despite the radical differences not only in style but in the feelings expressed in their respective letters? Others maintain that despite Stendhal's considered opinion on the matter, the courts of love never existed, being a pure fabrication on the part of a charming forger of the sixteenth century, Jean de Nostradamus, the younger brother of the famous prognosticator. It is admittedly quite probable that they were never institutions, strictly speaking. But even though they may have been only a sort of parlor game, that fact does not make the judgments pronounced by these ladies of any less interest as a psychological and social phenomenon, and moreover it totally disregards the fact that the contemporary

of these women, André Le Chapelain, mentions them by name in his description of these courts of love.

This fervent admiration or this scorn for the writings of women of the Middle Ages should come as no surprise: The very fact that they are relatively rare as compared to the many texts by men that have come down to us, the fact that they are a spontaneous, sensual, plain-spoken, and eager response to the love-smitten and frequently platonic writings of men, makes it impossible to consider them dispassionately.

All these lays and virelays penned by women nonetheless bear certain resemblances to each other. Without false scruples, we have inter-mingled Provençal writings of the twelfth century and texts from the north of France, a number of which were inspired by the oral traditions of Britanny. Our aim was not to write a literary history, but rather to set similar texts side by side in order to show the attitudes and styles of expression common to all these women.

The woman of this period thus can be seen to have assumed the role of the judge of men, the judge of their love behavior. As René Nelli remarks, this phenomenon has not had the place in the history of feel-ings that it deserves: "Its long duration, its persistence over a long span of time are surprising, as are the transformations that it has undergone as the result of successive cultural shifts, and also more or less inde-pendently of the intellectual and idealized philosophies of love that have been forthcoming from men."[1] The woman also calls forth and judges the form of behavior that is quintessentially masculine—valor— and puts her suitor to tests that go far beyond the framework of love. The birth of the man and particularly of the chivalrous knight becomes the handiwork of women, as though she were a sort of godmother who impels him to prove himself by confronting danger or death; she

[1] René Nelli, *Erotique et civilisations* (Paris: Weber 1972), p. 140.

remains the arbiter of this "service," indissolubly linking together manliness and ardent passion, in a sort of godlike judgment that will single out the proud heart, the warm heart, the worthy lover, after deeds of physical prowess. She thus sets herself up as the supreme recompense above and beyond all earthly glory and above and beyond death. One might also say that she seeks to amass such proofs before the act of love, doubtless because she is not at all certain as to what will happen afterward.

Hence the longest, the most passionate, part of love is the part that precedes the act of love, and it is over this period that women reign as mistresses and prophets. They force their suitors to undergo all sorts of trials, testing their fidelity, their discretion, which is so important in an era when secrecy took the place of virtue and discipline, and their refinement. Only this long period of unsatisfied desire, deliberately prolonged by the woman, allowed her to distinguish a passing infatuation from true passion, to excite the latter, and to then pass to the trial of the bedchamber.

At this point, everything does not suddenly turn topsy-turvy to the woman's disadvantage, as will happen later on in the seventeenth century; she herself sets the date of the single night that is to serve as a test, and invites the man to come to her if he so pleases, on condition that he will do "everything I should like," as Béatrix de Die puts it. In fact, it is she who takes the initiative and gives all the orders; it is she who embraces, caresses, and then asks for caresses and intimate embraces in turn. The lover[2] must be able at once to contain himself, for it would be unseemly to allow his sexual impatience to show, to give her pleasure, and to gain her confidence. This custom of the first night of tenderness and respect, entirely devoted to caresses and declarations of love preparing the heart for the act of love, is attested to by more than one woman writer. One can judge how long this custom lasted by reading the exquisite description of her wedding night written by Christine de Pisan in the last years of the fifteenth century. "Ah, indeed, the sweet man is fond of me," she repeats in the proud and happy refrain of the poem. Not only is she neither shocked nor disappointed that her husband has spent the first night with her merely caressing her and telling her of his love for her, but boasts of it as the supreme proof, as other women of her day know. It should not be thought that this rite was instituted by men. It was women who first dreamed of it and later elaborated the ritual, not out of fear of love but out of narcissism and out of love of love. For it was indeed a question of measuring their partner's love and not his virtue.

Virtue has, in fact, little place in the love experience of the Middle Ages. To begin with, love is scarcely conceivable unless it is adultery.

[2] Who may or may not be of noble birth.

Christine de Pisan, writing much later, is still aware of this when she attempts to persuade her readers that "we complain too much about our husbands," that hers "is happy with what I do," even if she distracts herself with a friend. As a general rule the husband is the enemy of love, and of marriage, of which it is said clearly that "in . . . the opinion of a great number of ladies" it "bears no relationship to love."

The rebellion against marriage, which is active and constant, is a notable characteristic of women's writings. Marriage imprisons them much more than it imprisons men, and the difference in ages is usually in the woman's disfavor. The young virgin is frequently delivered into the hands of a mature man, or even an elderly one whom she detests, and she innocently sings of how "sweet" she is and "prays death to come kill" her husband whom she does not "covet." She conceives a bone-deep hatred for him and does not appear to have the least pang of conscience in so doing, and cuckolds him without the slightest twinge of remorse. Many a husband dies in writings by women, as though they were taking revenge for the fact that they are unable to rid themselves so easily of their spouse in real life.

One must bear in mind, however, that marriage in the Middle Ages was not yet one of the sacraments of the Church. It was no more than a social tie, arranged by the family and made secure by the pooling of the two spouses' lands, movable property, and coin of the realm, duly recorded by a legal scribbler. On looking at it closely, one perceives, moreover, that even this sort of marriage that is merely a social institution is still rather vague, and bigamy was not at all uncommon. All the husband needed to do was to go off and begin a new life somewhere else. The civil registry did not exist yet, and anyone who moved only a half-dozen valleys away felt that he had entered another world. But this roving life was scarcely possible for women. Hence love for them was living in adultery, without remorse but in secret. Young girls are almost totally absent from love literature. They seem to have had neither a sensual nor a sexual existence: Doubtless they were married off at so young an age that they scarcely were aware that they existed while still under their fathers' dominion. It is only the married woman and her lover who constitute the ideal couple, to the point that Marie de France in her *lais* has the third party who might disturb the lovers—the husband or the lawfully wedded wife—gracefully bow out of the picture or politely disappear.

But far more often the need for secrecy takes the place of virtue. The lover's most prized quality is his discretion. Indeed, "he who cannot keep a secret cannot love." It is an exercise of will, it is a moral code, a discipline that enhances love, and not simply a banal sort of hypocrisy. Keeping silent, concealing, hiding one's love, replaces modesty, and feminine eroticism gains enormously thereby. We cannot read the texts to be found at the end of this chapter without being bathed in the light of these truths that seem scarcely conceivable to our twentieth-century minds. There is an absolute dichotomy between love and marriage. Love, which is experienced only in secrecy and concealment, nonetheless has nothing shameful about it. The woman does not seem even to know the words "modesty" and "virtue." Adultery is the field she chooses for her victory and her pleasure; it is she who gives the orders, who heightens the experience, who makes her lover serve her and glorify her.

We must not make the mistake of believing that hers is a platonic love. This woman who postpones giving her lover the gift of herself in order to stimulate his desire for her and strengthen his resolve, in order to better measure the stuff of which he is made, is not a frigid woman. Sensual abandon is in fact more clearly and forthrightly expressed in women's writings on love in this period than in men's. One is staggered at the thought that numerous scholars for some time were able to force upon their contemporaries the idea that *fin amor* (as it was once called, before the nineteenth century rebaptized it *amour courtois*—courtly love) was an "intellectual pastime," an "affair of the head and not the heart," whose goal was not at all the satisfaction of desire since that would be the beginning of the end of love. Even if we had from this period only the writings of the *trobairitz* (female troubadours), they would be quite enough to give the lie to this incorporeal view of courtly love. The *trobairitz* invites her lover to "steal beneath the bed-curtain" and remember all the mad things she has done with him "in bed or all dressed" (a clear indication that the woman went to bed naked with her lover). And if there still remained any doubt as to the nature of the love ties uniting the lady and her lover in certain of the *lais* that these *trobairitz* composed, the presence of their love child would be sufficient to demolish the hypothesis that theirs was a platonic relationship with the man.

This ardent sensuality is expressed in a way that comes as a surprise: It is not at all what we would expect from the psychoanalytic theories that were first propounded at the end of the nineteenth century and have subsequently ruled almost the whole of twentieth-century thought on the subject. Ingenuously, being familiar neither with Freud nor with Simone de Beauvoir, women express themselves as *subjects*, and speak of their lovers as *objects*, the objects of their desires, the objects of their fantasies, the objects of their daydreams. They "take him in their arms" (and never the contrary), they "make their breast a cushion for him" (and never the opposite), they "give him the kiss of love" (and never receive it first), they promise themselves to "hold him in their power," they take "their pleasure of him." Though certain of these expressions might be "in code," so to speak, the absence of the opposite expressions that would point to the man's taking the initiative are significant.

The manner of these ladies is direct and their language plain-spoken: They expect to be the leaders of this game and make no effort to conceal that fact. Restraint and false modesty do not appear until later, in writings of the fifteenth century, and even then there is no more than a trace of them. In the twelfth and thirteenth centuries, the affected airs of the coquette are ascribed to *la femme galante de métier*, that is to say, the professional prostitute who is trying to *s'enchérir* (to play hard to get in order to command a better price). The "right-thinking lady who knows and values herself (a quite different expression from the term *honnête femme*—well-bred woman—that will later take its place), on the other hand, gives herself when she feels like it, without beating about the bush. This lady of the Middle Ages does not waste a single word, a single line, to describe her tricks and her strategies, her calculations, her dissimulations, in order to please her lover: She declares her love, or rather her desire, without mincing words, like the fairy to Lanval or the princess to Eliduc in the *lais* of the same names by Marie de France, the moment she has chosen the lover who pleases her. She offers him presents, she sends her maidservant to fetch him, she invites him to sit on her bed, expresses her wishes, her love, and then subjects him to the trials that are a sort of ritual. Nothing of what follows belies these direct manners, this way of revealing her desire to the man and requesting that he bow to it, whereas for centuries to come the woman will endeavor to hide, and even to deny, her own desire. And nowhere do we have the impression that these extremely straightforward heroines are behaving contrary to the dictates of the manners and morals of their time—once their secret is kept.

But love is not only conquest, and the women conquerors of the twelfth century also suffer a thousand deaths—at being unable to keep the love of their lovers, of losing the beloved. But even then they express the torments of the senses forthrightly. Héloïse bitterly makes fun of her apparent chastity: "They praise my chastity; that is because they do not know my hypocrisy"; she writes from within the walls of her convent. She tells Abélard, become deaf to the senses, what he no longer wishes to hear. She tells him of the erotic daydreams that disturb her "during the solemnity of the mass." And although Christine de Pisan, the gentle widow left inconsolable by the death of her beloved husband, writes much later, in an era when decorum and modesty are becoming fashionable modes of behavior, stifling naturalness and spontaneity, she nonetheless still expresses, simply and directly, her delight in her beloved's body, describing it in detail, lingering on "his robust, imposing, stout, virile chest" whose memory makes her "sweat with pain," and speaking of the cruel chastity of widowhood she complains movingly of the "vain torture of a flesh that languishes."

But these women possessed of such ardent feelings and such clear consciences are not simply dominating females. Granted, they avidly seek the service of the lover and his fidelity by assuring him that only thus will he be a true chivalrous knight. They wish to be "queens and the man the servant," love to dominate and dictate, but they, too, are in love. And as they themselves have decreed, anyone who truly loves acquires "merit." This word is forever on their lips. They have rewarded the lover-knight who has proved his "merit" to them; they have faithfully returned his love; have they, too, not thereby acquired "merit"? Do they, too, not have the right to be rewarded for this "merit"? And yet he rides off, and is heard from no more: He has changed. And like every woman in love she feels herself to be dead, repudiated, nonexistent. And she appeals to her "master," as Héloïse addresses her lover, reminds him with touching naïveté of the "merit" that her sacrificial love gift of herself has earned her, her fidelity that demonstrates that "it was the voice of love I obeyed, and not that of pleasure"; she flatters him, humbles herself before him, with such fervor that this humility still bears traces of her deep pride and a masochism that is still full of sensual pleasure: "Although the name of spouse might seem both more sacred and more forceful, I would rather have had for myself that of mistress, or even that of concubine or woman of pleasure, with the thought that the more I humble myself for you, the more claims I shall have to your good graces, and the less I shall tarnish the glorious luster of your genius. . . ." No other way, no other strategy is possible for the woman who loves passionately, save this gift of self, this search for the absolute, even though she can foresee the futility of the goal that she has been pursuing: to be loved. But there is also the great temptation to test oneself to the limit, to double, as in a musical composition, the mystique of the man-as-vassal with that of the woman who has given herself totally, the servant of love, the mystical daughter of pleasure. And despite their fleeting moments of bitterness and blinding clear-sightedness, these women somehow communicate to us the dizzying rapture of the absolute in their consecration of self, which is a personal end, a self-glorification in their enduring love for the faithless lover, a way of pleasing themselves in their refusal to deny their feelings, of losing themselves in order not to lose themselves, of giving themselves, the better to remain the woman who has been loved, the woman who has loved herself.

You would have lost me forever
If this love were known
You would never have had me
Or possessed my body   /1*

Question: A chivalrous knight shamefully divulges certain love-
secrets and intimacies. All those who are members of the court of love
petition that such misdeeds be avenged, fearing that if they remain un-
punished the example will become contagious.

Answer: By the unanimous decision of the Ladies of Gascony it is
decreed that the guilty party shall henceforth have no further hope of
love. He shall be scorned and held deserving of scorn in every court of
ladies. Should a lady be so bold as to violate this decree, may she
incur the enternal enmity of every well-bred woman.   /2

In an orchard beneath the green hawthorn
The Lady holds her Lover in her arms
Till the watchman's cry, heralding the morn
O Heaven, O Heaven, how soon the morning dawns! . . .

Gentle, handsome friend, let us kiss, the two of us
There in the meadow full of the birds' melody
Despite my spouse's jealousy
O Heaven, O Heaven, how soon the morning dawns! . . .   /3

He who cannot keep a secret cannot love.   /2

Curséd be my parents
Who gave me that jealous husband
And married me to his body.
He will never die
When he was to be baptised
He was plunged
Into the fires and flames of Hell.
Hard are his nerves, hard his veins
Seething with hottest blood.   /1

* The number following each citation refers to the biographical sketch of its author:
see pp. 295ff.

Sweet and gentle am I, and hence sorely pained
By my spouse, neither wanting nor desiring him
For I am but a child still, a tender young maid
Sweet and gentle am I!
By all rights there should have been given me
A spouse who brings me joy
With whom I might disport myself and laugh each day
Sweet and gentle am I!
Heaven save me, I shall never be in love with him!
In no wise do I covet him
I feel such shame at the mere sight of him
I pray death to come take him from me.

But one thing there be to which I give my free consent . . .
And my friend has shown my love a new path to take:
Therein lies the hope to which I've given all my heart!
A ballad, this, of sweetest praise:
May it be sung by every lady I've thus apprised
Of that friend of mine I love and desire so,
Sweet and gentle am I!   /4

A rich old man, far advanced in years
Having a fine estate to leave
Took a wife to bear him sons
Who would be heirs of all he owned
The maid was of high lineage
And as she was most comely and fair
To guard her he took the greatest care:
He double-locked her in her tower
In a great chamber with floor paved in stone
And there kept her more than seven years . . .   /1

The attachment of husbands and the tender affection of lovers are
sentiments whose nature and customary manifestations are wholly
different. No just comparison can therefore be established between objects which bear no common resemblance or relation.   /5

She wishes to see her friend often
And her joy is to possess him
As soon as her lord departs
And by day or night, sooner or later
She has him just as she pleases.   /1

Question: Can true love exist between married persons?

Answer: We declare and assure, by these presents, that love's rights cannot extend to two married persons. In truth, lovers accord each other everything mutually and freely, without being constrained thereunto by any sort of necessity, whereas spouses are duty-bound to submit to each other's will and refuse each other nothing.

May this judgment that we have rendered with extreme caution and in accordance with the opinion of a great number of Ladies be for you an incontestable and ever-present truth. Thus decreed, the year 1174, third day of the Calends of May.   /6

The ease of carnal enjoyment diminishes its price, and difficulty augments it.   /2

Long have I suffered for love of a knight
I wish everyone to know
What excessive affection I bore him.
And now I have been abandoned
For not giving my heart away
And yet how often I lost my head
In bed or fully clothed!
How I should like one night to hold
My knight in my arms!
He would be overcome with joy
Were I to make a cushion of my breast
I am more smitten with him
Than Flor with Blancheflor.
Sweet gracious friend
If ever you are in my power
If one night I may sleep with you
And give you the kiss of love
Know you how pleased I should be
To have not my husband but you in my arms
Providing only that you first promise
To do everything I wish.   /7

Merciful heaven! We complain too much
Of our husbands . . .
For I have a husband who greatly pleases me
A good and handsome man. Without contradicting
He wants everything I want
Desires only amusement
And scolds me when I sigh
I please him much, or so he swears! . . .
He is happy with what I do
Everything suits him, and straight away
He wants everything I want.   /8

A sweet thing is marriage
My example proves 'tis so
To anyone whose husband is
As wise and good as he
Whom God made me find.
Praised be He who would save me,
For he has sustained me every single day
Ah, indeed, the sweet man is fond of me . . .

The first night of our marriage
He showed me forthwith how good a man he was
For he did attempt no violence
That might hurt me.
And before time to arise
He kissed me a hundred times, I remember
Without a single villainy
Ah, indeed, the sweet man is fond of me . . .

He spoke these tender words to me:
" 'Tis God has brought me to you
Tender friend, for your sweet use
Methinks He wished to raise me up."
He did not cease this reverie
The whole night through
Not once behaving in any other way
Ah, indeed, the sweet man is fond of me.   /8

Sensuality, simplicity, active viewpoint, with no modesty or coquetry

"Lady," he said, "praise be to God
Do not be angry if I say to you:
A harlot by profession
Plays the coquette in order to command
A higher price, so none may believe
That she is accustomed to such joy.
But the lady who thinks aright
Possessed of pride and good sense
If she finds a man to her liking
Will not be too haughty toward him.
She will soon love him, and let him be her joy
Before anyone may know or see
They will have profited.
Beautiful lady, let us leave off speaking now."

The lady sees that he has reason on his side
And promptly grants unto him
Her love. And he kisses her.
Guigemar is wholly at her ease
They lie together, in sweet conversation
And often kiss and couple.   /1

At night I cannot find repose
And cannot close my eyes to sleep
If out of love he wishes to love me
And assure me of his body's handsomeness
I shall do everything for his pleasure.   /1

And his gaze was so full of sweetness
That it gave me the hurt I complain of
When it penetrated full within me.
I do assure you
He could not hold or contain himself
And it seemed he said unto my heart. "Ah, come!"
He drew me to him as though everything belonged to him. . . .

His shining lips were red.
And full, though not too much so
Nor had he a mouth
That stretched from ear to ear
But rather, like a leaf
Flowering like a rose on a rose-tree.

His faultless neck
Was powerful, and solid at the base
His shoulders set off his waist.
They were large, tall, nicely shaped. . . .

Far from being gnarled
His long hand, setting the bait well
Tensed more tightly than tree bark.
Firm and nicely boned.
The splendor of his proud breast
Still moves me. And I sweat with pain
Remembering: Many times have I been received
In sweetest love there. The beauty
Of his robust, imposing, stout, virile chest
Surpassed everything.   /8

The maid was in the pavilion
A lily and a fresh rose. . . .
The knight came forward
And the lady summoned him.
He sat down beside the bed:
"Lanval," said she, "my handsome friend
It was for you I left my land
Of Lains and came here
No emperor, queen, or king
Ever had so much joy or contentment
For I love you."   /1

A lady who desires every merit must choose a gallant and valiant knight whose courage is known to her, and dare to love him freely. Of a lady who loves freely, the gallant and valiant will always have naught but good to say.   /7

I know that those knights do naught to advance their cause
Who court a lady's favor more than she courts theirs
For no advantage do they gain thereby
And fail to bend the lady to their will.
Quite the contrary: should a lady be disposed to love
She it is who must ask favor of the knight
If she sees nobility in him, and the wish to serve faithfully.   /9

      Borne to me by the perfumed aura that surrounds
      My friend, so handsome, courteous, and gay
      I drank in from his breath a fragrant ray.   /3

The whole night long I sigh and dream and waken with a start
Thinking my friend has roused me from my sleep
O Heaven! how soon my malady would be cured.
Should he chance to come to me one night. Ah me!
Into my curtained chamber he once stole
Like unto a thief
Into my chamber richly adorned.
Troubled, tormented, sore aggrieved
Have slanderers and false prophets left my heart,
Contemptuous of life and tender years
They have parted us and sent you far from me—
You whom I love before all else in this world,
And hence, unable now to gaze at you admiringly
I die of pain and my soul's aridity.
Those who reproach me for my love of you
Or forbid me to so love are able in no way
To improve my heart or make it stronger than
The desire, the hunger, and the thirst I feel for you.
No man there is, be he my avowed enemy
Not close to my heart, the moment that I hear
Him speak well of you, and he who can speak only ill
Can naught do that pleases me.
Far not, my lovely friend,
That my heart will e'er betray you or
Another take your place
For love of you has dominion over me
And keeps my heart only for you.
And were it in my power to steal back this body that belongs to you.
He who now possesses it would do so no more   /12

He was my captive. Ah me!   /10

Though it behooves me to bare all the weakness of my miserable heart, I do not find within myself a remorse capable of appeasing God. . . . It is doubtless easy to confess one's faults and accuse oneself of them, and even to subject one's body to outward mortifications. But what is difficult is to wean one's soul away from desires of the sweetest pleasures of the senses. It is not only what we have done, it is the hours, the places that were witness of them, that are so deeply engraved upon my heart, along with the image of you, that I find myself once more with you in the same places, at the same hours, doing the same things. Even sleep brings me no repose. At times the movements of my body betray my soul's thoughts, and despite me words escape my lips.

By calming in you the stirrings of your desire, a single wound inflicted upon your body has cured all the wounds of your soul. And though God may seem to have dealt harshly with you, in reality He proved merciful. For me, on the other hand, the fires of a youthful age burningly alive to pleasure and my experiencing of the sweetest pleasures of the senses fan the flames of these desires of the flesh. They praise my chastity; that is because they do not know my hypocrisy. My dissimulation long deceived you, as it deceived everyone. You took for a sentiment of piety what was merely hypocrisy. It is you far more than God that I desire to please.   /11

> The fairest one in all of France
> The very best and gentlest
> Why come you not my way?
>
> My love, my faithful trusted one
> My God on earth most adored
> The fairest one in all of France
>
> If in your power it may be
> Why do you not return to me?   /8

As for me, these sensual pleasures of love that we enjoyed together were so sweet to me that I cannot help loving the recollection of them, or erase them from my memory. No matter where I turn, they present themselves, they are there before my eyes, along with the desires that they awaken; not even sleep frees me from their illusions. Even the so-

lemnity of mass, during which one's orisons should be so pure, is filled
with the licentious images of these pleasures that so take possession of
this miserable heart of mine that I am more intent upon their turpi-
tude than on prayer. I ought rightfully to bemoan the sins that I have
committed, and yet I sigh for those that it is not possible for me to
commit.   /11

*Women who dominate, women who are dominated: women who love
deeply*
True love is always timid.   /6

My dearest lady, I do give myself to you
Hold me not to be your king
But for your man and for your friend,
I say to thee on my sworn word
That pleasure will I bring to you
I pray you, let me not die for you
You shall be queen, and I your servant
You proud and I your humble worshiper.   /1

It greatly pleases me that through love I vanquish you
O my friend, for it is you who are the most valiant.   /7

There is no savor to the pleasure that a lover steals from his partner
without her consent.   /2

I must sing what gladly I would not
So much rancor has my friend given me
I love him more than aught else in this world
But my beauty, merits, and intelligence
Earn me not pity or courtesy
And so I see myself betrayed, deceived
As I should be were I uncomely

What consoles me in such pain
Is that I failed you in no way
O dearest friend! Oh, I am pleased
To think I surpass you in tenderness
As you surpass me in brilliant qualities
I know no woman near or far
Inclined toward love who would not bow your way
But you, friend, are such a knowing one
That you must have for friend the fairest of them all
Remember how we said goodbye!

I ought to count on the merits that are mine
And on my beauty and my rank
More than on my tender affection
And so I address this song to you, my friend
As messenger and love's soothsayer
Why deal with me so barbarously?
Is it hate? Or is it pride?   /7

Alas, you are the death of me
And you, vassal, who have so tried me
May this be your destiny:
Never to have proper medicine
From root or green of any plant
Nor from potion or physician
Find cure for your affliction.   /1

To her master, or rather her father; to her spouse, or rather her brother; his servant or rather his daughter; his spouse or rather his sister; to Abélard, Héloïse.

At least it is not another, it is you, you the one subject of my sufferings, who alone can be the one to console me.

The one object of my sadness, it is only you who can bring me joy once more or offer me comfort. For I have blindly done everything you bade me do, to the point that, being unable to bring myself to offer you the slightest resistance, I had the courage, at a word from you, to wreak my own ruin. I did yet more: O strange thing! My love turned into delirium; it sacrificed what was the one object of its ardors without hope of ever recovering it. At your command, I adopted another habit, another heart, in order to show you that you were the sole master of my heart as well as of my body. Never did I seek in you aught but yourself. Although the name of spouse might seem both more sacred and more forceful, I would rather have had for myself that of mistress, or even, may I say, that of concubine or daughter of joy, in the thought that the more I make myself humble for you, the more I might acquire the right to your good graces, and the less I would tarnish the glorious luster of your genius.   /11

Tell me, if you can, why since my retreat from the world, which you alone decided on, you have come to neglect me, to forget me so that it has not been given unto me either to hear you so as to re-temper my courage, nor to read you so as to console myself for your absence? Tell me, if you can, or I shall tell you what I think and what is on everyone's lips: Ah, it is concupiscence rather than tenderness that attached you to me! It is the ardor of the senses rather than love. And that is why, once your desires were extinguished, all the demonstrations that they inspired have vanished with them.   /11

I had thought up until now that I had acquired many merits in your eyes, having done everything for you, and having continued to remain in retreat only to obey you. For it is not a vocation but your will, your will alone that has plunged my youth into the austerities of nun's vows. I have no recompense to expect of God: I have not yet—who is there who does not know this?—done anything for Him.

I who, with one word, God knows, would have preceded or followed you without hesitating into the flames of Hell! For my heart was no longer with myself, but with you. And if today more than ever it is not with you, it is nowhere.

So long as I enjoyed with you the pleasures of the flesh, well have pondered whether it was the voice of love I was following or that of pleasure. But it can be seen what feelings I obeyed from the very beginning. In accordance with your will, I have reached the point of forbidding myself all pleasures. I have held back nothing of myself, save the right to make myself wholly yours.

What an injustice if you grant less and less to one who merits more and more!

I end this long letter with one word: farewell, my everything.   /11

Anguished pain, rage past the measuring
Sore despair full of unreason
Endless languor, a blighted life
Full of tears, terror and torment
Painful heart that dully beats
Faint body on the point of perishing
Ah! continually and unceasingly
I can not be cured, nor yet can I die.

Bitter awakening, tremulous sleep
Vain torture of a flesh that languishes
Great torment concealed beneath a weary brow
Bitter chagrin, borne secretly
Life's dreary rounds with no rejoicing
Painful desire that dries up every good
These are in me, and will not depart
I can not be cured, nor yet can I die.   /8

He is dead, he for whom I mourn so grievously
And such sadness torments and gnaws at me
That I shall weep forever for his death.   /8

A source of tears, a river of sadness
A stream of pain, a sea full of bitterness
Surround me, and are about to drown
My poor overburdened heart.

They sink me, rudely overwhelm me
For within me runs a current stronger than the Seine
And their great waves wash over me
As the wind of fortune
Brings them crashing down on me. . . .

I curse my life as it goes on and on
I want nothing save to die
No reason have I for living still
When he for whom I lived lies dead.   /8

O love cruel and savage
Surely the one who pays you homage
Puts himself in durance vile
And can full well expect
Grief and mourning
As his lot thereby . . .

For your power is too strong
Rude and perverse
And so adverse
That every heart it pierces
Enters the port
Of mourning, and all honor dead,
Capsizes.

There where you sent my barge
Fortune made me descend
And there I find no help
Or good—only the message
Of death, about to turn me
Face and body both, to ashes.   /8

Love is a wound within the body
That has no outward sign.   /1

*In the fifteenth century, the sentiment of feminine "honor," and the
reluctance to commit adultery*

Although I kiss or embrace you
Ever even once in all my life
Do I wish or desire
To do a base thing
That will bring the least reproach
Down upon me.
Sweet friend, please know
That I have no wish
That you should even hint
I gave myself to you.
For never can I be so importuned
That I do a thing that will stain my honor.   /8

The more your hearts
Shall burn with love, as mine has done
The fairer shall you thus become
What sweet suffering these nails inflict!
The soul that feels their piercing points
Asks not deliverance from them.
They are like unto the unguents and the balm
Of paradise. Pain is forgotten by
The heart that they anoint
For far less sweet is honey in the comb.
If by a great burning traversed
Many a soul reels with ecstasy
How enraptured, how fulfilled that soul
By nails such as this transpierced!   /13

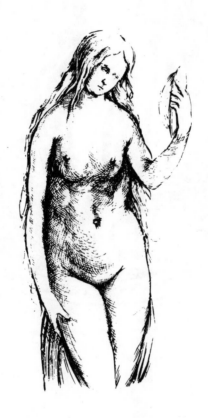

All at once I dry up and grow green.
Louise Labé

· III ·

The Renaissance
Diana or Lucretia?

This sixteenth century that rediscovered classical Greece and Rome is today considered "modern," closer in spirit to us than the seventeenth century. The "cultural revolution" that is throwing our civilization into upheaval has more than once been compared to these splittings at the seam, this "crisis of values" of the sixteenth century. It would nonetheless be dangerous to allow ourselves to be overly attracted by such supposed analogies. Nothing is simple, nothing is clear-cut, in this chaotic century—certainly not the moral code that rules the life of the heart, in any case. Any generalization that we might make could easily be countered by its very opposite. The frank, and at times downright bawdy, language of certain women, for instance, stands in direct contrast to the increasingly constraining moral codes preaching feminine modesty and decorum, to which women themselves willingly give their assent and carry to extremes; the frank celebrations of carnal passion stand at the opposite pole from the religion of feminine "honor," that is to say complete chastity; the marriage laws that impose so cruel a burden upon women are counterbalanced by the concept of the fatality of love, which is irresistible and hence easily condoned; the Christian idea of the taint of the flesh is countered by a triumphant paganism that is expressed by way of scholarly allegories and hides itself behind examples borrowed from mythology: "Bright Venus"[1] permits what horrifies the Virgin, "Gentle Dove."[2]

In its waning years, the Middle Ages had adopted attitudes that were harder and harder on women, a treatment of the two sexes that was more and more "unequal." At the time of the first crusades there were many women who set out with their husbands on the roads to the Middle East, accompanied by children, maidservants, household pets, beasts of burden, in litters if they were rich, on foot if they were poor. The great voyages of the sixteenth century were made by men alone. The famous learned abbesses of the twelfth century are now no more than forgotten memories. Knowledge in the sixteenth century is the province of males and the female religious orders decline. Even the day wages paid men and women who work in the fields or as weavers confirms this worsening of women's lot: Little by little the differences in earnings between the sexes become greater and greater.[3]

But what about love? What has happened to this *fin amor* that seems to have been invented for women's benefit, curing them of their profound feeling of inferiority by conferring such worth upon them and thereby allowing them such spontaneity in the expression of their desire?

Writings by women are ample proof that *fin amor* is by no means dead, but that its "style" has evolved and the "genres" in which it is expressed are becoming more numerous. The writings of women that have come down to us are far more varied. There would doubtless have been many more women poets if circumstances had been more favorable to them. In fact, the moment that a group was formed, a little coterie centered around a few men of talent (even among the nobility, it was only boys who received any sort of real education),[4] the women who took to frequenting these gatherings dared to play the lute, to sing the men's poetry, and gradually to improvise poems themselves, read the Italian poets, write themselves, and on occasion allow their verse to be printed. This was naturally more likely to occur in the case of princesses of the blood, inclined as they were to be patronesses of the arts, and encouraged by their court: Marguerite de Navarre, first and foremost, called by her high-born contemporaries "La Marguerite des Marguerites," the Pearl of Pearls, whose strange personality discourages oversimplified description, a spiritualist who demanded much of herself, a defender of "honest love," faithful to her spouse and holding herself

---

[1] Louise Labé, in one of her sonnets.

[2] Gabriel de Coignard, the author of spiritualist poems. "Make haste, arise, my fair one, my love / God bid the Virgin in the Divine Book by Him written / By your beauty I am divinely smitten / Hasten unto me, my gentle dove."

[3] See Evelyne Sullerot, *Histoire et sociologie du travail féminin* (Paris: Denoël Gonthier), 1968.

[4] See the chapter on education in Philippe Ariès, *L'Enfant et la vie familiale sous l'Ancien Régime*.

apart from the weaknesses of the flesh (before the "Précieuses" of the following century)—but a most indulgent realist when she observes others' manners and morals, in her *Heptameron*. Marguerite's daughter, Jeanne d'Albret, secondly, who corresponds with the poet Du Bellay, in sonnets. And finally, Marguerite de Valois, a much more complex figure than the reputation that posterity has given her (thanks first of all to Alexandre Dumas) as the licentious "Reine Margot." Each one of these princesses wrote. Yet their writings were not always published, or else they appeared anonymously.[5]

But more interesting developments take place in Lyons, where a number of intelligent men, among them Clément Marot, Olivier Magny, Pontus de Tyard, Maurice Scève, Peletier du Mans, meet and form a "school" that surrounds itself with pretty women who are not at all stupid and are eager to become cultivated. The group is a close-knit one, held together by intricate love ties and admiration for each other's literary talents. The women take turns receiving. There being no university in the city, the group constitutes an active literary "club," translating the classics, imitating and surpassing Petrarch, improvising songs and poems. The women introduced into this warm and intimate circle also dare to write: It is to these meetings, to the encouragement of this learned "band"[6] that welcomes the city's pretty women, that we owe the revelation of the talents of a woman who is recognized as one of the greatest poets of the time, Louise Labé, the beautiful wife of a Lyons ropemaker. We also know the names of a number of other women who frequented this circle, though their writings have disappeared: Claudine and Sibylle Scève, Clémence de Bourges, Lacqueline Stuard. And also Pernette du Guillet, to be sure, whose premature death at the age of twenty-five caused her husband such grief that he collected the songs that she had composed and published them, thus saving from oblivion a charming poetess. And it may well be that we owe the survival of the works of both these women to the fact that among their "band" of friends was a printer, Jean de Tournes.

[5] Marguerite de Navarre's *Heptameron* did not appear until nine years after her death, anonymously, thanks to the efforts of one of the queen's former manservants. Marguerite de Valois's *La ruelle mal assortie ou entretiens amoureux d'une dame éloquente avec un cavalier gascon plus beau de corps que d'esprit et qui a autant d'ignorance comme elle de savoir* (The Ill-Assorted Couple in the Bedchamber or Amorous Conversations of an Eloquent Lady with a Cavalier from Gascony Possessed of a Body Finer than His Wit, and as Ignorant as She Is Learned) was also published posthumously and anonymously.
[6] "I sought in it no more than a respectable pastime; some of my friends . . . had led me to believe that I ought to allow [some of my writings] to see the light of day," Louise Labé says, referring to the work entitled *Plusieurs Sonnets, Odes et Épitres que quelques-uns de ses amis lui auraient soustraits, et bien qu'imparfaits, publiés en divers endroits* (A Number of Sonnets, Odes, and Epistles That a Number of Her Friends Are Said to Have Extracted from Her, and Although Imperfect, Published in Various Places). (Royal imprimatur granted March 13, 1554.)

It was because Poitiers was a town where Grand Assizes were held that Madeleine des Roches and her daughter Catherine came to write, encouraged by the magistrates who presided over the "Great Days" when the court was in session. These distinguished gentlemen, finding time hanging heavy on their hands, often gathered at the home of the "dames des Roches" and spurred them in their literary endeavors.

It was because her brother had attacked women in an epistle that Marie de Romieu, of Vivarois, was inspired to write verses in their defense.

Though the poems of Anne de Graville were discovered in an attic, we would seem to have lost forever the writings of Antoinette de Loynes and her three daughters, Jacqueline de Miremont, Diane Symon, Artuse de Vernon, and many other women whose talents were vaunted by their men friends but whose works never reached print.

Whether queens, princesses, or mere commoners, the women of the sixteenth century do not make a career of writing (with the one notable exception of Mademoiselle de Gournay, a learned woman and a feminist). If they publish their works, they apologize for so doing: "Most beloved and honored Ladies, may no admiration move your chaste hearts upon considering my boldness in giving to this work the title that I have, alluding as it does to shameless loves, which in the opinion of a number of timid Ladies may be considered more worthy of being kept totally secret than of being published and vulgarized."[7] As with women writers of the Middle Ages, critics still consider this work to be extremely suspect. The name Hélisenne de Crenne was long regarded as a pseudonym of a male author, even though there were numerous documents capable of furnishing readily verifiable facts concerning the life and the work of the very first French woman novelist, the author of the first psychological novel in French, published in 1538. But such research was not undertaken until 1917, when the chance discovery by an antiquarian of her marriage certificate in Amiens proved that such a woman had really existed.

What, then, do these writings, whose publication and preservation are so often due to the sheerest of chances, reveal?

Fin amor, first of all, has not yet come to an end, but it has been practiced for so long that it has lost spontaneity, while at the same time it has taken on a greater perfection of form and greater subtlety. Literary critics would be inclined to stress the frequent borrowings from Petrarch and his imitators. Little harm will be done if we ignore this influence, for the feminine sauce that accompanies these borrowings has a flavor all its own. The principal theme: Love is a tissue of striking contrasts, experienced both as a union of opposites and as ambivalence

---

[7] Conclusion of Hélisenne de Crenne's *Angoysses douloureuses qui procèdent d'amours* (painful tribulations occasioned by love).

—as witness these women's celebration of the "dying" that "gives birth to another life," or such verses as "all at once I dry up and grow green," "I live, I die, I burn and drown," "My love is accompanied by jealousy," or "sweet is the pain" of the woman who feels "her eye to be contrary to her heart."

They are in love with love for love's sake—yearning only to part with their souls, which "in amazement" (a much stronger expression in those days, meaning "in bewildered stupefaction") will be led to experience both the keenest of joys and the most painful sorrows. Led by the lover? No, by love, rather—a malady personified. There are still traces of the simple, spontaneous celebration of the body and its fulfillment, "in sweet kisses and long embraces," living "one long rapture." But coquettishness has appeared on the scene, immodesty and chastity intermingled: leaping naked into a fountain in order to tear the philosopher away from his meditations, but at the same time throwing cold water on him if he reaches out to touch; a desire to dominate and a desire to submit: The woman wants the man to be at her mercy but does not want to "break him to her will."

Diana—the Diana who rules the heavens and the court of Henry II. Diana the proud, independent huntress, Diana the king's favorite from her forties to her sixties, still fair-haired and white-skinned and beautiful thanks to the ice-cold baths and early morning canters she is in the habit of taking—the goddess Diana and her earthly double, Diane de Poitiers, reign supreme in this century—mythologically, socially, and aesthetically.

Not all women, alas, can keep their lover's affections until past the age of sixty, and Pierre Ronsard was not the only poet in this century of upheaval to enjoin his readers to gather rosebuds while they might. Casting aside the embellishments of form, women nakedly reveal their real anguish, far worse than the fear of death (indeed the latter is often called a blessing by the woman in love), their real terror: growing old. In his famous "Sonnet to Helen," Ronsard confronts his mistress with the threatening reminder: "When you are one day an old woman . . . ," while speaking of himself only as a phantom who has disappeared, not as a decrepit body. In their writings, women are frightened at the thought of how ugly they will be one day and of the nameless horror they will feel should it be their lot "to burn with ardor in old age." To feel strong desire and not be desired is the exact opposite of the situation in which women usually feel most secure and most certain of themselves: not desiring too much while at the same time being greatly desired. And it is this terrible position that is presented as the punishment rightfully deserved by the woman who has rejected carnal love in her youth, out of "hauteur" or out of puritan frigidity. There are physical laws of love, and they must not be disobeyed—such is the naïve conviction of these ladies of the Renaissance, who seek no further explanation of the advanced cases of nymphomania that they describe: In their eyes they can only be the result of women's efforts to compensate for not having taken proper advantage of the joys that youth might have brought their way. Nature has foreseen everything, and the woman ought to profit from her beauty, as pagan wisdom teaches.

The woman's beauty, moreover, goes to her head. We find her beginning to celebrate her own beauty, to marvel at the "more inherent beauty" of her body, to echo her admirers' praises of her "golden tresses" or her rosy flesh, to make doubly certain of the truth of what they say. On the other hand, the defense of women, feminist theories, take up very little space in the love literature of this century. But we ought not to forget that there were numerous discussions of "the excellence of the female sex" or the equality of the sexes in the course of the sixteenth century: by C. de Taillement and Guillaume Postel, François de Billon, Poulain de Barre (the latter a true feminist), not to mention a number of anonymous works with such titles as "The Triumphs of Ladies." And finally, there is Mademoiselle de Gournay, who penned a defense of the female intellectual. These discussions were sometimes very ambiguous, and many an "Apology of the Female Sex" was really nothing but a stern treatise calling for the strictest feminine morality. Platonism is held in high esteem, and a woman fighting to further the cause of her sex does not preach sexual freedom to her sisters, but a rigorous platonism.

However beautiful and delightful she may be to herself and others, the fact nonetheless remains that women of the sixteenth century live a hard life in a harsh society that takes the strongest possible measures to keep in check the passions that traverse it and risk tearing it apart. Sudden violent, shifting passions that cannot help but amaze anyone who carefully studies the life of almost any Renaissance figure, or the fetes, the everyday manners and morals, the customs, the sports of the period. How could courtly love, whose refinement and formalism is now beginning to seem quaintly old-fashioned, have been expected to kill these lusty appetites, to sublimate erotic drives and impose fidelity through a subtle love ritual alone? The fear of hell itself never gained more than fleeting victories. Men made it a "point of honor" to fulfill their desire, even if it was necessary to rape the woman, deceive her, besiege her. "Love is a sickness. It is closely akin to rabies," Lucien Febvre notes in the description he gives of men's rage to satisfy their passions in this violent century.[8] "Victory is the one aim. And the means? Any and every

---

[8] Lucien Febvre: *Amour sacré, amour profane, autour de l'Héptameron* (Collection Idées) (Paris: Gallimard, 1971), p. 276.

possible one. Including murder. No false sense of decency. Women are forewarned. It is up to them to be on their guard."

They are indeed on their guard, carefully calculating the dangers. Hence they are evasive, suspicious of men, all men, even those in holy orders, and are prepared to exact a high price from them before bestowing on them "the fifth and final degree of love." Men speak of their "honor": Women, too, have theirs, which is also to "vanquish," that is to say, not be vanquished by "falsity" and "deception." Honor thereupon becomes a very narrowly defined concept. Not only must women not lose this battle, not allow themselves to be cornered in this pitiless chase to the death, for that would dishonor them socially; they also introject this concept of honor (which also includes the notion of living as one chooses and of winning a victory over another) and closely associate it with a refusal to engage in the act of sex and with chastity. "O flower of infinite price, chaste virginity," Anne des Marquets writes in one of her poems. Victory through refusal, victory through resistance, victory through abstinence: This rigorous self-discipline will torture and cripple women for centuries to come.

Neither the Church nor courtly love could hold back or stabilize these unstable and curious creatures who begin to question almost all the uses of the past. The link between past and future depended on institutions, of which marriage was one—which was all the more solid in that what was expected of it was not personal happiness but social continuity. It was necessary to force people to marry, and to resort to force within marriage. It was easier, naturally, to force women to obey than it was to force men: they were not able to fight with a sword or take to the highroad without endangering their very lives at this time in history, nor could they venture overseas in search of gold. They seek their fortune, social status, and power in marriage—or rather, their fathers, mothers, brothers, uncles, aunts, suzerains, and protectors of every sort arrange marriages for them, when they are as young as five or six. That is the only "career" they have.

From the end of the fifteenth century on, as society seems to lose patience with the search for new pleasures and extravagant behavior of all sorts, women are more and more often reminded that the harsh laws of marriage rule their lives. Adultery, once the general practice so long as it was committed in secret, and so greatly prized as the only possible social expression of true love, is now constantly denounced as a mortal sin for women. *Griselda*, the sado-masochistic model of feminine resignation, is again held in great esteem and published in 1495 with the title: *A singular and profitable example for all married women who wish to do their duty within marriage toward God and spouses and earn the world's praises: The Story of Lady Griselda.* The 1546 edition is more threatening still: *Here begins the story of Griselda and her wondrous fidelity and is called the mirror of married women.* In the Middle Ages, the obsessed king who tortured Griselda had been presented as a ferocious monster, "filled with error." In the sixteenth century he has become merely an example to teach women to "put up with their husbands."

Fin amor had long held that marriage, which was merely a means of saving society, an instrument of the Church to control morals, was incompatible with love. Had not God favored Isolde, an adultress and a liar? Had not God brought the princess in love with Eliduc back to life, and inspired the latter's wife to politely remove herself from the scene? In the eyes of the troubadours and the *trobairitz*, God was on the side of the lovers, and it mattered not at all what monks and priests might think. The situation became a dangerous one, from the moment that the self-restraint imposed on men and women by courtly love began to lose its powers of sublimation, much as a religion on the wane sees its rites being bastardized and pharisaism and hypocrisy taking root. In such unsettled times, the Church seeks to firmly establish the primacy of the spirit over the flesh, and an entire century was soon to see men gaily ripping each other's bellies open as they fought to the death over theological subtleties. A social order holding the passions in check through religious faith: such is the ideal that is never attained. Christian marriage, imposed by force, assuring the purity of the family's bloodlines and the survival of the social order, is a much more powerful and efficacious instrument, a straitjacket whose necessity for the good of the group as a whole is vaguely perceived by its individual members. It is more useful for maintaining order than the religious orders, which in this sixteenth century were corrupted by simony and a source of disorder. As evidence of this, we need only note the fear that women have of Franciscan friars, who are more than ready to rape them if they find themselves alone with one of them.

Women, then, are divided on the question of marriage, not only among themselves but in their own hearts and minds. They denounce the cruelty of marriage one moment, and the next they extol its "sanctity and decency." They feel themselves to be at once imprisoned by it, and safe and secure because of it. They aspire to adultery, especially since they see that men permit themselves every liberty. But they live in terror of the dread punishments that these same men are capable of inflicting upon them when they are their husbands. This terror ought not to pass unnoticed, for it is ever-present as the background of the love-life of married women; we have therefore included in this anthology of writings on love a number of texts that express it. Jeanne Flore alone rebels against this savagery, in no uncertain terms. The abductions, murders, threats of death, shaving of women's heads, and other macabre and sadistic practices employed to punish adultresses call forth no condemnation on the part of women. Curiously, the women who are the victims of such acts of cruelty appear also to be the allies of the moral code that sanctions them. They raise their voices in violent protest only against "marriages between unlike partners," the unnatural union of an old man and a young virgin, and the pictures they paint of the repellent ugliness of certain men in their mature years or in their old age possess an unusual intensity of feeling: that of sheer physical disgust.

How oddly unsatisfying it is to draw up a list of influences—Petrarch, Ovid, Platonism, Boccaccio, and so on—to explain the outcries of these passionate women! After the sixteenth century, three or four hundred years will go by before the woman who is in love dares to express the love of her body for the body of the man. We see the inhibiting influences grow more and more powerful from century to century. Hence it behooves us to stop to listen to woman sing of the mystery of man, the mystery of the seductive spell he casts over her, which fascinates and intoxicates her—a mystery which proves as powerful as that of the woman for the man, that eternal refrain that we have heard so often through the ages. Knowing that there is no answer, she ponders the question of the size and stature, the hair color, the complexion, that make the man most "venerable," that is to say, worthy of being loved to the point of veneration. She enumerates the charms that attract caresses and exclaims: "So many torches to set a woman on fire!" Even when she refuses the advances of a great lord who has sought to "dishonor" her, she cannot help remarking that the woman who "possesses the body" and the love of such a prince will be the happiest woman in the world.

Accepting her adoration of the man as being as natural a thing as her own beauty, and finding it as natural to be in love with love as it is to breathe, Louise Labé is the perfect expression of the vision of life, the emotions, the suffering, the feminine experience, of the woman in love. A highly sensual woman, first of all, who feels herself to be a body of which her lover is the soul, she knows that as the bow reveals what is hidden within the violin, so the violin reveals the masterly touch of the hand that holds the bow. She will give her lovers a soul by amplifying their song with her own body. Then, having discovered that seeming certainties learned from experience turn out not to be certainties at all, yet still persuaded of her charms and her gifts, living the life of the mistress no longer desired by her lover, all the more deeply tormented because of the intensity of feeling she has invested in her beloved, forced to cry in her pain "the whole night through," Louise remains the prototype of those women lovers at once highly passionate and lyrical. Like others whom we shall meet in these pages, she was beautiful, venturesome, a woman of action ("He who had seen me go proudly off in arms / To bear the lance and send bucklers flying / To do my duty in the heat of battle / To wield a pike, to caracole the glorious steed," she says of herself, recalling the siege of Perpignan in which she participated as a "woman warrior"), and as such a feminist, calling upon "virtuous ladies to raise their minds somewhat above their spindles and distaffs." Moreover, like all great women lovers, she had more than one passionate love experience, for feminine monogamy would appear to be not at all typical of those women who have deeply loved the bodies, the intelligence, and the love of men, of those "ardent" women who know what it means to "burn" with passion. Like all great women lovers, her writings have an intensity and a breadth that make the great sixteenth-century poets Ronsard and Du Bellay seem precious by comparison. Like all great women lovers, finally, her name has been dragged in the mud, beginning in her own lifetime, and she has been accused of being a "courtesan," when in point of fact as a rich married woman (whose husband was twenty years her elder) she was merely free, cultivated, creative, charming, and in love. She simply did not trouble to hide her desire—which was more than sufficient reason for her contemporaries to pin upon her the label of "shameless woman" which has so long been attached to her name.

As for Hélisenne de Crenne, she herself describes herself as shameless. This young Picard wife burns with desire as she bends down to kiss the mark left on her white satin petticoat by the foot of the young man of low estate that has brushed against it at mass, after he has seduced her "at a distance" from a window across the street. All society's taboos loom large in her mind, but her body refuses to remain silent. It calls her toward the fulfillment of her desire, toward the bed, her mind in a daze.

It is only one short step from this point to the description of love as a fatal physical malady that is as contagious as the plague. (It is an image that comes all the more readily to mind in this century in which the classics of Greece and Rome are rediscovered and enthusiastically imitated, among them Ovid's writings on "the malady of love.") Passion is the work of fate, which in this period is a concept that is a strange blend of Christianity and paganism. It makes its chosen victim act against his own interests and against his own common sense. That is why the writings of these women describing "the anguish occasioned by Love" are always dedicated to the "most beloved Ladies" who are their sisters, begging them to shed "a few tears of pity" or asking their indulgence for an irresponsible creature branded with the mark of shame, who has paid dearly for her indiscretions: "When you read, O ladies of Lyon / These writings full of love-complaints / When my regrets, trials, disappointment, tears / You hear me tell of in sad songs / Do not condemn my naïveté / And the young error of my mad youth / If error it be," Louise Labé writes. If men, even the strongest of them, are "unable to resist the charms of love," how can a mere feeble woman be expected to resist them?

The feminine world, however, is divided by the strange boundary separating sensual women from sensible women—a line of demarcation that would appear to have little to do with social status and cultural conditioning, since in all times and places it has served to establish a dichotomy between women who are "hot-blooded" and those who are "lukewarm." These two feminine types are simply unable to understand each other and never cease envying each other and condemning each other. The problem was to reconcile Christianity, the "triumph of the female sex" through modesty and chastity, and the "amorous excesses" of certain women—without making womankind appear to be a "front" that was hopelessly disunited, and above all without overemphasizing the heterogeneity of the female temperament (the idea of woman and her destiny, of personal moral standards that are different for each woman, was far more common currency than the idea of a single, unquestioned way in which a man lives his masculinity). And the best solution seemed to be to embrace the idea of the fatality of passion visited upon mortals by pagan deities. These latter—Venus first of all, and Cupid and Diana, too, of course—appear to be incarnations of Nature, while Christianity on the other hand affords the means to "overcome" Nature, to separate the soul from the body and permit it to reign supreme. Thus Marguerite de Navarre, a woman who has wisely opted for the soul and God, writes on behalf of all other women that "reason was never the mistress of love." The seed from which Romanticism will one day spring has already been sowed.

And yet, within this disequilibrium between men the pursuers and women the pursued, birth and power allow these roles to be reversed by creating social disequilibrium as well. Marguerite de Valois treats her lover as an object of pleasure. Yet a revealing turn of phrase escapes her as she thus haughtily disdains him: She refers to her affable, good-looking gallant as "the mute one"—in the feminine. . . .

I live, I die, I burn, I drown
I endure at once chill and cold
Life is at once too soft and too hard
I have sore troubles mingled with joys

Suddenly I laugh and at the same time cry
And in pleasure many a grief endure
My happiness wanes and yet it lasts unchanged
All at once I dry up and grow green

Thus I suffer love's inconstancies
And when I think the pain is most intense
Without thinking, it is gone again.

Then when I feel my joy is certain
And my hour of greatest delight arrived
I find my pain beginning all over once again.   /17

He who has love can desire nothing better
He who knows love knows everything
He who sees love has ever-laughing eyes
He who loves love does but his duty
He who can embrace love, take it, and see
With solemn grace will filléd be.   /18

In keenest pleasure, gayest disportment
At feasts, contests, and tournaments
In joy and peace, desire and happiness
So spent Palamon his days with his mistress
She in honors, rich accoutrements
Dances, songs, exquisite instruments
Took her delight, and hence her youth was spent
            In keenest pleasure.
Their thoughts, as on one thing bent:
Sweet kisses and lingering embrace,
All cares banished, all sadness
Long enjoyment abating not their eagerness,
For like new lovers their hours were spent
            In keenest pleasure.   /19

My body enraptured, my soul marvels
At the great pleasure I feel
On being ravished by love, that awakens all
And for that sole reason is called god.

Oh, how full of good it must be
If, in keenest desire,
One would die if it came not soon
Yet this dying engenders another life.   /14

Sincere, my desire, my heart, my life to me
Forgive me, I pray you, and take not offense
If, in the course of these verses I've commenced,
I accompany my love with jealousy.   /15

Consumed am I by fire: furnace-hot, I own
As it slowly spreads from bone to hollow bone
From vein to vein, circling the maze
Of my poor body, night and day, until at last
It settles in my heart, setting it ablaze.   /16

Sire, let not the poor this day forgotten be
Nor yet my heart pierced with love's wound, said she.   /16

How many times have I wished
To find myself in the summer's heat
Beside the clear fountain
Where my desire strolls with him
He exercises in his philosophy
His fine mind that I trust so much
I would not fear to leave my retinue behind
And find myself alone in his company.

There, when I had tarried long with him
And let him hold long discourse
I would little by little draw apart
And plunge naked into the water.

I would sing him a song
To see what gestures it would bring
But if he walked my way
I would let him draw nigh,
And if he wished to touch me
I would throw at the very least
One handful of water
From the clear fountain
In his eyes or in his face.
Oh, would that the water had the power
To change him into Acteon,
Not to cause him to be devoured
By my dogs, like unto a doe:

But to feel himself my servant
To such a point that he would think
Diana envied me my power. . . .

Let him go serve the nine Muses
Without entering my service
For I am without grace or merit. . . .

He who hopes by his writings
To be happy and pleased in my company!   /14

For a brief span, you showed that I was one
Of your sweet friends; and then, more swiftly than the moon
Your aspect toward me changed
And lingering is my pain.

If within your heart there is the slightest store
Of mercy and of pity, I sue for your grace:
Cease to turn toward me your darker face
And that aspect from me hide forevermore.   /21

I see some quite content
Others full of suffering
I hear the first laugh
And the second complain
I see both these passions
Reigning within me.   /14

If serving merits recompense
And recompense is the aim of desire
I should like to serve more than one thinks
So that my pleasure never ends.

To whom is a lover most obliged:
To Love? Or in truth to his Lady?
To love he owes his heart, to her his Soul
The one to honor, the other to pleasure invites him
And yet there is one great point to remember
Which satisfied my mind:
Without a Lady, there would be no Love.   /14

Those stupid fools who scorn love
Without once knowing it their whole life through
I swear by God and my conscience
They are wrong to fault such pleasure!   /18

And round about the hour of midnight, I returned in great melancholy, for all things appeared to me displeasing, sad, and hateful. But the following morning, I went to hear mass in a little church. And as I turned to leave, I saw my friend, whose eyes met mine with such a piercing gaze that my heart was transfixed thereby. I felt such perfect joy therefrom that I promptly forgot all the torments and grievous pains that I had suffered because of him. I began to look at him, without shame or modesty, caring not at all that a companion of his was in all likelihood quite aware that I was casting most indecorous glances at my friend. . . . This, my dearest Ladies, is how I have been dealt with in matters of the heart, constrained at times to sigh and lament as I suffered extreme pain, while at other times great joy and consolation was granted me through the pleasing glances of my friend.   /20

The fear of old age: one must make the most of youth, the time for love

Never was she willing to allow the hauteur of her hardened heart to yield, and ever did she persevere in pleasing herself and priding herself

upon her unbending refusals. And thus it was, my dear love-smitten Ladies, that the poor creature somehow lived through her days of finest
flower, I know not precisely how, but surely most woefully, failing to
bear in mind that the most joyous thing in this world is to share youthful love with a partner who is one's equal. But in order not to tire you
with too long a story: burdened with this blindness of spirit, she went
each night to sleep all by herself in her cold bed, with no one to keep
her company until the twenty-eighth year of her life. . . . Then love
took its revenge, and the lady began to burn with her secret fires in a
most dreadful way, like one suffering from a deep and terrible wound.
And sorely tried by this unwonted bridle and rein she was obliged to
impose upon herself, she began to languish. Her miserable heart, become a fiery furnace, constrained her to desire the embraces of young
and handsome men who had importuned her in the past, and in impatient lust she could scarcely keep herself from soliciting the attentions
of base men of the lowliest estate, possessed of no respect. She would
fain have invited them into her bed in order to satisfy her ardent, pruri-
ent concupiscence. Had a hideous Egyptian or an extremely ugly
Ethiopian made overtures to her, she would in no wise have refused
him, for she was in a state of extreme languishment, burning with the
heat of raging flames, spurred on by lubricious illicit desires and pruri-
ent appetites.

Take the greatest care, dear Ladies, not to offend true love, not to
scorn heaven's dispositions and perfectly ordered causes, in accordance
with which young persons are meant to experience the warmth of love
at the proper age. For it is only the most foolish of maidens who
rigorously resist these venerable mysteries. They fail to consider—O
vast misfortune!—that they insult heaven and offend benign Nature
most grievously.   /21

> So long as my hands can pluck the strings
> Of the sweet lute to sing your graces
> So long as my mind will be content
> To wish to understand nothing save you
> I do not wish yet to die
> But when my eyes have dimmed
> My voice has broken, my hand lost its power
> And my spirit in this mortal abode
> Can show no sign of its love:
> Then will I ask Death to darken my brightest day.   /17

Beautiful crowns are woven, quite naturally, from the twin strands of narcissism and the defense of womankind

As I persevered in loves of this sort, my body grew, and before I reached my thirteenth year, I had an elegant figure, and all of it was so well proportioned that the beauty of my body surpassed that of any other woman. Had the beauty of my countenance been as perfect, I would not have hesitated to number myself among the most beautiful women of France. When I found myself at a place where great multitudes of people had gathered together, a number of them would flock about me to look at me as though wonderstruck, all of them exclaiming in chorus: "There is the most beautiful body that I have ever seen," and then, on looking at my face, they said: "She is indeed fair of countenance, but it is not to be compared to her body."   /20

And what shall we say of women, whose dress and bodily adornment are meant to give pleasure? Is it possibly better to set off the beauty of a head than Ladies today do and ever shall do? To have hair better highlighted with gold, better crimped, better curled? And what care they take, moreover, of their faces! If it be beautiful, they guard it so well against rains, winds, heat, the ravages of time, and old age that they remain very nearly forever young. And if it be not at all beautiful by nature, they make it so by diligent care. . . . And in addition their garments are clean and fresh, like the foliage round about the fruit. . . . If there be a bodily perfection or a lovely curve that should or could be seen and shown off, the adjustment of their dress conceals very little of it. . . . The breasts in their high roundness give a certain elegance to the large stomach. Moreover the well-fitting gown, the body nipped in where it should be, stockings pulled tight and a slipper molding the little foot, for most frequently the amorous curiosity of men makes them search for beauty even down to the tips of a woman's toes.   /17

Is not there more inherent beauty in
This flesh from which, without a model, woman's body was
   fashioned?   /16

My freedom I hold dear, and do not care to lose
And to lie dead I would sooner choose
Than to trap you in my love's noose.   /21

Though a lady on another may take pity
Mayhap she treats herself most cruelly
Sweetness, friendship, courtesy
Are virtues of the woman of nobility
And the true dwelling of sympathy
Is in the heart of a fair lady.   /19

I love my body—do you ask why?
Because in my eyes 'tis fine and comely.   /18[1]

What is like a fine-wrought jewel
Fashioned by a master craftsman's hand
And finished perfectly?
The outline formed
By your twin curving thighs
With their lovely convexities.

What is like a perfect cup, pray tell me
Overflowing with a sweet liqueur
Made from a subtle recipe?—
Your tiny navel.

And your belly, as is meet
Is like a little mount of wheat
Bordered with lilies resplendent
Giving forth most fragrant scent.

And the nipples of your breasts
Mindful of a wild doe
Are like unto a pair of twins
So splendid is their burnished glow.   /24

[1] Lines spoken by the "woman of the world" in the comedy by Marguerite de Navarre performed on Shrove Tuesday of the year 1547.

Men are prepared to go to any lengths to have a woman; hence it is necessary for woman to be on her guard at all times; her "honor" becomes a cult: it must be defended, safeguarded against the man's dangerous onslaughts. The introjection of this idea of the woman's "honor," which originates in a fear that is social in nature, gradually gives rise to a new and powerful sentiment: modesty

"Kill? Would you have a lover be a murderer then?"

"Were I to find myself in such a situation, Hircan replied forthwith, "I should consider myself dishonored if I did not attain my goal."   /18

> By such honeyed words who would not be deceived?
> Bold, importunate, disturbing, daring—a flood unrelieved:
> That is how a pretty maid, one among a hundred others
> Allows the finest of her fruits to be gathered
> By being duped and ravished, rather than
> Truly moved by amorous affection.   /16

When one is dealing with a clear-thinking woman, whom one is unable to deceive, and so good that one cannot win her over either with sweet words or gifts, is that not sufficient reason to seek to gain a victory over her by every other possible means?   /18[2]

> From what I'm told, it would appear
> That once a man has found a love martyr
> He must himself pretend consuming passion
> Feign sleepless nights, pace restlessly by day
> Cast adoring secret looks the lady's way
> Think only of the goal, pursued in ruthless fashion
> Feign to love no other . . .

> Invent, compose, write out love-sonnets by the score
> To prove she is the one he cares truly for,
> Cast wary glances all about, as does the savage wolf,
> At times assume the mask of blissful happiness
> At others show naught but a face in tears engulfed,
> Post servants. Have a thousand stormy arguments.   /16

[2] The speaker is a man.

Men freely yield to love, considering themselves not to be worthy of blame in so doing, for among their sex this is not taken to be a vice, but on the contrary they are vainglorious and boast of it when, through their deceptions, pretenses, and adulations, they get the better of your sex, which is too credulous and too eager to lend an ear.   /20

And as I might have supposed from evident signs, he divulged and bruited about the secret of our love. I learned of this for certain from one of my maidservants, who had overheard him in conversation, speaking in this wise to one of his companions: "The lady in question is madly enamored of me. You can see the seductive look in her eye. I presume that by continuing to pursue her, I shall easily have my way with her."

I remained long lost in thought, and then raising my eyes I looked at my friend reproachfully, and said to myself: "Alas, Fortune, thou art bitter, adverse, hard, and cruel to me! I now know that all was but simulation and pretense on the part of him who I believed loved me with all his heart, but alas, his sole aim is to rob me of my honor in order to tell his friends and laugh of it at my expense. But though I now see him at his true worth, my heart belongs so wholly to him that it is not within my power to take it back from him. But henceforward, I shall not allow my eyes to stray in his direction, at least in public, for it is easy to cast aspersions on a person's reputation, in particular that of gentlewomen, when they are not modest, as befits their highly respectable station." Having so decided, I retired to my apartments and spent the entire day alone. That night, as I lay in bed at my spouse's side, my mind was in a whirl as I began to conceive of various new fancies, which caused me such grievous pain that I was unable to sleep.   /20

When you hear tell that a man has taken a woman by force, you may be certain that the woman has made him despair of attaining his goal by any other means. And do not esteem the less the man who has put his life in danger in order to pave the way for his love!   /18[3]

Good heavens, said Oysille, shall we never hear the end of these troublesome gray friars?—It seems to me, sage Parlemente said, that a woman abed ought never to allow a man of the cloth to enter her chamber, save to administer the last rites of the Church; and if I should chance to summon one, you may be certain that I am on my deathbed!   /18

[3] The speaker is, naturally, a man.

I wish to call to your mind and urge you to follow the example of ladies who risked death rather than compromise their chastity. Among others, you should be mindful of Penelope's continence. . . . and the pudicity of the Roman matron Lucretia ought not to be forgotten, she who had no wish to live following the intimate congress forced upon her. I find a great contrast and difference between your resolve and that of this noble lady, who prized her honor more than her life; whereas you, more willful than wise, stubbornly follow the dictates of your sensuality, and would sooner give up your life than fail to satisfy your voluptuous desires and your unruly appetites, without regard for the offense you give to God and to your spouse.   /20

I am not so foolish, milord, or so blind as not to see and appreciate the beauty and the grace that God has given you, and not to hold the woman who will possess the body and the love of such a prince the most fortunate woman in the world. But what is all that to me since it is not meant for me or any other woman of my humble condition, and desiring it would be the sheerest folly on my part? What reason can I find for your addressing yourself to me save that the ladies of your household are so virtuous that you dare not ask, or hope to obtain from them, what the lowliness of my estate causes you to hope to obtain from me? And I am certain that should you have what you ask from persons such as myself, it would be simply a means of entertaining your mistress for the space of two hours more, telling her of your victories over those weaker than yourself. . . . It is not a lack of love that causes me to flee your presence, but rather having too much of it to sit easily upon your conscience and my own, for I hold my honor dearer than my life.   /18

Alas, I tried my best to resist, endeavoring to chase love from my heart, for that night as I lay in bed at my spouse's side distinct thoughts came to me of the great friendship that I had always felt for him, and I remembered that heretofore my reputation had been blameless, with not a single blot upon my honor. "How can you wish to take the bad, disgusting, fetid downward path, straying from the beautiful upward one? . . . O my poor lady, would you choose illicit, lustful love rather than married love, which is chaste and modest?   /20

The prison of marriage, the fear of one's husband, the distaste for one's
spouse, the horror, stronger than ever, of being wedded against one's
will to an elderly man

As he thus reproached me, my spouse drew closer to me in order to take
the pleasure of Venus with me, but with great haste I moved far
away from him and spoke these words to him: "My friend, I beseech
you to allow me to take my rest, for because of the sadness and anguish
that continually burden my heart, I have a weakness in all my members
such that I have no further hope of living out my days save in languor
and infirmity." And so saying, I sat down upon my bed, feigning having
been stricken with some grave malady.   /20

And so saying, my spouse took the letters that I had left upon my
bed because fear had clouded the clarity of my mind; and when he had
read them his fury waxed yet more intense, and in great indignation he
drew closer to me and gave me so hard a blow on the face that it threw
me violently to the floor, from which I found myself suddenly unable
to rise.   /20

The moment that I arrived, I was shut up in the largest tower and
locked in, accompanied only by two chambermaids, one of them far advanced in years, who was sent for by my spouse because she had been in
his service ever since I had been married and he had found her a most
faithful domestic.   /20

He led him into his house, where he lodged and feted him most
fittingly. It being the supper hour, the gentleman led him into a hall
hung with a handsome tapestry, and when the meat was brought to
table, he saw a woman come out from behind the tapestry, the most
beautiful creature imaginable. But her head was shaved completely
bare, and she was dressed all in black, in the German fashion. After the
gentleman had rinsed his hands with the aforementioned Bernage, the
water was brought to this lady, who washed her hands and went to sit
at the end of the table, speaking to no one, and no one speaking to her.
After she had eaten a bit, she asked for something to drink, and it was
brought to her by one of the household servants, in a vessel that was
most passing strange: the skull of a dead man, with the holes stopped

with silver. And the young lady drank from it two or three times. After she had supped and rinsed her hands, she bowed to the lord of the manor, and retired behind the tapestry, without so much as a word to anyone.

"I can see that you are surprised by what you have seen here at this table. That lady is my wife, whom I loved more than ever a man shall love his spouse, to such a point that in order to wed her I threw caution to the winds and brought her here despite the wishes of her parents. . . . But in the course of a journey that out of honor I was obliged to undertake, she so forgot her own honor, her conscience, and the love she bore me that she became enamored of a gentleman to whom I had offered hospitality here in this house. . . .

"The love that I bore her was thus turned to rage and despair, and hence I watched her so closely that one day, concealing myself in the chamber where she now dwells, I saw this gentleman enter, at her invitation, thus enjoying an intimacy that I alone have the right to share with her. And when I saw that it was his intention to climb into the bed beside her, I leaped out, tore him from her arms, and killed him on the spot.

"And since my wife's crime appeared to me to be so monstrous that a similar death was not sufficient punishment, I locked her up in that chamber to which she was in the habit of retiring to take her keenest pleasure, in the company of that gentleman whom she loved, to her sorrow, far more than me. I put all the bones of her friend in a wardrobe, hung up like precious garments in a closet. And in order that she not forget his memory as she eats and drinks, I have her served at table before me from the skull of this villain in place of a goblet, in order that she may see alive him whom she made her mortal enemy through her misdeed, and see dead him whose friendship she preferred to mine. She hence sees at dinner and at supper two things that must most displease her: her enemy alive and her friend dead, and all through her own grievous fault. For the rest, I treat her as I treat myself, save that she goes about with her head shaved, for the ornament of hair does not befit the adultress, as the veil does not befit the woman without shame. If it please you to see her, I shall take you to her." /18

The heinous duke, not content to see his enemy dead, the dignity of his handsome golden hair stained and sullied by the blood mingled with gunpowder, proceeded to slit his belly and remove his heart, which he then carried off with him. He thereupon ordered it to be boiled in the soup and served to his wife. When she had eaten, he asked: "What say you of this meat? Is it tasty?" "In my opinion, milord, it is indeed most tasty," she replied. "It is the heart of your friend Gullain," the duke said. Upon these words the lady was overcome with such pain that she resembled a babe in arms as the tears began to flow, and then she burst into bitter lamentations: "You have just now made me eat such delicious meat that I shall never taste any more savory!" Whereupon she clutched her heart and fell to the floor.   /21

Since I see that your iniquities are inveterate, I must proceed immediately to remedy the situation by obliging you to absent yourself from this house, for it would be impossible to guard against that vulpine female craftiness of yours. I see that at present your heart is disposed to love, and I am certain that you are being sought after by more than one gallant. . . . I must bend you to my will. For perhaps your gestures and your lustful demeanor will one day constrain me to wreak my vengeance upon you, without its being in my power to contain my wrath. Prepare hence to leave, and I shall arrange for your departure.   /20

She was married to the aforementioned Pyralius, a brutish man not fit enough to serve a lady such as Rosemonde in the delightful tournaments and jousts of love, his natural heat having waned as a consequence of long illnesses and finally died out altogether due to his advanced age. . . . He resembled not so much a man as some sort of monster, for he had a huge heavy head, bristling with coarse, rough hair now old and gray, a brow furrowed with wrinkles, thick bushy eyebrows, rheumy cheeks gaunt and drawn, a nose so long it almost touched his chin, a very short fat neck perched atop miserably hunched shoulders. . . . His color was habitually pale and pasty, as though stinking Harpies had breathed upon his face. From his belly there issued a fetid breath, through a putrid, black, sunken mouth.   /21

The old man merely kisses her and it is as though a slug had dragged itself across her charming face. Neither her seductive gestures nor the potions brewed to warm his vitals that she had him drink were of any avail. . . . Her every hope was thwarted, for despite all her arts she was never able to excite his prostrated members that extreme old age had numbed and drained of vigor.   /20

> Marriage of the ill-matched here will faulted be
> For there is ample reason why I must
> If the fruit it bears so tastes of gall
> That pleasure, through the spouses' disparity
> Soon turns to sheer disgust.   /21

The moment they come home, they bar the door, close the windows, eat most untidily and without company, and sleep hunched over like a chicken. And in bed they wear great nightcaps two fingers thick, a nightshirt held together with rusty pins down past their navels, heavy wool stockings that come halfway up their thighs, and as they rest their heads on a warmed pillow that smells of melted grease, their sleep is accompanied by coughs and emissions of excrements that fill the bedcovers. In the morning they arise sluggishly. . . . Skullcaps and great bonnets covering their unkempt hair: creatures duller and more insipid to the eye than the flavor of soup without salt to the tongue. What think you? If all men were such as thus, would there not be scant pleasure in cohabiting with them?   /17

In this pagan century which takes up arms over theological questions, women as yet feel no need to conceal their sensuality, their love of a man's body, their passion

But my awaiting
Is desire for him
To be all his
As he will be all mine.   /14

O accursed woman, you have always denied me that which there are evident signs that I might have enjoyed had I not lost all reason. I am certain your friend has been bringing a number of musicians here with him to revive your spirits and lead you into temptation and bend you to his nefarious will. But if he knew your heart as intimately as I, he would not suffer such pangs of anxiety. For your unrestrained lust assuredly has the power to cause you to be the one to lead the way and rouse his passion, and seeing the ways in which you comport yourself, were he expert in love he would have been well aware of the great ardor that continually holds you in its sway. Your venereal appetites have poisoned your heart, you are so led astray by love of him that your entire behavior, all your manners, gestures, and desires, your most modest and upright conduct have become the very opposite of what they once were, but you may rest assured that I shall no longer tolerate this, for your dissolute life causes me such anguish and suffering that I shall be constrained to use cruelty and ignominy against your person.   /20

He chanced to pass by so close to me that he stepped upon my white satin skirt. I was most meticulous about my dress, it was a thing that gave me singular pleasure, but nonetheless his action did not displease me; on the contrary, I would willingly and gladly have kissed the place his foot had touched. /20

Promptly breaking and failing to keep my promise, I looked at him most affectionately, despite the fact that I had not forgotten in the slightest the griefs and torments that I had suffered at my husband's hands because of him: but I was like a woman heavy with child who is afflicted with grave and excessive pains before the birth of the infant, yet forgets them the moment she lays eyes on the fruit of her womb, such is her joy and happiness; in like manner the intrinsic sweetness and gentleness that I felt well up within me as I looked with delight upon my friend made me forget all my past pain and anguish. /20

> Do you complain? I'll heal the hurt
> By giving you ten others, soft and sweet
> Thus mingling our kisses full of happiness
> Let us enjoy each other at our ease.
>
> I am unhappy leading the discreet life
> And cannot find what pleases me
> Unless I go outside myself. /17

> What height maketh a man venerable?
> What size? What hair? What complexion?
> Who has the most charming pair of eyes?
> Who soonest makes the wound that will not heal? . . .
>
> But I know well and for a certainty
> That no matter what beauty one elects
> And despite all art in Nature's aid
> No one my desire could increase. /17

> When you see me ever one
> Suffering for you, hiding her pain
> Allowing myself to be consumed by it,
> Should you not love me?

When you see that I'm less fair than you
I find no reason to quarrel with you
And wish only to claim you for my own,
Should you not love me?

When for some other new love
I shall never treat you cruelly
And give voice to no complaint,
Should you not love me?   /14

Upon these words he commenced to look at me as though dum-
founded, taking pause to ponder, as I later came to realize, how the im-
petuosity of love had burst the bonds of temperance and moderation
within me, causing me to exceed the very limits of feminine audacity. . . . After uttering these words he took his leave of me, and I accompanied him to the door with eyes gleaming with amorous desire, for
I was burning with venereal fire, and love was waxing so powerful in
my heart that what I might say of it would be incredible to those who
have not experienced such a thing.

My sweet friend, I know for certain fact that it is not within your
power to forswear love, since from the beginning you have failed to
resist it, and indeed have nourished the lustful love in your bosom by
long and continual thoughts and willingly yielded to your sensuality,
whereby the power of your love has constantly augmented, to the point
that you would now choose rather to lose your life than to lose your
friend. But you ought to consider that were your soul to be separated
from your miserable body, a sad abode would be assigned it for all eternity in view of the enormous and execrable sin you would have committed by becoming the murderer of your own self.   /20

Alas! the thoughts and regrets that torture and torment me are not
pain I rightfully deserve as punishment for my heinous sins: they are
occasioned by the countless desires and amorous temptations of which I
am a victim, and it is impossible for me to resist them, for I am so passionately in love that I would far rather be deprived of my life than of
the sight of my friend. . . . O woe is me! What prayer might I address
to God to keep me from loving? For you may be certain that I would
be unable to constrain my heart to forswear love. Although I have
suffered inestimable pain and anguish, there has been a certain
sweetness, if only at the sight of him. If I am pale, one look from my
friend can bring a blush to my cheeks; if I am sad, he can raise my
spirits; if I am weak, he can fortify me.   /20

When I pondered the inconstancy of my friend, it brought me inestimable pain. Yet even though I knew him to be villainous and wicked, it was not within my power to love him the less; love was so deeply engraved upon my heart that every moment of the day and night my melancholy memory conjured up the image of him. And so it happened that the following night, having gone to bed at my husband's side, feeling weary and comfortably warm beneath the coverlet . . . I felt such drowsiness steal over me that finally I gave in to it and fell fast asleep. And I must confess that my slumber was far more pleasant than lying there awake, for I dreamed that I was with my friend in a lovely and delightful garden, and openly holding his hands, without the least fear. . . . Hearing his sweet and honeyed words, it seemed to me that his voice often broke off in order to kiss and embrace. But alas! what pain was mine! For in order to settle an affair of great importance, my husband awakened me, thus leaving me in a most melancholy state.

I was most eager for it to be night again, in order that while sleeping I might be granted that pleasure of which I was deprived whilst awake. But never again was I able to enjoy delight. On the contrary, a number of times I seemed in my dreams to see my friend in a frightful state, so pale and wan that it horrified me to see him, so that as a consequence on several occasions I cried out in a loud voice and my husband awakened and inquired as to the reason for my fear and alarm. . . . In such travail of spirit I arose, sought out augurers, diviners, soothsayers, and fortunetellers in order that they might interpret my dreams and tell me their true meaning.   /20

If in holding him in my arms
As the oak is circled with ivy
Death came, envious of my pleasure

And he then kissed me more sweetly still
And my spirit took flight on his lips
I would die happy to have lost my life.   /17

I endure my pain in the sun's light
And when I am almost broken on the rack
And take to my bed in weariness
I must cry in my pain the whole night through.   /17

I live by and for you as for myself
I live by and for me as for yourself:
We shall have but one life and one death.
I desire not your death, but mine own
But my death is your death and my life yours
Thus I wish to die, and yet do not so wish.   /22

This is your belief, my dear heart, you have confessed as much to me in your last letter. But you may rest assured that your pleasure in so believing is less great than that which I receive thereby, deeming as I do that my perfection depends upon the perfection of my love. Not that I thereby share the opinion of Plato, who considers the lover to be filled with a divine fury and more excellent than the beloved. For being both the one and the other, I shall always give each of these two qualities their rightful due, while still preferring the cause to the effect. And it is our beauties that have engendered our loves, which in an endless circle will pursue their immortal round, for the essence of their cause is likewise immortal.   /22

Thus filled with this divine rather than vulgar passion, I lavish in my imagination a thousand kisses on your handsome mouth, which shall be the sole participant in the pleasure reserved for the soul, this being its just reward for serving as the instrument of so much eloquent and lofty praise, which I hope may soon delight me again. Farewell my everything, my life, and my sovereign good.   /22

As the heavens revolve and are in perpetual movement round about a motionless point, my thoughts, my desires, my affections, governed by this great daimon, revolve and move continually round about the idea of you, the principle and end of all my intentions. Corporeal actions may be impeded, but the spirit can neither be turned away nor diverted from that for which it conceives an affection. Be my love then, since love there is in this world. Be my only pleasure, my only angel, and my only life.   /22

I went to sleep last night to the music of the ballet, with my chamber full of all the gallants of the Court. Such diversion, which would gravely disturb any other passion, had on mine for you no more effect than the waves of the sea beating upon an immutable rock. It merely caused me to awaken earlier than usual, marveling at my great good fortune. . . . And so it is, from everything that I see, with my spirit bent upon but a single goal, I extract only that which is apt to feed my fire that I cherish and preserve as the true vigor and the very life of my life. Farewell, my beautiful sun.   /22

O laughter, O forehead, hair, arms, hands, and fingers!
O plaintive lute, viola, bow, and voices!
So many torches to set a woman on fire!   /17

You alone are my evil and my good
With you I have everything—without you nothing.   /17

The idea of love as the work of destiny; a fatal and ineluctable power contrary to reason and one's best interests; all efforts to resist it are of no avail: romanticism

In order to take his pleasure with Bath-sheba, David committed murder. In matters of the heart, wise Solomon was guilty of idolatry. Aristotle, the prince of natural philosophy, was smitten with a blind love for his adored friend Hermias. . . . I pray you to reflect on the fact that since love had such great power over our forebears, it cannot help but hold sway over their descendants. Would it not hence be a great folly on my part to consider that I had triumphed over love, when men have never been capable of holding out against it? And hence, putting all fear behind me, I must yield to the same desire as in my youth, or die.   /20

Other than we, despite their high station
Have endured love's pains
Their proud hearts, their beauty, their lineage
Have not preserved them from being slave
To cruel love. The noblest spirits
Are but the sooner and more strongly in its grasp.   /17

For even though he who is the possessor of my heart is not my equal in nobility or wealth or opulence or worldly possessions, he is sublime in my eyes whilst I am lowly and mean. Love is nothing save a forsaking of reason, which is best avoided by the prudent person, for it warps the judgment, and likewise it is the downfall of lofty and generous spirits. It saps one's every power; it makes a person melancholy, wrathful, prodigal, rash, arrogant, quarrelsome, mindful neither of God, the world, nor himself. . . . Alas! I speak of it not as one who is ignorant, but as one who has experienced everything, and nothing new awaits me save death. But despite my being intimately acquainted with all such trials and torments, I cannot resist it, for my mind, my reason, and my free will have been surprised, conquered, and enslaved by that which, from the beginning, I surrendered to, offering scant resistance, and an easy thing it is to vanquish one who will not do battle.   /20

Alas! Why did I see him this day
When his eyes were to set my soul on fire
So then, Love, must our happiness
Be turned to despair by your burning flame?
If I had known his fatal power
How soon would I have fled from him!
Alas, what do I say? If that sweet day
When first I saw him should again appear
I would fly to him, swift as any bird!   /17

Do not reproach me, Ladies, if I have loved
If I have felt a thousand torches' flames
A thousand labors, a thousand gnawing pains
If I have spent my days in love-laments. . . .
But conclude that love at a certain point
Without excusing your ardor of a Vulcan
Without possessing the beauty of Adonis
Can, if it wishes, make you still more amorous.   /17

Masques, tourneys, games to me are wearisome
Without you nothing doth seem good
As I endeavor to extinguish this desire
And set before my eyes a new object
And distract myself from thoughts of love
I wander in the loneliest forest
But perceive the thousandth time around
That if I wish to be free of you
I must live outside of my own self.   /17

Meanwhile, I one day saw my friend walking down the middle of the street. I was taken with the desire to inquire about his estate and manner of living, which were revealed to me. He was of lowly condition, which made me sore aggrieved. Yet the great fury of the love that possessed me and ruled me so clouded my mind and so deprived me of my powers of reason that even though this greatly vexed me, my love did not diminish.   /20

Not that I wish to deprive of freedom
Him who was born to be master over me.   /14

If I love him whom I should hate
And hate him whom I should love
One should not be surprised
Or blame me in any wise.   /14

Reason was never the mistress of love. . . .
For love lives on pleasure and distress.   /18

But Love could no longer stand to see
My heart, loving but Mars[4] and learning.
Wishing to give me other cares
Smiling it said to me:
So you think, milady of Lyon
That you can thus escape my flame
You shall not do so. . . .
Let us see if you persist
And flout my will by following him. . . .

The breach made, Love enters the place
Banishing from it all repose.
Giving me endless travail
Keeping me from drinking, eating, sleeping
Neither sun nor shadow falling to my lot:
I have only love and fiery courage
That distinguishes me and makes me appear different
Till I do not even recognize myself.

[4] She has just recounted her war exploits, when as a woman warrior she took part in the siege of Perpignan.

I was but sixteen winters old
When these diverse cares overburdened me:
And now it has been thirteen summers
Since love stopped my heart. . . .

But alas! it seems to grow in me
With time, tormenting me the more. . . .

If you wish me to love to the end
Make him whom I esteem to be my all
Who alone can make me weep and laugh
For whom I so often sigh
Feel in his bones, blood, and soul
An ardent or an equal flame
Your burden on me then will ease
When there is someone sharing it with me.   /17

And Folly will guide blind Love, leading it where it pleases.   /17

Love and social status; a queen to her favorite; a favorite to her king

"I should like to inform you that a true lover must ever be impatient, burning with desire to see his beloved, and not await a message, a summons, a set hour for a rendezvous, as you do. . . . But let us put an end to such argument: You look too splendid today for us to quarrel. By my faith! how handsome your Roman collar looks on you!"

"You're taking all the curl out of my hair in back and spoiling it!"

"It will but look the better the whole day through because my lovely hands have stroked it."

"You look like fair Venus to me."

"And you look to me like her little Adonis, assuredly far more spoiled and self-indulgent than he, though far less amorous. What is the real truth of the matter? Am I to believe that you love me and that your demonstrations of affection are out of love for me, or are they out of love for yourself? For young men these days are most circumspect in their designs and tendor philapthy has great power over their souls."

"And what is philapthy?"[5]

"Viands that never appear on the table in your part of the world. Ask those silly little idiots of whom you're so fond. But my little treasure, when I look at you I find you most preciously dressed! You must wear long hose, a ruff, a sword, a plume, and speak out if you wish to appear a man."

"It seems to me that I've a man's size and stature."

"You fancy that you resemble a grown man, and no one claims the contrary. But the many occasions which you say not a word, which is the greater part of the time, you will see how little difference there is between you and a statue."

"I see others who never say a single word."

"It is also true that one sees many birds and few parrots. The more a thing is rare, the more it is desired, and what is more, in this respect I for my part resemble weasels and doves, and like them find great pleasure in making love with my mouth."

"Not always."

"That is because I wish to satisfy your bestial desires, and offer your body that certain something of which it has need. For my natural inclination leads only to those little pleasures offered by the eye and the spoken word, which are incomparably more delicious and sweeter than that other pleasure that we have in common with stupid beasts."

"I take great pleasure in playing the stupid beast. . . . I love the body far more than the spirit."

"Yet the spirit is far more worthy of love. Have I not bade you to speak often enough? Is it an excess of love that causes you to be tongue-tied and occupies your senses, so that what another less amorous than you would employ to speak out, you employ in desiring?"

"That is the pure and simple truth of the matter. . . ."

I must avow that I now see no disadvantage in deeming you a beast, confessing that I am in the wrong to make you speak, since you have many more charms if you are silent. You must now employ your mouth for another use, and take a certain pleasure in so doing. Reserve your fine language for your mistresses, and silence for me. And whilst my alcove remains empty of tiresome visitors who will soon interrupt my pleasures, I wish to have some satisfaction from this mute creature who answers not a word. . . . Come hither, my treasure, for you please me more close at hand than at a distance. And since you are more suited to satisfy my taste than my ear, let us seek from an infinite number of various kisses the one that will be the most savory to prolong. Oh, how sweet and how well seasoned to my taste they now are! They fill me

[5] Philapthy: love of self.

with ecstasy and there is not the slightest part of me that does not participate in them, and into which some spark of lively sensual pleasure does not steal.

I could die of rapture! I am moved to the very heart of me, and blush to the roots of my very hair! Oh, you have done far more than was asked of you and anyone at the door will learn of it! Well then, you are now in your proper element and appear to be much more at your ease there than in the pulpit. Ah! I am panting and cannot catch my breath! With all due deference to the powers of speech, I must avow that however fair words may be, this frolicsome sport surpasses it. There would be nothing sweeter, were it not so brief. /22

For my felicity depends more upon you than upon the power of destiny, to which I shall not attribute the cause of my suffering, since it is your will that such be the price of the publick wishes of France for your marriage. A suffering, in truth, that I am constrained to avow, not because you must fulfill the wishes of your subjects, but because your wedding feast is the funeral ceremony for my life, and because it subjects me to the power of a cruel discretion that is about to banish me from your royal presence as well as from your heart, in order henceforth not to be offended by the disdainful glances of those ladies and gentlemen who have seen me enjoying your good graces, preferring as I do to suffer in freedom in my solitude rather than breathing fearfully amid the great press of highborn company. It is a disposition of my spirits that your generosity has sustained, and a courage that you have inspired in me, which taught me not to bow to misfortunes or yield to them, does not allow me to return to my former condition.

I herewith speak to you only in sighs, my king, my lover, my everything. For as to my other secret griefs, Your Majesty may hear the dimmest echo of them in my mind, since you know my soul as well as you know my body. . . . If it be the habit of kings to keep the memory of what they have loved, I pray you remember, Sire, a young girl whom you possessed, and one who (a thing which only your sworn word allowed her to believe) held her honor as much in her power alone as Your Majesty holds life in his.

Sire, from your humble servant, a creature your subject, and I shall add, your forgotten beloved. /23

Your royal majesty has still less power in this respect: for Love is pleased at equal things. . . . Hence when you wish to be loved, descend below, leave your crown and your scepter here, and do not say who you are. Then you will see, in serving and loving some Lady well, that she will willingly love you without regard for your wealth and power. Then you will feel a quite different satisfaction from those that you have had in the past: and instead of a single pleasure you will receive a double one. For there is as much pleasure in being kissed and loved as in kissing and loving.   /17

"You have expected of me things as impossible as those I
expected of you."

Madame de La Fayette

·IV·

SEVENTEENTH CENTURY

The Baroque Century of Classicism

Women now write their myths, so teeming with symbols that if a psychoanalyst were to embark upon classic (and reductive) Freudian analysis of them, he might well die of exhaustion before finishing his labors. These women had little knowledge of grammar and none at all of spelling, but at the same time they are capable of inventing a steady stream of emblems and signs: palaces and grottoes, lovers and torturers, nets that paralyze the victims caught in them, scaffoldings towering upward, dwarfs, giants, miraculous pregnancies and children named Miracle, as well as offspring that are monsters, toads, pug dogs, serpents, or green fish, fathered upon them against their will by frightful elderly sorcerers. They are thereupon consoled by birds that kiss them with their beaks and speak eloquently of love, by rose trees that bow to them and break into speech, by soft waves that lap against them and tenderly lick them in endless delight. Tortures and pleasures intermingle, undergoing unexpected metamorphoses against backgrounds even more schizophrenic than Hieronymos Bosch's most boldly telescoped scenes, but these landscapes are curiously, richly studded with minerals: emeralds, turquoises, and pearls hang from the trees, spurt from lovers' eyes, as walls made of diamonds are vainly scratched at by the fingernails of the helpless female captives trapped within them.

Fairy tales are the very essence of feminine love in this century. The majority of these tales, and the strangest and least well known of them, were written by women. A number of the stories collected in Charles Perrault's Mother Goose tales were in reality simply adaptations of these stories by women. Ladies of quality and a number of middle-class women invent fabulous tales that bear little resemblance to the peasant tales told by grandmothers that we find in the folk tradition. Delirious, baroque fantasies, impossible to cite from in an anthology because their rich symbolism defies excerpting, these tales remain an almost completely unexplored continent, the garden of the feminine erotic imagination.

How little the symbolism of this baroque seventeenth century resembles the "classic" imagery we remember from our schoolbooks! We find ourselves confronted with a "powerful diversity"[1] that cannot be reduced to the overrefined perspectives of the grand staircases of Versailles, or to the confines of the famous "three unities" of time, place, and action that ruled over the classical tragedies of this century.

During the Regency, before Louis XIV came of age and ascended the throne, a rebellion of the nobility, "La Fronde," takes place, led by great ladies of the realm. A dangerous, turbulent, grandiloquent spirit of revolt rages through the land until the Crown successfully quells the uprising. Poverty and misery are also abroad each winter as the grain supplies give out in rural areas overrun with bands of marauding soldiers. Crude, ungracious women deal highhandedly with their servants, who are sometimes their lovers, stride through their households with their great bunches of keys clanking, keep a sharp eye on the pantries and cupboards, spin and weave, do the household accounts, cure hams and bacon, delight Molière with their talents, "so long as they are kept within bounds," as Fénelon put it in his treatise on the education of young girls. But despite the fact that Guez de Balzac exclaims in one of his famous letters: "By my faith! If I were the head of police, I would ship off all women who write books, make a travesty of wit, and desert their rank in the world," the fact remains that the star, the woman called the "marvel of the century" or "the *prima donna* without peer in this world," the woman who enjoyed the most glorious reputation of any in her day, was not a raving beauty but a downright ugly spinster who lived with her long-tailed pet monkey, her parakeet (to whom Leibniz wrote verses in Latin), and three chameleons from Egypt. Madeleine de Scudéry, known to her contemporaries as "the incomparable Sapho," wrote endless novels "policing" society after her own fashion, celebrating "glory," delicacy of speech, and the delights of fervent but asexual love. At the same time, however, the good friend of this prudent prude, Ninon de Lenclos, is as highly sexed and sensual as one could wish, a collector of lovers, a selfless, cultivated woman and a

[1] Émile Henriot.

libertine, no more afraid of the "poppycock" she considered necessary to converse with males than she was of the boldness required to be a religious unbeliever, proclaiming that love "is a taste based on the senses, a blind sentiment, which in no way presupposes any merit in the object that gives rise to it, and in no way binds the latter to feel gratitude."[2] And meanwhile at the abbey of Port-Royal amid solitude and a complete withdrawal from the world, the Jansenists, the "Puritans of Catholicism," invent an austere new prose style as they summon their contemporaries to renounce the world.

What an odd mixture, and what extremes we find in this century! Jansenism, quietism, and black masses all exert their attraction on women. Death, moreover, makes its presence felt everywhere, and morality takes the form of maxims. And as language is purged of its excesses and excrescences, elegant bad taste triumphs at Versailles, in dress as in interior decoration. Obeying men's wishes, women remain ignoramuses. Yet it is they who will give this shaky age (which out of cowardice nearly everyone wishes to be more stable than the preceding one, even at the price of absolutism) the outward appearance of harmony and refinement. For these women *fin amor* is a concept that has been totally forgotten, yet they nonetheless reconstruct the very same ideology of the emotion. It is through them that the man's path to worldly or mystical perfection must pass, for it is by remaining a "lover," that is to say, submissive, attentive, a devoted servant, a slave, that he will attain a higher state. Only by following this path does the male become a gentleman. The tales that women invent bear naïve witness to their belief in this feminine power over the "lower appetites": The Pig-Prince will lose his porcine fleshly envelope only when he falls truly in love with a princess and gives up baser loves.

Forcing nature in order to obtain more "subtlety," "decanting," "sublimating" (all of these alchemical terms suited their purposes), choosing what was most valuable and disdaining the rest—such was the essence of the women's movement known as the school of the "Précieuses." Feminist in intent, it is founded on the affirmation of the woman's powers and the pursuit of her freedom, in a game whose rules the "Précieuses" invent in order to keep men's coarseness in leading strings and deflect men's efforts to surpass themselves by way of religion or warfare by causing them to seek their perfection by way of tender, refined courtship of the beloved.

The "Précieuses" attempt to discipline the man's amorous inclinations through a psychological ritual that is at once rigid and tortuous. They invent "typical portraits" and "typical situations" and "itineraries" marked out according to the "geography" of love. In so doing, they give proof of the same pitiless ardor and imagination as the gar-

[2] Cited by Claude Dulong, *L'Amour au XVIIᵉ siècle.*

deners who laid out the formal plantings of this age. Admittedly, we are tempted to trample upon these overly neat flower beds, but we must stop short of dismissing these rigors as nothing more than insipid fantasy and pointless formality. Despite the "Carte du Tendre," an imaginary itinerary laid out by Mademoiselle de Scudéry for the Tender Lover to follow to win the affections of the Beloved (who for her part need do nothing), there is no tenderness whatsoever in this world of the "Précieuses." The master-slave dialectic has the force of law, and women seek only to turn it to their profit.

They have discovered that they can do so in the rarefied air of endless refusals and postponements of the lover's ultimate pleasure. They make a fashion, a rather gratuitous parlor game, of saying no, but at the same time they occasionally surpass themselves. Being neither willing nor able to renounce the passion that makes this entire fragile construction worthwhile, they sometimes find themselves cast up on deserted shores that they had not at all expected. One of them discovers religious ecstasy, another fainting spells, yet another death, and still another the less worldly rigors of religion.

The ideal lover, the one who brings gratification, is in the eyes of these "Précieuses" not the lover who brings the woman to climax, but rather the one who is ever-attentive to his beloved's needs and wishes—and the one who, above all, talks and talks to her, never tiring of so doing. Like the Bluebird the color of Time, who speaks of love for night after night, never tiring, never experiencing satiety, boredom, or flagging powers of imagination. . . .

The "Précieuses" are queens in a deck of cards: seen in profile, with big eyes, tiny little mouths and plump little hands, holding the mystic rose of recompense.

Their hair shirt is modesty, Modesty with a capital M, the absolute Queen, so completely introjected as to become inhibiting. Have they themselves not contributed a great deal to her enthronement? It is a question well worth pondering. Madame de Maintenon, the prudish mistress of Louis XIV who wishes to educate young ladies, gives the following advice with regard to the boarding schools in which they are to be housed: "Do not allow any man, be he rich or poor, young or old, priest or layman, or indeed even a saint, if there be such on this earth, to enter therein." And she finds women willing and eager to embark upon this enterprise with her!

But this tyrannical restraint called modesty, whether imposed by force or freely chosen by the woman, has none of the hypocrisy of the Victorian era. It still has the naïve vigor of a prideful show of strength that it began to acquire in the sixteenth century, and in this sense it makes the woman not shy and sweet and retiring, but harsh and demanding. It is also a necessary strategic weapon. The man's desire is all

the more keenly aroused if the woman refuses to give any sign of desire
on her part and instead devotes all her attention to showing off her
"charms." It is as though she deliberately sets out to be a trap, knowing
full well that she is simply the man's prey. And in point of fact, the
fate of the woman who is courted changes dramatically the moment
she gives her body to the man. We have forgotten today both the profound joy experienced by women in those days thanks to the flattering
gratification of their narcissism that "courting" represented, and the
panicked fear (one that had not the slightest tinge of remorse about it)
of "seeing ardor such as this change into icy coldness," and "these flattering and respectful attentions into scorn and mockery" after the satisfaction of the man's senses. Hence the penetrating conciseness of
Ninon de Lenclos's letter to the young man who asked her advice on
how to seduce a mistress. We must not be misled by the bantering tone
of the beginning of the letter, for the final words are tragic: "She puts
into your hands her life's happiness and makes you the arbiter of her
fate."

The fear of love is everywhere to be found. A purely intellectual fear
for what in this century women called their "glory," a fear forever incar-
nated in the story of the Princess of Cleves, but also the naked fear that
their pleasure will not be accompanied by emotional security. After
making her "lover" treasure her charms, even the greatest coquette risks
having them deemed no better than her sister's, or perhaps even more
banal, once she has been bedded. "Once the marquis had possessed this
beauty, it seemed to him that perhaps he would have found its equal in
a person who would better have served his purposes," Madame de
Villedieu says sadly.

Young women today hear it said, and are themselves inclined to believe, that mutual sexual satisfaction is the secret of happiness for a
couple, the guarantee that such happiness will be lasting, and a sign of
a more profound mutual harmony of the spirit. It is difficult for them
to conceive of an age when sexual enjoyment seemed to women to be
the beginning of the end, and pleasure the danger that threatened lasting happiness. Hence we have a tendency to make them the victims of
our worst suspicion: they were frigid. But this is to leap to conclusions.
Certain of them were undoubtedly frigid, just as some of their sisters
today are, even after undergoing a barrage of social conditioning whose
aim is to reassure them of their "right to orgasm." However, the majority of women in the seventeenth century were not frigid at all, but
rather, were terrified of paying the price for their physical enjoyment by
being thereby deprived of other intellectual, emotional, and sensual
joys. Possessed by a polarized, dichotomized idea of love, they were the
victims of a thousand terrors.

Those who accept their sexual appetites as the prime need to satisfy deliberately renounce loving affection and its gratifications, deliberately choose libertinism and say so openly. Neither jealousy nor fidelity enter the picture: "I for my part wish to love free of care and free of envy, free of fear and free of illusion"[3] or "I have told you a hundred times that pleasures are the only chains by which I would keep you prisoner. I wish to have a lover, not a slave."[4]

Women such as this view the possibility of taking a lover optimistically. They suffer no remorse, and very little censure in the eyes of others. Their one fear is of being made mock of in a lampoon or a ditty if they are known to have come out the loser in the affair. They sometimes swear their partners to secrecy, but just as often they openly boast of their love affairs: not because they are rebelling against the heavy hand of social reprobation, but because it is to their tactical advantage to do so. The woman of the seventeenth century must not be measured by the same yardstick as the rebellious or repressed women of the nineteenth century or the beginning of the twentieth.

What they do rebel against is the institution of marriage, however. Their hopes of independence and dignity find their expression in the hyper-refined gallantry, seasoned with the strictest decorum, of the "Précieuses"—though it is not accompanied by the slightest remorse as regards the forgotten husband. In the case of the "libertines," these hopes take the form of sensual gallantry—and they too have no scruples about deceiving their husbands, either in secret or openly. "Sent out on life's way without their consent," they have only scorn or hatred for marriage. The two women, moreover, who rule over society and best represent their century in the eyes of their contemporaries, Madeleine de Scudéry and Ninon de Lenclos, are both spinsters. No one would dare to call these two women "remaindered goods"! They express the aspirations of the others, the married women, and avenge them for the stifling bourgeois prison of marriage based on Roman law, of unions between an innocent virgin and a domineering spouse many years her senior, for bride prices which men, with magistrates and notaries leading the way, haggle endlessly over. Little by little men of the peasantry and the middle class are making their way up in life. Their view of women is practical, crude, utilitarian, and frequently sadistic. Possessed of common sense, power, and talent sometimes as well (Molière!), they resist the liberation of the woman that already has received the tacit approval of the world of literary salons and the nobility. These bourgeois have not yet arrived at the point of enhancing the joys of conjugal love and setting it up as an emotional and aesthetic value (as we shall see hap-

[3] Madame de Villedieu.
[4] Ninon de Lenclos.

pening in the eighteenth century). Hence marriage is ridiculed, scorned, hated by aristocrats, who see in it only a social necessity and a mere business affair.

Among the women, Catherine Meurdrac, born in the lower reaches of society and the wife of a soldier, is the only one of her century to defend the joys of married life, such as she herself has experienced. The smell of gunpowder on the field of combat plays a large role in her feelings for her husband, but so do caresses, and she expresses in no uncertain terms her disdain for those who do not have a strong physical love for their husbands, who are "all prim and proper [and] very much to be mistrusted." Between each military campaign, after each of their reunions, she finds herself "big with child" once again, and informs us in one concise phrase brimming with health that she thus bore her husband ten children, "all quite respectable." Her husband's love for her, which she describes as "most extraordinary," is expressed by shouts, threats, the violent acts of a naïve Caliban. She takes them in stride and rules his heart.

But what about the others—all the miserably toiling, joyless women who never wrote a single line? And their exact opposite, the prostitutes, the "strumpets," the "tarts," the Good-Hearted Marys and the Dirty-Ass Jeannes, the professionals who sold their charms to feed their bellies, continually in danger of being perverted by the noble lovers of the "Précieuses" who were not above going to the bordello, women in danger of being beaten, burned, marked up, disfigured by the procurers, panders, ponces, and pimps of the day? And the hundreds of thousands of chambermaids, often forced to remain spinsters by the masters and mistresses whose property they were ("I belong to Madame X," they say), "occasional" prostitutes who were manipulated by the footmen and used by one and all, seeking through cleverness and shrewdness, should they be fortunate enough to possess any, to make up for the wrongs that love had done them? Were they even aware of the definition of love of one of their contemporaries, the Duc de la Rochefoucauld: "In the soul, it is a passion to rule supreme; in the mind, it is a sympathy of feeling; and in the body it is but a tender, hidden desire to possess what one loves after many a mystery"?

Metamorphoses of courtly love: the "Précieuses" hold themselves in great esteem, and aspire both to polish the man's manners and to affirm their own dignity; the casuistry of these "Jansenists of love."

"So then you wish the man to love you without hope?" Cnydon retorted.

"I wish him to hope to be loved, but do not wish him to hope for anything further," Sapho replied.

"But would you be so kind as to tell me a little more precisely how you wish to be loved and what sort of love you expect?"

"I expect the man to love me passionately, to love only me, and to love me respectfully," she said. "I also wish this love to be a tender and sensitive one, capable of finding the greatest pleasure in the smallest things, to be as solid as friendship and be founded on esteem and affection. I wish this lover to be faithful and sincere; to share with no confidant or confidante the secret of his passion, and to lock so tightly within his heart all his feelings of love that I may pride myself on being the only one to know of them. I also wish him to tell me all his secrets, to share all my pains, to find all his felicity in my conversation and the sight of me, to be sorely aggrieved if I am absent, to tell me nothing at any time that might cause me to suspect his love of faltering, and to tell me always everything that is needful to persuade me that it is ardent and will long endure. And finally, my dear Cnydon, I wish to have a lover, without wishing to have a spouse. And I wish to have a lover who, content with possessing my heart, loves me till death do us part. And if I do not find one of this sort, I wish to have none at all."   /25

> With such qualities I would have esteemed him.
> But I would not love him had he not loved me.   /26

The last of the emblems was one of those tableaux made up of various separate, formless parts, which when viewed through an optical lens come into focus as a perfect whole composed of a number of imperfect parts. The general sense of this emblem was that there is nothing so imperceptible to our senses that science or art cannot make it perceptible. But the mystic sense was that the attentions, the glances, and the words that those who are indifferent take to be useless parts of love that bear no relation to each other trace the portrait of a most ardent passion when looked at through the eyes of a mistress.   /27

What! yield to love? What? be wanting in bravery?
Abandon my freedom for cruel slavery?
Fail to do battle, and hence see
A tyrant conquer my virtue in spite of me?
Oh no! Myself and my glory shall I ever defend
And my victory snatch from my conqueror's hand! . . .

There is respect in his love, and without self-abjection
I may give ear to his sighs, return his affection
He knows that virtue impresses my heart
Sees that my rigors will yield to his art
And patiently waits the day he can prove
How worthy he is of enjoying my love.   /28

There are persons to whom one dare give no other marks of passion than by way of things which do not concern them; and not daring to show them that one loves them, one would at least like them to see that one does not wish to be loved by anyone. One would like them to know that there is no beauty, of whatever rank it might be, that one would not look upon with indifference, and that there is no crown that one would seek to acquire at the price of never seeing them.

Women ordinarily judge of the passion that one has for them, she continued, by the care one takes to please them and to seek them out; but this is not a difficult thing providing that they are lovable; what is difficult is not yielding to the pleasure of keeping them company; avoiding them out of fear of allowing the sentiments that one has for them to appear in public, and perhaps to themselves as well. And what marks real attachment is to become entirely opposite from what one was, and to have no more ambition or pleasure after having devoted one's life to the one and the other.   /29

After that, madame, it is necessary, by your leave, to return to *New-Friendship* in order to see what path one must take from there to *Tenderness-by-Gratitude*. Take note, I pray you, how one must first make one's way from *New-Friendship* to *Complaisance*; and next to this little village called *Submissiveness*, hard by another most pleasing one known as *Little-Attentions*. Note, I beg you, that from there it is necessary to pass by way of *Assiduity*, thus proving that it is not enough to devote oneself for only a few days' time to all these courteous little attentions which give rise to so much gratitude, but rather, that one must do so assiduously. And then you see that one must proceed to another village, called *Eagerness*, and not be like certain indolent souls who cannot be hurried, no matter how one importunes them to press on, and who are incapable of this eagerness that at times so greatly obliges another.

As you see, it is thereupon necessary to proceed to *Great-Services*, and pray note that, to indicate that there are few who are capable of rendering them, this village is smaller than the others. One must next proceed to *Sensibility*, thus demonstrating that it is necessary to share even the slightest pains and sorrows of those whom one loves. And then, in order to reach *Tender*, one must pass by way of *Tenderness*, for friendship leads the way to greater friendship. One must thence go on to *Obedience*, since there is almost nothing that more obliges the heart of those whom one obeys than to do so blindly; and in order to arrive at last at one's destination, it is necessary to go on to *Faithful-Friendship*, which is beyond all doubt the surest way to reach *Tender-by-Gratitude*.

I am obliged to confess, however, that it is women who are to blame for men's lack of true courtesy; for if women knew how to take advantage of all the privileges of their sex, they would teach men to become truly courteous and would never allow them to lose the respect that is a woman's due. Indeed, they would refuse to permit a hundred discourteous familiarities that most untutored gallants seek to introduce into worldly society, for when all is said and done, there is a vast difference between formal courtesy and incivility, and if all gallant ladies properly understood the role that is theirs to play, their gallant lovers would be more respectful and more gracious, and consequently more pleasing. . . . Men would be more attentive, more submissive, and more respectful than they are, and women would in turn be less self-serving, less mean-spirited, less hypocritical, and less faint-hearted than we now see them to be. As a result, with everyone occupying his rightful place, that is to say, with mistresses behaving as mistresses and slaves as slaves, the world would soon be full once again of a multitude of pleasures. /25

[*The Pig-Prince, at times a man and at times a pig, sheds his swinish skin and becomes wholly a man only when he experiences a noble love for a noble lady.*]

The fairy saw that her Pig-Prince was unhappy.

The clever fairy, pursuing her own ends, gave him her permission to wed the Grisette[1] without the Queen's knowledge. His joy was boundless, and the following day he married her, with the fairies Charity and Tranquillity as witnesses, whereupon they led the newly wedded

---

[1] A working woman of easy virtue. (*Translator's note.*)

spouses to a chamber and saw the bride to bed. Then as soon as the prince had undressed they left the room. But to his great surprise, when he climbed into the bed he found therein not his newly wedded bride, but a life-size paper doll!

The same ceremonies were observed with a second Grisette, save that when he climbed into the bed he this time found therein not a doll, but a huge cat that immediately fled through the casement windows, breaking the glass. . . . The fairy came immediately to see what had happened, and found the prince in the bed, on the point of drowning in his tears. She spirited him away against his will, and when he had again taken on his swinish form, she brought him a draft of the waters of the River of Forgetfulness and made him drink.

[*The Pig-Prince finally experiences true love, for a true princess.*]

With no ado, the fairies led their majesties to their palace, where the prince and the princess were wedded in a simple ceremony, following which the bride was seen to her bed. The fairies hastened to the stable where the pig's skin had been left, tore it to shreds, and burned it in a fire of verbena, ferns, and herbs gathered before dawn. Then, having gathered the ashes therefrom together, they had them thrown by a dwarf into the frozen waters of the river Pactolus, which thereupon became as liquid as before.   /32

"No, my princess, the lover who addresses you is not capable of betraying you," he replied. And after uttering these words, he flew off through the window. Florine was terrified at first of such an extraordinary bird, who spoke with as great intelligence as would a man, though in a voice as faint as a nightingale's; but the beauty of his plumage and the words he uttered reassured her. "Have I your permission to see you again, my princess? Will it be granted unto me to know such perfect happiness without perishing of joy? Yet it is a joy, alas, marred by the thought of your captivity." . . . "Can it be possible that this little bird I hold in my hand is King Charming?" "Alas, beautiful Florine, it is only too true," he replied, "and my one consolation is that I preferred this pain to that of renouncing my passion for you. . . . And in the end I chose to be a Bluebird for seven long years rather than betray the fealty I vowed to you." Florine experienced a pleasure so intense at hearing the words of her gracious lover that she no longer remembered the sorrows caused her by her imprisonment. How many things she said to him to console him for the sad fate that had befallen him and persuade him that she would do no less for him than he had done for her! Dawn came, most of the officers had already risen from their beds, and still the Bluebird and the princess continued their sweet

conversation together. They took their leave of each other with a
thousand regrets, after having promised each other that they would
thus converse each night.

Two years went by thus, without Florine's ever once lamenting her
imprisonment. And what cause to lament would she have had? She had
the satisfaction of conversing all night long with the one she loved. So
many sweet words have never before been exchanged. Though she saw
no one and though the Bluebird spent the daylight hours in the hollow
trunk of a tree, they had a thousand new things to tell each other. The
material was inexhaustible, their hearts and minds provided abundant
subjects of conversation. . . . Bluebird, the color of time, Fly to me,
this moment! And immediately the Bluebird came, and the second
night went by like the one before, quietly and without incident, to our
lovers' great delight; they hoped that the woman who kept watch
would so enjoy her peaceful rest that she would sleep as soundly every
night. And indeed the third night was spent together as happily, but on
the following night the guardian, having been awakened by some sound
or other, heard their voices. Still half asleep, she looked, and in the
moonlight saw the most beautiful bird imaginable speaking to the princess, caressing her with his foot, gently kissing her with his beak. She
then heard part of their conversation, and was most surprised, for the
Bird's words were those of a lover.   /36

The fear of love, the condemnation of love

Love in its effects to fever is akin.
Fever sets the blood aflame
Brings on dreams, delirium, mad visions:
The God of Cythera does the same. . . .

Fever lays the spirit low
Drains away strength and appetite
Poisons the heart, occasions metamorphoses:
Love, though most trivial it may be
Does likewise, in excessive degree. . . .

The sole and single difference:
Fever gives us some respite,
Moments when the mind is free of it
While those whose brain by love is set awry
Lose all reason, irremediably.

And hence, my dearest Amaranthe
I should far rather afflicted be
By this raging fever that torments me so
Even should it wax more violent
Than feel the tenderest love's first fatal glow.   /30

Madame Paul, the widow of the gardener at Livry, has lost her head
and fallen head over heels in love with a great ninny twenty-five or
twenty-six years old whom she had hired to do the gardening. He has
made a really good match. The woman is about to marry him. He's a
brutish young fellow, quite mad; he will soon beat her, as he has already threatened to do.

It is of no great moment; she is quite willing to put up with it. I have
never seen such passion: all the most marvelously violent sentiments
imaginable enter into it. But they are laid on like thick paint: all the
colors are there, and they have only to be spread out. I was extremely
diverted by these love caprices, and I myself became frightened at such
attacks. What insolence! Attacking Madame Paul, that is to say, austere, old-fashioned, solid virtue! What is there to save us? But
master Paul's widow is outraged: there has been a hitch in her wedding plans. She weeps like a fountain. Her great simpleton of a lover
doesn't love her, he finds Marie, the daughter, very pretty, very sweet.
My dear, I tell you frankly, all that is worth nothing: I would have hidden it from you if I had wanted to be loved. What is happening here is
what goes to make up all novels, all comedies, all tragedies. . . . If you
were here, this gross original would vastly amuse you. As for me, I have
occupied myself with the matter and am taking Marie away, in order
for her not to cut the ground from under her mother's feet. These poor
mothers!   /31

Most mothers imagine that it suffices never to speak of gallantry in
the presence of young persons in order to keep them from it. Madame
de Chartres was of another opinion; she often painted pictures of love
for her daughter; she showed her what was pleasant about it in order
the more easily to teach her what is dangerous about it; she told her of
men's lack of sincerity, their capacity to deceive, and the infidelity, the

domestic cares in which one is plunged if one gives one's heart; and on the other hand she also persuaded her of how tranquil the life of an upright woman was, and how noble and brilliant a person was who had beauty and was highborn.   /29

Of the sad adventures of a hundred beauties we've been warned
The Kingdom of love is full of thorns.   /26

What means is there to love violently and to love with all the circumspection that the law of Christendom demands, and to love with pleasure when one is persuaded of the inconstancies and displeasures that must follow love? Could you decide to love a man, even though he had more merit than an angel, if you were certain that his ardors would change in no time to icy coldness, his tenderness into cruel indifference and horrible displeasures, his regard and respect into scorn and offensive mockery, and the fidelity that he had sworn was eternal, taking heaven and earth as his witness—if, I say, this fidelity changed into a horrible inconstancy, could you allow your heart to be taken in such conditions? . . . As delightful as is the possession of what one loves tenderly, in like measure privation of it is painful and unbearable; but if the involuntary privation that comes about when some accident takes away a beloved object is felt so strongly, what pain must there not be in losing this object that abandons us of its own accord, that scorns us and has only disgust for us? Certainly nothing is so cruel; but since there is almost no love that is not subject to this horrible defect and this extreme misfortune, I believe that the best course is to live without attachments.   /29

Modesty is "Queen"; those who have chosen to obey its law find it a tyrannical one

I feel that fear, modesty, and reason
Have united in my soul, conspiring to kill
But theirs is a vain effort, out of season:
How could I heed their counsel, when they wish you ill?

Then I shall surrender to you, love: my reason gives consent
What have I said! Alas, 'tis the opposite, in sum:
To what you counsel, love, it refuses its assent.
I dare not speak, yet cannot keep myself therefrom.

My mind grows clouded as good argument I seek,
The peril is extreme, no matter how I choose;
I shall lose my lover should I fail to speak
And if speak I dare, 'twill be myself I lose.   /28

I fear for my repose, I fear for my liberty
Yet without a murmur would I suffer as I do
Were it vouchsafed me to speak of my slavery.

Over my desires modesty extends its reign
It overawes my eyes, my voice, my every sigh:
In such respect do they hold this queen's law

They dare not reveal the reason for my pain
And though to my rescue they wish they might fly
For fear of her displeasure, they will let me die.   /26

Alas! though we burn with desire without measure
Modesty robs us of all of love's pleasure.   /26

It is a most amusing irony that modesty has been made the rule for
women, who respect in men only shameless boldness.   /33

You allow the lover, whose heritage
From the day of his birth is strength and courage
To disclose without blushing his secret grief.
And the frail Mistress alone would you oblige
To conceal her pain from the world's eyes.
And prefer death to seeking relief.
And if of her love the extreme violence
Constrains her to speak, despite your command
Her mind is troubled by her heart's sentiments
And her every word bespeaks her misery
She quivers with fear as she speaks of her slavery:
Give her other laws to obey, or another heart!   /26

Thus Cyrus sought, in order to express his sentiments, the strongest and most passionate terms, whereas Mandane in her conversation searched for words which would be neither too kind nor too unkind, and which, without betraying the tenderness of her feelings, would preserve entire that strict and rigorous modesty to which she adhered.   /25

Feminine narcissism, in all its ambiguity

Sir,

It is only through marks of respect, constant attentions, countless courtesies, and eternal compliments that you may succeed in sharing the extreme love that your mistress has for her beauty.

Speak to her constantly of herself, and rarely of yourself. You may be certain that she is a hundred times more enchanted by the charms of her person than by any possible display of your affections. If, however, she one day yields to your ardent entreaties, pray remember as you accept the gift of her heart that she is placing in your hands her whole life's happiness, that she is making you the supreme arbiter of her fate.   /33

> On her bosom:
> A little twin mound of snow
> That in a motion full of grace
> Gently rises
> And as gently falls
> Continually moving thus
> In manner comely and felicitous
> As though drawing closer to the eye
> Its beauties to display, and then
> Slowly disappearing once again
> So as to arouse desire.   /27

> "I've some delightful muscatel: come sup."
> Seeing you, my tenderness wells up:
> Would I were a man just now, or later when
> Your voice rings out in merriment
> Mingled with a bottle's soft gurgling sound.   /34

Marriage: it lasts longer than love and kills it: how to make the best of it?

"I take it then that you do not look upon marriage as a blessing?"

"It is quite true that I regard it as an endless slavery." Sapho replied.

"Do you take all men to be tyrants then?"

"I at least take them as capable of so becoming. I know full well that there are those of them whose comportment is most courteous and gentlemanly, but then again, the moment I consider them as husbands I see them as masters, and as masters so inclined to be tyrants that it is not within my power not to hate them at that moment, and I must thank the gods for having made me by nature strongly opposed to marriage. I know not whether my feeling in this regard will one day change, but I know full well that unless I fall so passionately in love as to lose all reason, I shall never give up my freedom."   /25

Embarked upon life without my consent.   /31

Do men remain faithful to their passion after swearing these eternal vows? May I hope for a miracle in my favor, and look forward to a definite end of this passion, thus assuring my entire happiness?   /29

You have expected things of me as impossible as those I expected of you.   /29

The young princess took no notice of these miracles. Her melancholy would have roused pity in the heart of anyone save these pitiless fairies. They nonetheless appointed from among their number the least cruel to watch over her, a certain Serpent, though they enjoined this latter to make certain that the princess had no commerce with anyone. . . . And finally she gave her in abundance everything that she believed might please a young person, while forebearing to speak to her of the monster to whom she had chosen to give her in marriage. But she postponed the day of this most unsuitable marriage, hoping to bend her to their will before apprising her of the misfortune that awaited her.

From time to time she took her walking in the lovely spots that I

have heretofore described, and pointing out their many delights, told
her that if she were obedient to their will, she would one day be
the mistress of them, while at the same time warning her to beware of
arousing her hatred, since she was as capable of punishing as of reward-
ing. As the fairy spoke these words, spying on the water's edge two
turtledoves that seemed to be so tame that they did not take wing as
they approached, Philonice asked her permission to catch them and
take them to her chamber. "I cannot allow you to do so," the fairy
replied.   /35

Monsieur de Clèves was perhaps the only man in the world capable
of preserving love within marriage.   /29

I told myself that marriage would diminish the affection that
Bélisaire felt for me, that henceforth she would love me only out of
duty.   /29

She crossed several great courtyards where the grass and brambles
were so high that it seemed as though no one had walked there for a
hundred years. She pushed them aside with her hands, scratching herself in several places, and entered a hall where the daylight entered only
through a tiny opening: its walls were hung with bats' wings. Twelve
cats serving as chandeliers were suspended from the ceiling, mewing
most piteously. . . . As the princess was contemplating these tortured
creatures, she saw the magician enter, clad in a long black
robe and wearing the most frightful headdress imaginable, a live croco-
dile. This old man was wearing spectacles, and in his hand he carried a
whip made of some twenty live serpents. Her one thought was to escape. And without saying a word to this terrifying man, she ran toward
the door: but it was covered with spider webs. She brushed one away,
only to find another and yet a third; brushing away this one, she found
yet another: these frightful portals were made up of countless, endless
spider webs. The poor princess was overcome with weariness; her arms
were not strong enough to brush all of them aside. She decided to sit
down on the floor to rest for a moment, and immediately felt great long
thorns piercing her flesh. . . . Finally he called her to him and said to
her: "You could well spend the rest of your days here and still all your
efforts would be in vain; you are younger and more beautiful than anything I have ever seen; if it please you, I shall marry you . . . "I have resolved never to love anyone," she replied. "Oh how foolish you are!" he
answered. "I will feed you the most marvelous viands, I will spin tales

for you, I will give you the most beautiful garments in all the world; you will journey only by coach and by litter and be addressed as 'Milady.'" "I have resolved never to love anyone," the princess said again. "Ah far too indifferent creature that you are," he said, touching her, "since you do not wish to love me, you must have a most singular nature. Hence in the future you shall be neither fish nor fowl, neither blood nor bones: you shall be green because you are still in the green years of your youth."   /36

Marriage is a state that makes three quarters of humanity wretched.   /37

> I know of more than one charming spouse
> Still a lover after the wedding vows
> When a tender soul through artfulness
> Conjoins duties, and is spouse-mistress
> Her lover-spouse will conjoin his.
> If by the heart's law a hand is given
> Marriage is not by heaven's decree
> The grave of love 'tis said to be.   /27

"I am not Adonis, agreed; I am nonetheless a most redoubtable boar. Supreme power is worth quite as much as a few natural charms!"

"We shall disguise you so that you are handsomer than Cupid himself," the queen said, "and when the marriage has taken place and we have her in our power, she perforce must remain with us!"

"I am incapable of engaging in such trickery—I would be overcome with despair were I to cause my wife to be unhappy!"

"Can you possibly believe that the one on whom your heart is set will not be unhappy living with you?"

"Alas, what you say is all too true," Marcassin replied. "But if I may dare say so, you should be the last to remind me of my misfortune. Why did you turn me into a pig?"

"I am not reproaching you," the queen added, touched at his words. "I wish merely to remind you that if you wed a woman who does not love you, you will be most unhappy; and you will cause her great pain. If only you understood the suffering a woman must endure in such forced marriages, you would not wish to cause her to risk suffering such tortures." . . .

The bride danced with Marcassin. He was indeed frightful to look upon, and it was even more frightful to be his wife. The entire Court

was so sad at heart that the ball ended at an early hour. The princess
was taken to her apartments after the disrobing ceremony. . . .

She trembled. The idea of losing her lover by being deprived of her
reason was so painful that she resolved to renounce him. "Well then, if
such is your decision, I must give myself to you!" she said to the
gnome.

Crested-Cricket leaped upon this chance, and married her forthwith.
The powers of reason of the princess grew greater by virtue of this marriage, but her unhappiness grew in like proportion. She was horrified at
having given herself to a monster. [*The princess decides to betray
Crested-Cricket and sleep with her lover. But Crested-Cricket touches
the lover with a magic wand, thereby causing him to take on exactly the
same appearance as himself.*] She could no longer tell which of them
was her lover and which her spouse. She saw two husbands instead of
one, and was never certain which of the two of them she should confide
her griefs to, fearing that she would mistake the object of her hatred for
the object of her love. But it may well be that she lost little thereby.
For in the end do not all lovers become merely husbands?   /39

My father listened to him attentively and thanked him most politely,
telling him that he had already pledged his word to another. . . . But
since Monsieur de la Guette was the most violent man in the world, he
took this refusal in a most strange way. He began to curse and rage
most frightfully, saying that he would force my father to break his
word. My father, who was in no mood to tolerate such transports of
anger, replied immediately that he had not the slightest intention
of so doing. The uproar in his study continued for more than an hour
as one of them roared out his violent feelings in the matter and the
other shouted him down. My mother and I were in the parlor waiting
for the chevalier. He finally burst in, in an unimaginable fury, saying
that my father had refused him, but that he would have his revenge,
and was resolved to kill unto the seventh generation, beginning with
me. These sweet nothings would not have been at all pleasing to one
with a timid heart. But their one effect upon me was to make me respect
him the more, for I took this as a sign that he loved me in a most extraordinary way. . . .

One day he came to the house most unexpectedly, since the servants
had been given strict orders not to admit him. He went straight to my
father's study, pistol in hand, threw himself at his feet, and said to him
straight out: "Sir, I must have your daughter's hand in marriage, or die.

There are three bullets in this pistol. You have only to press the trigger." My father was not at all moved thereby. . . .

Seeing the prospects of marrying growing no brighter but instead becoming more and more remote, we were greatly distressed. After having left no stone unturned, as the saying goes, we decided to marry and have done with this state of affairs. . . . We were wed at two hours after midnight, and afterward mass was said. The church was just opposite our house: my father, who had not the slightest idea of what was happening, was inside in his bed, slumbering peacefully. Once the mass was over, my husband and brother-in-law took my hands in theirs to escort me to my house and then immediately took their leave of me, for they had just been party to a bold and dangerous act, against a man who could easily be their undoing. I for my part went off to bed without a single fear. Fifteen days went by without my father's discovering what had happened. He ordered me not to leave my room without his permission. I was thus a prisoner—not of war, but of love, for it was love that was responsible for my being treated in this way. But it was a most chaste and modest love, for during his quest for my hand my husband had always led me to expect that we would live as brother and sister and that my virginity would remain intact. Such was my belief, and because of it I allowed myself to go on. For had I thought that I would be obliged to sleep with a man, I should never have married. This is proof of how naïve I was, and how trusting.

[*The young lady is carried off one day by her chevalier on his horse, as the Duc d'Angoulême keeps her father from pursuing them. They live in bliss, but then one day the husband is obliged to go off to war.*]

It was a cruel separation, for I must say that he loved me in a most extraordinary way, and that I worshiped him. As had never happened previously, I had the time to shed as many tears as I pleased, to behave as most women do, to the detriment of those noble inclinations and that resoluteness of soul that were so natural to me and that even caused me to have an aversion for those of my sex who are weak and fainthearted. I have always been of a disposition more suited to combat than to such tranquil occupations as settings hens to brood and spinning. . . .

[*She sends her portrait to her husband at the battle front.*]

He showed my portrait to his intimate friends, and feasted them forthwith. A number of toasts were drunk. They turned my face in the portrait toward the city that was under siege as soon as they heard the enemy begin firing their cannon. They were right to do so, for the original has never turned her back in moments of peril. My husband pretended to himself that the portrait was myself, and thought I ought to see what was happening. . . .

When he returned from the war there was naught but tender caresses on both our parts. I shall speak out plainly here, for a woman cannot love her husband too much. People may say what they please, but I for my part do not think much of those who are prim and proper because they are very much to be mistrusted. . . .

[*The following year.*]

I was big with child again and will say once and for all that I have had ten children, five boys and five girls, for which I thank God. . . .

[*Ten years later.*]

As he was the most violent of men, he turned to his lackey in a rage and said: "Go tell your mistress to come at once, for I am of a mind to shoot her with my pistol." The poor lad, a German boy, ran to me as fast as his legs would carry him and announced, in the presence of my father and his friends: "Madame, come quickly. Monsieur intends to shoot you with his pistol!" "Do tell! What an amusing bit of news!" I replied. I then went gaily off, though the others tried as best they could to stop me. Several of them followed after me, and I came across Monsieur d'Angoulême in a hallway: "Damn my eyes! Your husband is behaving like a madman! Where are you going?" "Sire, I'm off to get shot by him!" I answered. "Don't go! A hundred men would not be enough to bring him to his senses!" "Sire, I have a secret for so doing," I said, and went on. I found my husband on horseback, surrounded by a crowd of people attempting to calm him. "My chevalier, I pray you dismount! I wish to have a word with you. As for shooting me with your pistol, we shall speak of this matter another time."

He leaped off his horse immediately to speak to me, and in a few minutes climbed back in the saddle again as docile as a lamb.   /38

Lady libertines: philosophers and sensualists

Leave sublime discourse and lofty sentiments to the Céladons[2] of this world. Let them enjoy perfect love if they will. Speaking on behalf of women, I can assure you of this: There are moments when they would rather be rushed off their feet than dealt with too gently. It is more because of men's maladroitness than because of women's virtue that the latter's hearts resist capture.   /33

> The lot of all true lovers, we are told
> Is to fall prey to raging jealousy
> But this mere excess I do hold to be:
> Passion become but pure frenzy.

[2] Name of the hero of *L'Astrée*, a popular serial novel of the day. (*Translator's note.*)

I for my part aim to love heedlessly
Without envy, without fear or pretension
I shall indulge my every fantasy:
My charms are my sufficient surety. . . .

If one would change one's lover or mistress
One spends a month in conversation
And then the change is simply made
Without blame or recrimination
But there will still be tenderness
Small attentions to be paid:
For two lovers, when a great love ends
Should for all that remain friends.   /27

Your conduct reveals more and more of the truth to me, and you show yourself to be not at all clever: You have given up everything for me since the beginning of our liaison, you tell me. But that is what a man always does, not only for the woman he loves, but for the one he merely desires; he makes sacrifices for the woman he wishes to possess, and ceases to make them for the woman who adores him. If her heart suffers, if her health is affected, he relies on time to heal her. This is behavior worthy of the fickle men whom you resemble. I have long been aware of this; there was no need to fill up four pages telling me this yet again. . . . Since you are capable of such cold reasoning, this reply will serve to prove to you how inappropriate your letter was. Keep your sublime ideas to yourself henceforth, and should you be still capable of making a sacrifice in my behalf, I pray you to spare me your icy sermons.   /33

I swoon as a sweet languor steals over me
I die in the arms of my faithful lover
And by this death am restored to life.   /27

I have told you a hundred times that pleasures are the only chains by which I would keep you my prisoner. I wish to have a lover, not a slave.   /33

It does not suffice to be well mannered. One must also please.   /33

The senses' rebellion, innocent happiness . . .
There is a time to love—and a time to die.   /27

I suppose that I shall love you for three months. That is all eternity for me.   /33

The sweet but extremely dangerous pleasure of being loved; love as bitter combat; the terrible anguish of being no longer loved

Such a strange gesture on the part of a rose tree astonished the princess. This miracle she had been privileged to witness; it was a sort of homage paid her that touched her heart; she walked round the garden several times; the rose tree bowed to her each time she passed by. She tried to gather a rose whose crimson color pleased her, and pricked her finger most painfully. The deep prick kept her from sleeping all night long. The following morning she arose much earlier than usual and went out to take a walk in the garden.

The rose tree bowed again, so promptly that the heart of the princess was filled with joy, causing her to forget the painful prick and think only of this wondrous miracle. Finally, lost in thought, she drew too close to the rose tree and found herself trapped by its thorns, unable to escape. As she struggled to free herself, she felt its extraordinary resistance. . . . A certain feeling of deep displeasure took the place of the joy she had experienced on seeing the rose tree bow so respectfully; she felt that it had taken an impermissible liberty by having dared to lock her in the embrace of its branches; she then took her leave of it, though not without casting several backward glances at the garden.

Her mind was assailed by certain sentiments that bore a more or less close resemblance to each other, even though she considered them to be quite different. The boldness of the rose tree astonished her; the prince it concealed aroused her pity; she was somewhat vexed that it had dared to speak to her of love, but in the end she pardoned this Lover, since it was merely a plant. One could surely not allow oneself to be vexed by a rose tree!   /39

I suffer, not knowing the reason for my pain
The means to cure myself I seek in vain.
Alas, my fate is sealed, my life but misery
What once was pleasure today is anxiety
My spirit, wearied by battle without pause
Ponders its state, unable to discern its cause
Alas, it is not certain I'm undone
For all I know, the battle may be won:
My heart, you've risen in rebellion against me. . . .   /28

There are no passions save those that overwhelm us at first and take us by surprise; the others are but liaisons to which we freely give our hearts.   /29

Wherever it makes its appearance, love is always the master. It seems, indeed, that it is to the soul of the one who loves what the soul is to the body of the one whom it animates.   /40

Sweet and secret peace of a blissful lover,
To my loving heart will you never return? . . .

I would be ever in love, or if not cease to live. . . .

Since becoming a slave to love unrequited
I have discovered the secret of dying each day. . . .

Fire and ice were thereby conjoined.
Their antipathy causes continual strife
That drains my heart's strength without ending my life. . . .   /26

"I have spent my time chasing after the loveliest doe that I have ever laid eyes on," the prince said. "Her wondrous agility has enabled her to trick me a hundred times, though I took such accurate aim that I do not understand how she could have possibly escaped me."

As he had become overheated by the chase, he was delighted to come across apples whose color pleased him greatly. He ate of them, and almost immediately thereupon he grew drowsy and lay down on the cool grass beneath the trees. As he slept, our timid doe, seeking one of the remote haunts of which she was fond, chanced upon this one where he lay slumbering. O love, love, what is your intention? Is this soft-eyed doe to risk her life at the hands of her lover? Indeed she so risks it, without a thought for her safety: she lies down just a few steps away from him, unable to turn her delighted gaze from him. She sighs and gives plaintive little moans. Then, growing bolder, she draws him so close she almost touches him, when suddenly he awakens.

She flees with all her strength and he follows her with all of his. But alas, it grieves me to say that what slowed the soft-eyed doe in her flight was the pain of fleeing this lover whose merits had touched her heart far more than all the arrows that he shot at her. . . .

He saw that she had lost all her strength: she was lying there like a poor half-dead creature, awaiting the coup de grâce at the hands of her victor. But rather than dealing with her so cruelly, he commenced to caress her. . . . He took the doe in his arms, pressed her head to his bosom, laid her down tenderly on the green boughs, and then sat down beside her, reaching out for handfuls of soft grass which he offered her, and which she ate out of his hand. . . . After finding a spring, the prince came back to where he had left his beloved doe, but she was no longer there. He looked all about for her, but was not able to find her. "Well then! will this deceiving and faithless sex ever bring me aught save cause for complaint!" he cried. . . . Dawn broke once again, and the princess again took on the appearance of a white doe. . . . He found her in the densest part of the forest. She immediately bounded over the bushes, and as though understanding him the better after the trick that she had played on him the evening before, she fled more swiftly than the wind. But he took such careful aim this time that he sent an arrow into her leg. She felt a most grievous pain, and so drained of her strength that she was unable to make her escape, she fell to the ground. O cruel and barbarous love, where were you then? Can it be that you permit such an incomparable maid to be wounded by her tender lover? The prince caressed her a thousand times: "How it grieves me to have wounded you! You will hate me, when I wish you to love me!" /36

The Devil or God; or love without a lover

I, Marie de Sains, promise thee, Beelzebub, that I will serve you all my life and give unto you my heart and my soul and all my corporeal senses, and all my works, all my prayers, and all my thoughts. /41

But this is not yet the kiss on the mouth. The essential union and the kiss on the mouth are the spiritual marriage wherein God takes the soul for his spouse and unites it unto Him: not personally now, or through some intermediary act or means, but immediately, reducing everything to unity and possessing the soul in its very unity. There follows thereupon the kiss on the mouth and real and perfect possession. . . .

One can be united without being commingled. It is the union of powers. But commingling is essential union, by which is meant the loss of all propriety and an amorous remelting of the soul. . . .

The Beloved, seeing the docility of his mistress in allowing herself to be crucified and instructed by him, is charmed by the wondrous beauties with which he has endowed her. That is why he caresses her and praises her, calling her beautiful and beloved. "If I am beautiful, it is because I am beautified by you. It is you who are beautiful within me. Our bed, that intimate place within me where you dwell, which I call ours, to invite you to come give me therein that nuptial kiss that I asked at first from you and that at present is my end, our bed, I say, is readied now and decked with the flowers of a thousand virtues.". . .

"I am the lily of the valley that grows only in souls reduced to nothingness." . . .

She is the sealed fountain that no one can open or close save himself. She is then the walled garden for her Spouse that he closed and that no one opens, that he opens and no one closes. For love is as powerful as death, saith the Spouse in order to do as he pleases with his Beloved. It is as powerful as death, seeing that it has made her dead to everything in order that she may live for him alone. . . .

O Spouse worthy of the angels' jealousy, you have found your beloved at last. . . . You are so wholly his that nothing prevents you from losing yourself in him. Since you have been altogether melted by the heat of his love, you have been disposed to flow into him as into your appointed end.

I find you the mansion prepared for me: you shall dwell in me and I in you.   /42

> My beloved little Master
> I am wholly yours
> Can greater bliss be asked for
> Than loving your whiplashes?

I feel no more pain
All becomes pleasure
No more constraint
All becomes infinite
All becomes pleasure
No more constraint
All becomes infinite.   /42

I live, and with my life am one
I am nourished, though I know not by what
I feel neither hunger nor desire in my heart
All is empty and yet full, it seems to me.
Who wreaks these effects so contrary?
Ah! who but you, Love, can be their cause?
Who my already contented heart doth satisfy?
Is it *Nothingness?* Can it be my Spouse?   /42

I love you as though I were only fifteen
and the world were in the Golden Age.
Éléonore de Sabran

·V·

Reason and Sensibility

Why do we keep insisting that "modern times" began in 1453? The fall of an already shaky empire was merely a passing episode in history, while the socioeconomic background remained largely unchanged. The seasons followed one upon the other, sometimes good and sometimes bad, and subsistence and hence life and death depended more upon the harvests than upon treaties and wars. Societies experienced changes, but change as an underlying principle—that is to say, the concept of "progress"—did not yet exist. In the eighteenth century, however, especially in its second half, change becomes a characteristic of Western society, which values it, seeks it, and deliberately provokes it, even though there are those who are terrified by it. Technology begins to profit from the birth of modern science; chemistry frees itself of the alchemical rubbish from which it emerged; agricultural production increases, more and more new food crops are grown, the quality of livestock and meat improves; there are more manufactured products, more mills and factories, all presaging the Industrial Revolution, which is already under way in England.

Progress and development cannot take place unless the spirit of the age is favorable to change, receptive to change. And this is the case in the eighteenth century. The death of women in childbirth and the death of young infants are no longer accepted as the workings of fate; there is increasing interest in the techniques of delivering babies, though this research is still haphazard and naïve; married couples seek to have fewer children and begin to practice coitus interruptus, which heretofore had been strictly forbidden by the Church; the children that couples do have begin to be loved for their own sake, rather than merely being considered to be offspring who will continue the family line; and as a consequence parents begin to be concerned about their children's education. Even though they are straying further and further from it as they free themselves of its constraints, nature appears to them to be both good and beautiful. Women of the world, enamored of Jean-Jacques Rousseau and his philosophy (despite the fact that he is an extremely antifeminist prophet who is convinced that woman's only vocation is to serve the man her entire life long), are converted to the "vanities of the breast," as Madame de Genlis puts it, and nurse their infants in the drawing room, where they have never before been seen.

The *philosophes* of the age attract many disciples. To study "philosophy" in the eighteenth century is not so much a question of learning to read Descartes or Spinoza or being interested in man's appointed ends, and it has even less to do with theology. It is, rather, a certain turn of mind, a spirit of curiosity and a questioning of all received ideas, a frank humanism, and a search for a personal ethic that is more social in nature than religious.

Reason is expected to bring about moral progress once it has freed itself of what would soon come to be called "medieval horrors." But sentiment, too, is given free rein at last; it is valued and plays an important role in this renewal that is felt to be imperative if society and the individual are to be freed of their chains. It is indeed the "age of enlightenment," but it is the heart as well as reason that is responsible for the radiant light that gave this century its name.

Women are a perfect mirror of the age, and for the first time we shall read texts that, except for two or three old-fashioned turns of phrase, sound surprisingly modern to our ears. We had sisters very much like ourselves in the eighteenth century.

There are some things, of course, that remain unchanged. As in the preceding century, women continue to write fabulous tales. This century sees the publication, in forty-one handsome volumes, of the precious collection of fairy tales entitled *Cabinet des fées* that so appealed to Balzac's imagination—as it did to countless numbers of his contemporaries and successors. Madame Leprince de Beaumont, the author of a collection of "moral tales," creates a world of white cats and fluttering hands that disrobe and caress distraught wandering princes.

In the salons, as the Goncourt brothers assure us, it is women who reign, the queens of idle pleasures and of what has not yet been given the name culture. The Marquise de Rambouillet had invented the salon in the seventeenth century, giving birth to it in her famous "blue alcove," where under her aegis the rough edges of the language of the age were polished off and formal courtesy became capable of generating psychological subtleties. In the eighteenth century, regarding these accomplishments as territory already conquered, Madame de Tencin, Madame du Deffand, and Mademoiselle de Lespinasse tended to encourage intellectual brilliance instead, choosing as the guests at their salons the mathematicians and philosophers of the day. Since this fact is well known, let us speak instead of things that are less matters of common knowledge, though they are entirely new, developments and most fruitful ones.

The child is finally recognized as a person in his or her own right, and for the first time little girls and adolescents are no longer faceless creatures, for grown women begin to speak of their childhood and by so doing attract the attention and touch the hearts of those who listen to them or read their writings.

At the age of seven, Hélène Massalska, an orphan and a wealthy heiress, arrives at the convent of the Abbaye au Bois in Paris, having journeyed there from the remote Baltic estate in the wild forests where she was born. During the eight years that she is boarded and educated at the convent, she faithfully keeps her diary, illustrating it with caricatures in the margins. She carefully preserves this document, and her father-in-law, the charming Prince de Ligne, finds it delightful and has it published. The reader discovers in its pages proud, boisterous, unruly little women, who fence with each other with meat skewers, play at riding to hounds, write anonymous epigrams on the walls of this "cloister of Souls" (just as the students at Nanterre wrote revolutionary slogans on the walls of the university in May of '68), rise up in revolt when a nun displeases them, and even go so far as to organize a conspiracy and occupy the kitchens "so as to starve their ladyships" and hold them at their mercy. They are anything but sweet and submissive, flirt through a little window with the young baker's helper next door, but immediately mend their ways when it is pointed out to them that they will not be proud of such goings-on when they leave the convent. Marriages are arranged for these highborn young ladies when they are about thirteen or fourteen; though they often view the spouse chosen for them with horror, they look forward to marriage itself with the most passionate joy, as a symbol of freedom: fine carriages, pack animals, a life of luxury await me as soon as I speak my vows at the altar and am addressed as "madame." These cloistered adolescents are not at all prudish, even though they are completely innocent. We find them copying love letters out of novels and sending them to grown men, intoxicated at the thought of soon being able to exercise their "dominion over men."

A new creature begins to take form, with charms all her own: the young lady, who heretofore did not exist. Her life begins in the eighteenth century, in the convent or at home—a life that is more inde-

pendent than we might have thought. Manon Phlipon (later to become Madame Roland) makes her way all by herself through the
streets of Paris to visit her idol, Jean-Jacques Rousseau. Though her
mother has died and her father is not at home, she receives men in the
drawing room—and exchanges letters with them. Geneviève de Malboissière delights in telling her best friend of her own sex how she
spends her days in the country with a boy cousin of the same age, in
whose company she spends all her time, from morning till night. She
knows German and English as well as Greek and Latin, and Italian as
well, of course—and all of the passages in the letters that she writes to
her best young lady friend and confidante at the age of sixteen in which
she describes her sentiments are composed in Italian.

Even though these young ladies are carefully kept under lock and key
to ensure that they will be virgins when they marry, they are aware of
the liaisons between grownups, of which they speak in the turns of
phrase that were fashionable at the time, leading us to wonder if they
knew precisely what was meant by them: "Monsieur de X belongs to
Madame de Y," "the word is going around that the Count de R no
longer belongs to the Marquise de C," etc.

We also note a new phenomenon: as they prepare themselves for
marriage, they hope to love their husbands and share with him their
thoughts, their ideas of life, their reading, their profound aspirations, as
well as their beds and their money.

For the first time there is a concerted movement in favor of marriage.
Harsh words are said on every hand of couples who are at odds with
each other or bored by each other's company. "When you see a carriage
go by with a man inside who is looking out one window and a woman
who is looking out the other, you may be certain that they are husband
and wife," the *Journal des dames* notes. But such criticism implies that
this is a regrettable situation, that there are hopes that things may
change. The aristocracy, an institution whose façade is cracking, is everywhere obliged (even in the best convents and in the classes of the
best tutors) to make room for the rising bourgeoisie, the elite of the
third estate—the magistrates, tradesmen, bankers, administrators, man-
facturers who are also beginning to give their daughters an education.
Among this class, marriage is neither a farce nor a façade. Its function
is no longer merely to pass on a name, a title, a hereditary office, and to
assure oneself a place at court. Husbands and wives go over the household accounts together, sleep in the same bed, know how the other's
day is spent, take meals with their children, go on family outings with
them on Sundays. The two of them grow old together, and thus sharing
their lives and interests they often love each other deeply and wax in-

dignant at the loose morals and sophisticated revels in novels. This faith in marriage as an unquestioned good finds fervent expression during the Revolution: the year 1790 sees the appearance of a most revealing journal, *Le Courrier de l'hymen* (The Wedding Courier), whose aim is to make marriage "moral," and in particular to denounce "husbands who take on aristocratic airs with their wives," by which is meant what today's American women's liberationists have labeled "male chauvinism." Young ladies write in to this paper in search of a husband; a number of them have just fled the convent, where they have been forced to take the veil, since their father has been willing to give a dowry only to the oldest girl in the family. The aspirations of these young girls are the same as those of Manon Phlipon, Geneviève de Malboissière, Lucile Desmoulins, and all the others who yearn for true union with their spouses, a union of the heart and of the mind. It is curious to note that as religion loses its hold over a society which is becoming rapidly laicized even though it remains vaguely deistic, marriage as a sharing of life becomes more and more valued. It is no longer a religious sacrament that defines the institution, but rather the shared interests and feelings of couples who belong to the most dynamic social class: the bourgeoisie.

We should not forget that in the last years of the eighteenth century husbands and wives who cherished each other were held in the greatest esteem. Fervent conjugal love attracted not sarcasm, but the most fervent admiration, thus giving rise to a sort of contest to see who could love his or her beloved spouse the most, who could best prove to the world the unshakable fidelity felt toward one's life partner, toward the father or mother of one's children.

Camille and Lucile Desmoulins, separated by the guillotine, remain a symbol of these young couples who are deeply in love with each other. The incomparable, angelic Adrienne de La Fayette, so passionately attached to her husband ("How many thanks I owe God for the fact that such a violent attachment was but my duty! What joy has fallen my lot to be your wife!") that she asked to be locked up with him in the same miserable dungeon at Olmütz where he was rotting away, thereby becoming a heroine to all of France, immortalized in prints of herself accompanied by verses celebrating the glory of conjugal love. But it is just as revealing that Madame Roland expressed, till the day she died on the guillotine, her respect for marriage and her horror of adultery, despite her secret passion for a man not her husband.

In the novels of Madame Riccoboni, admired by Napoleon, there are countless examples of conjugal devotion. There are countless examples in real life as well. Couples and families found themselves swept up in a great wave of affection and devotion. One married for love at the end of the eighteenth century, and believed in the family as an institution, particularly in the most liberal and progressive sectors of society.

Was this a "reasonable" ideal?

Not if we mean by that term what the word "reason" implied in the course of this century. In the first two thirds of it in particular, rather than listen to reason and refuse to be carried away by passion, one tried to reason out the consequences of love. A cultivated, well-bred lady, that is to say, attempted to marshal all her powers of intelligence and be as clear-sighted as possible in affairs of the heart, in order not to make a fool of herself and be made a fool of. For love around the year 1750 was defined as "a vast emptiness of words and a vast stupidity of the heart."

Hence one must "keep one's mind on reality," which at the time meant experiencing sensual pleasure while at the same time not losing one's senses. Above all it meant being witty, and how better to be so than to know how to keep one's distance from one's feelings and see oneself clearly, so as to be the first to laugh at oneself? Wit and humor are closer cousins than we are inclined to believe, and humor begins with a loss of illusions about oneself, even before the loss of illusions about others. One must hold all the right cards and know the rules of the game, which one wins by not surrendering to one's partner.

But this is a game that is hard for tender-hearted women to play, and even hard for women who are passionately in love. Certain women, incapable perhaps of great passion, play it supremely well. Most women play it as best they can, out of pride, even when passion unexpectedly overcomes them, as was the case with Madame du Deffand, who became love-smitten at around the age of seventy—already gone blind and believing herself safe in the fortress of her mordant wit and clear-sightedness. Most women simply make of reason a vague moral virtue and transform it into a sort of loosely defined wisdom that they then call philosophy. A rather pompous sort of ideal that falls far short of being realized takes the place of what at the beginning of the century was a trenchant spirit of criticism that knew no bounds, an icy laughter.

Yet this wit is not brittle, for very soon it is softened by a gentle tenderness. All is sweetness and light: pastel colors are the fashion, as are nature and delicate sensibilities. Graceful necks, little turned-up noses, subtle compliments and nicely turned phrases, saccharine-sweet shepherds and shepherdesses in porcelain who bear no resemblance to real ones, and great liquid eyes about to brim over with tears—all this, too, is the eighteenth century, the century of the Marquis de Sade and the

Beast of Gévaudan,[1] but also that of the most insipid poetry ever penned in France, of vapid opera ariettas, of the *Journal des dames*, whose editor, Dorat, was a former musketeer become a poetaster, who wrote pale imitations of Richardson's Pamela, full of descriptions of rural landscapes and swooning ladies, which sold well from Dakar to St. Petersburg.

All this saccharine sentiment was more than enough to exacerbate the mordant sense of irony of the most intelligent women of the time. Nonetheless, coyness and daintiness are not the only things we find in this complex century—far from it. It also sees the birth of the most beautiful, the most enduring sentiment of all: tenderness. It takes the form of a spontaneous outpouring from the heart that seeks to create a climate of gentle, intelligent understanding, accompanied by light-hearted shared laughter—a complicity between men and women who share their hopes and their trials, their laughter, their opinions, their interests, with each other. Tenderness is an art of the heart, as conversation is an art of the mind. Both arts blossom and flourish in this period, each nourishing the other, since both stem from a supreme politeness: that of truly listening to one's partner and responding with feeling and intelligence.

Coldness of heart or mawkish sentimentality are considered to be glaring defects in women whose charms are mere affection. And, to be sure, we frequently read of prostitutes (some of them powdered and perfumed, others not), mistresses, battles to win men worth thousands of livres who treat the women who fight to possess them as one might expect these pitifully inadequate males to treat them. But such phenomena merely enhance the victory won by the most sensitive, most generous women of the age, thanks to this new quality, a faithful, unfailingly kind tenderness that leaves room for both laughter and tears, and creates lasting ties between lovers who have both the greatest indulgence and the greatest esteem for each other. Though the letters of Sophie Volland, with whom Denis Diderot corresponded for twenty-five

[1] Between 1764 and 1767, more than sixty persons, mainly women and children, were devoured or seriously mauled by a ferocious beast of which survivors gave a terrifying description. Asked for help by the frightened peasants, the king sent his own master of the wolf hunt and his best hunters. For two years they tracked down wolves and killed them, and thought several times that they had destroyed the fantastic "beast." But the creature continued its depredations, and moreover it tended to kill human beings rather than sheep. The matter became common knowledge, and fascinated people. Songs and laments were made up about the fabulous beast who killed poor peasants in a rough and wild region. A statue to the "beast" was erected, which can still be seen in the principal city of Gévaudan, Mendes (in the modern *département* of the Lozère). Many theories have been invented to explain these events, the most curious of which has it that the beast was none other than the Marquis de Sade disguised as a fantastic animal, for it was known that the Marquis lived in Gévaudan at the time.

years, have disappeared, as have all but two of the letters of the delightful Adrienne de Noailles to her husband, the Marquis de La Fayette,
we fortunately have those of the Comtesse de Sabran, every one of
which would merit inclusion in these pages. It is, in fact, an example of
a love literature that has not attracted sufficient attention: it is the
story of a long and happy liaison, though not without its ups and
downs, the story of a mutual love that endures despite the ravages of
time, intrusive third parties, minor infidelities, long absences (her lover
spends two years in Senegal, which in those days was wild jungle territory, in order to acquire the title and the pension that will permit him
to marry his countess, whose considerable fortune keeps him from asking for her hand immediately), and all manner of trials (the Revolution, exile), finally ending in a happy marriage. These letters of the
comtesse deal not only with the kisses and embraces the two of them
yearn to share but also with such subjects as her viewing of the moon
through a telescope, her climbing a mountain in Alsace in a burst of enthusiasm for nature, and above all her children from her first marriage,
their tutors, their progress, their illnesses, their games, her worries as to
their upbringing, the problem of finding the proper husband for her
youngest daughter. Everything is told to the lover, put before him, in
order that he may help her to make the proper decisions, in order that
he may share her life from day to day. Should I have a word with my
daughter before her wedding night or not? the mother asks her lover,
posing the question in the most charming manner imaginable. We
might well have chosen other collections of letters just as full of wit
and feeling, of esteem and joyous enthusiasm. The letters of the
comtesse are nonetheless quite representative. Even her choice of words
is revealing of the true sensibility of her era: She calls her lover "my
child," not because she is a possessive, castrating woman who wishes to
"mother" him, but because this was a customary form of address between two people who loved each other, quite naturally and without
hidden complexes, happy at having discovered the comparable power of
the two "tenderest possible bonds": that between mistress and lover,
and that between mother and child. This in fact became so much the
fashion that the "ladies of the evening" who sold themselves in the ar-
cades of the Palais-Royal asked their clients to address them as
"mama," whereupon Sébastien Mercier called upon the French Academy to drop the words mama and papa, thus sullied, from the official
dictionary of the French language. The fashion soon became out-
moded, the words papa and mama remained in the dictionary, and little by little they came to be no longer used as terms of endearment or
gallant compliments.[2] We should note, however, that there is nothing

---

[2] Thirty years later, however, we still find Julie Charles pretending to be the "mama"
of her lover-child Lamartine.

unusual in the fact that Rousseau called Madame de Warens "mama," a fashion likewise followed by Stanislas-Augustus of Poland in addressing Madame Geoffrin.

The mother in this century is not suspected of being a castrating, destructive, man-devouring female, as is so frequently the case today. Maternal sentiment being a recent discovery, the century made it the symbol of tender and unselfish love. Women in general, moreover, were considered to be nature's purest and best creation, and in this era it was a compliment for a lady to write "You have a woman's heart" to her lover. Yet poor tender-hearted Madame de Sabran, who wrote those words quite naturally and spontaneously, believed that she lived in "a century hard as iron!"

This calm intensity of feeling, this goodness without sickly sentimentality, this love accompanied at once by esteem and playful teasing, this Mozartean music, is not to every woman's liking, or rather not every woman has a talent for it. Bored by their own wit, weary of courtly compliments, inclined to be disbelievers (with the exception of Aïssé and the incomparable Adrienne de La Fayette), the women of the eighteenth century stand on the very brink of love as fatal passion, and will soon become the first to succumb to it. Already women can scarcely wait to get their hands on translations of Ann Radcliffe's gothic novels. As Voltaire's towering shadow falls over the century, passion is about to storm both heaven and hell, ravage and sabotage everything, excuse everything, put everything in question, lay bare the white-hot core of love that rages uncontrolled, contained by neither esteem nor tenderness nor the sharing of everyday life: suffering.

Following her philosophy of measure in all things, Madame du Châtelet had led a most satisfying life, dividing her time between her intellectual pursuits and her attachment to Voltaire, yet at the age of forty-two she allows her passion for St.-Lambert to overcome her, humbles herself, suffers, throws everything overboard: "If only I can spend my life with you. Let all the rest take whatever course it will." Julie de Lespinasse, crucified by her passion for Monsieur de Guibert, writes that she loves him "to excess, in madness, ecstasy, and despair." And on another occasion she writes: "My friend, I am perfect, for I love you to perfection." "Heaven and hell" are what she cries out for in the clearest possible language: "That is the climate that I should like to inhabit, not this temperate state in which all the slaves and all the automatons who surround us live." Passion makes its nest in discontent with life in general, which inevitably begins with a contempt for one's fellows, disguised as a feeling that one is more clear-sighted than the vulgar run of humanity and hence the possessor of superior wisdom. This contempt for others suddenly surfaces, with passion serving as the excuse: "I have neglected my friends, broken off intimate relations . . . burned the shared secrets, confidences, assurances of tender affection of my child-hood friends," Hélène Massalska, now the Princesse de Ligne, writes to Compte Potocki. She has also abandoned a loving husband, a very young child, a delightful father-in-law—everything. But what causes the worst suffering of all is the fact that this scorning of everything and ev-eryone, justified in the name of passion, is such a difficult thing to live with that it continually casts a dark shadow upon the image of the be-loved: does he deserve the sacrifice that I have made for him? Surely not, but it is too late now, I refuse to admit it, and what is more I adore him, since I have sacrificed everything for him. Powerless to take back the tremendous gift that she has laid at the feet of her beloved, the woman gripped by her passion is tormented by the hate that is the complement of love, and in particular by the feminine form of this hatred, contempt. Her contempt for the one she loves goes hand in hand with his sanctification. "You have taken everything from me and then abandoned me," Hélène Massalska writes accusingly (and un-truthfully) to her lover, only to immediately reassure him: "Nonethe-less you shall forevermore be the object of my eternal love." "You have led me to the most desperate extremities; I was convinced that I would die of your most peculiar behavior toward me," Adrienne Lecouvreur complains, thoroughly disgusted yet still ready to yield to her lover's will. "You are not my friend. You cannot become so. I have no sort of trust whatsoever in you," Julie de Lespinasse writes implacably, still madly in love. "Do you not know that a man cannot seduce those women he has charmed?" Julie Talma writes, bewitched but not se-duced. And Madame du Deffand uses her razor-sharp claws to tear to pieces her beloved Walpole, whom she loves not wisely but too well. And Sophie de Condorcet seeks to lower herself to a point below even that to which her esteem for her lover has fallen, in order to still love him even though she despises him. In any event I am obliged to love him, the woman tells herself, and at each moment she is torn between two possibilities: Shall I be eternally saved or eternally damned by my love? "You praise me for loving you! Ah, it is a crime, and even the ex-cessive degree of my love does not justify me. But I shall horrify you: I abandon myself to crime, knowing that I am a criminal. Loving you or ceasing to live: this is the only *virtue* that I know." It is confusion that transcends everything—or alternatively, the form of transcendence con-fuses everything.

Julie de Lespinasse has been faithfully loved by D'Alembert for twenty years, but what do his genius, his friends, his salon, his reputa-tion, matter to her? What does it matter to Sophie that she has been the beloved and the wife of Condorcet, the first and the greatest of feminists? What does it matter to Hélène Massalska that at the Bel-Oeil estate of the Prince de Ligne perfect goodness and the most lively intelligence reigned? What does it matter to Madame du Châtelet that she has shared with Voltaire ten years of their lives and a carefully practiced philosophy of mastery of oneself?

Whether it be a young man twelve years her junior, who is seeking his place in the world and takes a wife during their love affair; or an actor who is as spineless and dissolute as he is handsome; or a mysterious character who has already had two children by a married woman whom he has taken off with him to the remotest reaches of the Ukraine; or a foppish womanizer and third-rate poet—what these women want is the impossible, a mad affair, a dramatic break—what they will come to call their fated destiny. The great outcries of these women in love come from the darkest depths of their hearts, from beyond good and evil, or rather torn between the two, for they never succeed in forgetting this good and this evil, and endlessly re-create them, in order to accuse, to excuse, to accuse themselves, to excuse themselves. Even before the Revolution they have begun to declaim phrases that sound straight out of the works of Hugo or Dumas. They have suffered, in short, the Romantic *mal du siècle* half a century too early, before it had become the reigning fashion.

Three of these women died still passionately in love, and wrote till the very moment of their death, which all three of them clearly saw approaching. It is they who sum up the eighteenth century, far more than that age's porcelain shepherdesses and vapid pastorals.

All three of them are in their forties, the age of great passions, of great loves, the age of maturity in this century that was not yet fascinated by youth.

The first of them lived in the rakish, rotten, refined sophistication of the years of the regency. The Regent himself courted her assiduously, to no avail. As a lovely, innocent four-year-old, she was bought in a slave market in Constantinople by the French ambassador, and reserved for his own personal pleasure. She fell in love with the Chevalier d'Aydé, and had a daughter by him—whom both of them loved dearly and contrived to raise and educate in secret. Poor Aïssé, who loved truly and was truly loved in return, knowing that she was being unfaithful to God! A Swiss Protestant lady, possessed of a moral piety that can only be described as disgusting, meets Aïssé and causes her to be deeply ashamed of her conduct. Aïssé seeks desperately to obey God's will, tries her best to cease to love her adorable lover, fails to do so, coughs, spits blood, slowly destroys herself, and dies a creature torn in two, after a last-moment confession, with her lover at her bedside, helping her to pray. (Their daughter, thank God, is a miracle of grace and charm.)

Julie de Lespinasse learns one day, at the age of eighteen, that her real name is not "de Lespinasse" at all. Her "benefactress," who has raised her, is in fact her mother. The daughter of her benefactress, whose employ she has entered as the governess of her children, is in reality her half sister, and her little charges are her nephews. As for the husband of her employer, she learns that he is not only her brother-in-law but also her father! On the day following these revelations worthy of the Astrides, Julie leaves for Paris with Madame du Deffand, and for twenty years serves as hostess of her salon, and then breaks with her and becomes hostess of her own salon, rivaling that of her former mistress, and the Encyclopédistes worship at her feet. She is still a virgin. At the age of thirty-seven, she falls in love with a young Spanish grandee twenty-five years old, Monsieur de Mora, who adores her. He leaves for Madrid on family business, still madly in love with her—and stricken with tuberculosis. At this point she falls in love a second time, again with a young man twenty-five years old, Monsieur de Guibert. The night that she gives herself to him, in Paris, Monsieur de Mora, journeying back to her, has a lung hemorrhage and begins to die a lingering death. Julie is heartbroken and accuses herself of being the cause of his death. Her remorse quickens her passion for Guibert. Mora dies. Julie, tormented with grief, suffering from insomnia, delirious with passion for Guibert, which she has fought desperately but in vain, begins to take enormous quantities of opium. Guibert marries. Still in love with him, she writhes in pain, and dies after having written one last letter to him. D'Alembert, who has adored her for more than twenty years and lives in the same house, then discovers her letter to Guibert and is devastated. She has been driven mad by love, love has been the death of her, and he has noticed nothing!

Manon Phlipon worships intelligence and reason, to the point of passion. She occasionally gives proof of a dull, bourgeois turn of mind, but how devoted to her ideals she is, and how upright her conduct! She has enormous moral fervor, and unhappy in her craftsman-father's workshop after the death of a mother she adored, she searches for a husband who is a *philosophe* like herself. She finds him, in the person of Jean-Marie Roland, the future leader of the revolutionary Girondin party, with whom she lives in "perfect understanding"—an expression that is a most exact description of their relationship. Like her husband, she is a passionate advocate of the new revolutionary ideas, and comes to be the muse of the Girondins. The two of them are arrested and guillotined. As every French schoolchild knows, it was Manon who cried out on the scaffold: "*O liberté! que de crimes on commet en ton nom!*" (O Liberty, what crimes are committed in thy name!) What is less well known is the cause of her extraordinary serenity in prison. There in her cell, this perfect example of rectitude can allow herself to think of her

love for another leader of the Revolution, Buzot; in prison her thoughts, her dreams, are free! She knows that she is condemned to die; she will never be physically unfaithful to her husband; he will never know. She may thus love Buzot without remorse. Her death will simplify everything. She dies for her ideas, for her husband—treasuring in her heart her beloved who was never her lover. She is happy. She is loved. She is in love. She has fulfilled herself.

The Cabinet des Fées *will delight the entire Age of Enlightenment, and women, "queens of leisure," continue to invent tales in which they are at once indispensable and inaccessible*

The prejudice that the fairy had aroused in Doudou, a fatal aversion for women, soon manifested itself. The moment that he was able to impose his will, he forbade women to enter his Court. The tribulations that resulted from this order gave rise to that phrase that all too often comes to the lips of oldsters: "Things were not like this in our day." And in truth young men became rude, slovenly, given to drink and to hunting. The ministers yawned in Council, supped in melancholy, and retired scolding their servants. The courtiers fell asleep in all the corners; ambition could scarcely rouse them. . . . One day when the king had strayed some distance away from the rest of the hunting party in over-hot pursuit of a fallow deer, to his vast surprise he found himself in a sort of enormous hall, and saw in one of the corners a young person sitting beneath a canopy of silver gauze, next to an old woman who appeared to sleep. The young person lay her book down on her knees, and began to adjust her coiffure, which the wind had ruffled slightly. A few flowers tucked into the most beautiful hair in the world were its only ornament. A thick lock was readjusted and put back in place across her breast with a care that was proof not only of modesty but of a desire to please. Doudou dismounted, and drawing closer with a feeling of confusion and discomposure that he had never before experienced, he exclaimed: "How fair you are! How worthy of adoration I should find you, were you not a woman!" "I am not a woman. I am Azerolle, and the fairy Sévère whom you see here beside me is taking me to an inaccessible castle."

THE AGE OF EIGHT

I was eight years old when this passion began, and at the age of twelve I teased myself about my fondness for him, though not the fact that I found Monsieur de Gesvres most likable, but I found it less of a joke that I was so eager to go and talk and play in the gardens with him and his brothers. He was two or three years older than I, and the two of us seemed to be much older than the others. As a result we would talk together while the others played hide-and-seek. We behaved most properly, and saw each other regularly every day. We never talked of love; for in all truth neither of us had any idea of what love was. The window of the little apartment was opposite a balcony on which he often appeared. We smiled at each other; he took us to all the Midsummer-Night bonfires, and often to St.-Ouen. As we were always seen together, the tutors and governesses began to joke about it among themselves, and this eventually reached the ears of my Aga,[1] who, as you may well imagine, fancied all sorts of things when he heard it. I learned of this, and it greatly distressed me; as a reasonable person, I believed it was my duty to examine my heart, and this examination caused me to conclude that I might indeed be in love with Monsieur de Gesvres. I was most devout, and went to confession; I first recited all my minor sins, and finally the moment came when I was obliged to avow this major sin; I found myself most reluctant to do so; but as a properly educated young lady I was eager to conceal nothing. I said that I was in love with a young man. My confessor seemed surprised; he asked me if the young man loved me, and if he had told me that he did; I answered no; and he continued his questions. "How do you love him?" he asked me. "As I love myself," I replied. "Well then, do you love him as much as you love God?" he asked. That angered me, for I found it most unfair of him to suspect me of such a thing. He burst out laughing then, and told me there was no penance necessary for such a sin; that I had only to continue to be good and well behaved, and never let myself be alone with a man; and that that was all he had to say to me for the time

[1] She is here referring to Monsieur de Ferriol, the French ambassador to Constantinople, who had bought her when she was four years old. Though she frequented the most elite circles at Versailles and was treated as though she were a girl of high rank at court, having received the education of one, Aïssé was in fact nothing more or less than a slave, the property of her "Aga," who had reserved her for his own personal pleasures.

being. I also admit that one day (I was then twelve years old, and he fourteen or fifteen), he ecstatically announced that he would be going off on the next campaign. I was shocked that he expressed no regrets at leaving me, and I said to him bitterly: "Your words greatly displease us." He immediately apologized, and we discussed the matter for considerable time. That is the most there ever was between us. I am persuaded that he was as fond of me as I was of him. But we were both very innocent—I because I was devout, and he for other reasons. And that is the end of the story.   /46

THE AGE OF TWELVE

The reading of novels caused me to reflect on things that until then I had understood only vaguely. I learned by reading them that there existed a passion that gave women absolute dominion over men.

And I felt great joy at the thought that I had as much right as any other to lay claim to such dominion, and that I might perhaps even have had the occasion to exercise it already. I recalled, in fact, that in the days when I was still living with my grandmother there was a man of quality who loved me and used to call me his "little queen." I remembered all the affection he had shown toward me, and was certain that this was an effect of the passion so well described in novels. . . . I resolved to make him come to visit me so as to enjoy the glorious triumph of making a man submit to my rule. I was far too young (I was twelve at the time) to have any other motive for so doing than sheer vanity. I had no notion that Love could be anything else than this flattering dominion that I would exercise. The way I contrived to get the Marquis de Blossac to come seek me out at the convent was to write to him. I copied out of the novels all the passages that seemed to me to be the most inviting, which is to say that I wrote a most passionate, most tender letter without having the least idea of what I was saying and without so much as surmising that there was any harm in writing such a letter. This is doubtless the perfectly innocent effect that the reading of novels is capable of producing in the mind of a young person. But ultimately this effect is most dangerous, for in acquiring the habit of speaking the language of love, one exposes oneself to the risk of coming to like the word and hence feeling its effects. Having learned from novels that one was obliged to resort to secret and mysterious devices to dispatch one's letters, I conceived the idea of putting mine in a packet of religious works that I said I wanted to give to Blossac as a birthday present. . . .

The abbess told me that since I was capable of writing such letters, I deserved being locked up inside four walls. I began to weep, telling her that I had no idea it was wrong to write such things. She answered me in such a way that I was apprised of everything that I had previously been totally ignorant of. . . .

Of all the things that the abbess told me, nothing impressed me so much as the reproach of having allowed a man to believe that I loved him. She told me that this was the most despicable behavior imaginable, and that girls who acted in this way were held in contempt by the very men whose love they sought. This truly impressed me, and I was not so much filled with horror at the disorders to which she assured me I had exposed myself, as filled with shame at having done a thing which apparently would cause the person I loved to hold me in utter contempt.   /51

Mademoiselle de Bourbonne came back to the convent after a visit outside in the saddest of moods . . . announcing her marriage to Monsieur le Comte d'Avaux. We all flocked round her to ply her with questions. She was barely twelve years old, was to make her first communion the following week, marry the week after that, and then return to the convent. She was in such a grave state of melancholy that we asked her if her future husband displeased her. She told us straight out that he was terribly old and terribly ugly. She also told us that he was coming to see her the following day. We asked Reverend Mother's permission to have the windows of the Orléans apartment opened for us, since it overlooked the convent courtyard and we could thus see our companion's future husband, and our request was granted. Monsieur d'Avaux arrived next day. It was only too true: he was awful! When Mademoiselle de Bourbonne came out of the parlor, everyone said to her: "Good heavens! Your intended is certainly ugly! If I were you, I wouldn't marry him. You poor thing!" And she replied: "I have to marry him, because Papa wants me to, but I won't ever love him, that's certain."
. . . Her intense hatred merely burned the brighter, and once when her intended asked her to come down to the parlor, she pretended to have sprained her foot so as not to be obliged to go downstairs.   /61

FIFTEEN YEARS OLD

I heard talk of a fine gilded coach, handsome livery, nice horses. And the idea of a freedom soon to come so pleased me that had my father proposed to me the least likable man in the world, I do believe I would have married him to have a coach and diamonds, and wear rouge and mules.   /64

Imagine being married six months, and still loving each other after living for such a long time together! They will most certainly become an example for posterity. By my faith, a husband who loves his wife— it's a breath-taking miracle! They are right to marry us off young, for I am persuaded that if one waited till we were older, we would find it most difficult to make up our minds to enter upon an engagement in which it is morally certain (oh, excuse me, I forgot to add the word "almost") that one will be risking one's happiness and freedom. A young person of fifteen or sixteen, already enjoying in her heart an imaginary freedom, imagining that her every desire will be satisfied when she has a gleaming carriage and horses and lots of diamonds, believing in all good faith that the man whom she marries will behave toward her in the same way after the wedding as before, eagerly accepts an offer of marriage. But what a world of difference between a suitor and a spouse!   /62

SEVENTEEN YEARS OLD

My little cousin is very kind, gentle, polite, affable, and obliging. He loves me with all his heart, and I really love him a great deal. An amusing thing happened to us yesterday morning. He came over to me, took my hand as usual, and kissed it. Without even thinking, I drew closer to embrace him. He started to move closer to me too; there then came an instant of reflection, and immediately we both drew back, blushing and laughing. This "dramatic turn of events," for that is what it was, was most amusing. . . . How mad one is at his age and mine! Don't scold me, I am being most sensible nonetheless, and grant him nothing that he does not swear he sees no harm in doing. . . .

I really love him with all my heart, and I shall be most vexed when he leaves. I see him almost all day long. At eight in the morning he is already with me, helps me with my toilette, powders me, puts my shoes on, fastens my necklace, slips my rings on my fingers. As we take walks together, he always offers me his arm.

At night, when Mademoiselle Jaillé comes to fetch me to go to bed, he comes upstairs with me, takes off all the things he has put on me that morning, and as soon as I've done up my hair for the night, he leaves. It is like that every day. Two people fall into the habit of seeing each other constantly, and then . . . Good heavens, what a most unusual young man, I swear!   /62

EIGHTEEN YEARS OLD

From the age of fourteen to sixteen, I wanted a polite man; from sixteen to eighteen I wanted a witty man; and since turning eighteen, I have been wanting a true *philosophe*, so that if things continue in this fashion, at thirty I shall require an angel in human guise, and shall never have anyone.   /49

The couple united by tenderness and a true meeting of minds, the lawfully wedded couple, the marriage, in short, of two persons who have freely chosen each other, is now celebrated for the first time in this history of love: as a consequence, a certain aversion toward adultery, and even an outright opposition to it

I leave it to you to decide everything: be my master, my support, my crown; may your soul animate me, elevate me, and make me ever better, more kindly, and more worthy of you. Your will shall be my law; my fond inclination is to follow it, my aim to divine it and read it even before you express it; my life's work to satisfy you and continually add to your satisfaction. I have no fear that I shall lose my way, for I shall but follow in your footsteps: guide, command, voice your desires. My worth lies in your esteem, it is my merit in your eyes that is its true measure, and it is for you, for you alone, that I shall exist.   /49

> Cécile to the convent is led
> And there welcomed with open arms
> Gold changes hands, hastening the day
> When she will be locked away.
> Alain knows all. For in tears
> Cécile has plotted with him

And love prepares to outsmart
A father's inhuman heart.
The doors of the church open; the victim's steps falter
"My child," the priest intones at the altar
"Why are you come to God's House?
To vow to obey His will?
What seek you?" "A spouse!"
At her words, Alain leaps to her side
And puts his arms round her, glowing with pride
And here in this holy of holies
Hand clasps hand; the priest recites then:
God, receive the vows of Cécile
God, receive the troth of Alain."
All dowager nuns, sore distressed
Flee the chapel, angered and vexed
The priest offers a different prayer
And that night the new-wedded pair
Enjoy supreme bliss by a hearth
As humble as their humble hearts.   /52

I beg Monsieur de La Fayette to kindly serve as the executor of my
last will and testament. Its provisions are not complicated, but it is
most gratifying to me to commit to his keeping all the objects, however
small they may be, that will perpetuate my memory. It seems to me
that this is a way of prolonging our union, which it will surely cost me
dearly to see severed. . . . The letter that I enclose herewith will inform him further in this regard, but I cannot forbear from repeating to
him once again, in the last act of my life, that I have been sensible to
the merits and the delights of my lot, and that I can but wish that I
might in all ways have proved myself deserving of them, as I have done
through my deep tenderness.   /65

I dare not tell you, though you are the only one in the world who
would understand, that I was not very angry at having been arrested.
It will only make them that much less furious, that much less savage
with Roland,[2] I said to myself; if they subject him to some sort of trial,
I will find some way to help him that will enhance his glory. It seemed
to me that I was thus discharging a debt I owed him because of the
suffering he was undergoing; but do you not also see that by finding my-

[2] Her husband.

self alone, it is you with whom I dwell?—hence by being put in prison I sacrifice myself for my husband, keep myself for my friend, and owe to my jailers my having reconciled duty with love: do not pity me!

Others admire my courage, but know nothing of my joys; since you however must be aware of them, I pray you to sustain all their charm through the constancy of your courage. . . .

The most glorious moment of my life, the moment when I felt most passionately that loftiness of soul which braves any and every danger and causes one to congratulate oneself on exposing oneself to them was the one when I entered the cell in the Bastille that my jailers had chosen for me. . . .

I found it delightful to have found a means to be useful to him, and at the same time a manner of living that allowed me to belong more wholly to you than ever. I would like to sacrifice my life for him in order to earn the right to breathe my last breath for you alone. Except for the terrible distress caused me by the decrees against those who have been proscribed, I have never enjoyed greater calm than in this strange situation.   /49

Thus I am free, my dear heart, since here I am on the path that will bring us together again. I feel such surpassing joy that I can only describe it by telling you that I reproach myself for still being capable of such passionate feeling after all the misfortunes that have befallen us.

The memory of them will poison the rest of my life,[3] but I feel that the one whose loss might have been the end of it has been spared me, since I shall soon be with you again.

It was this hope that restored me, almost at the very foot of the scaffold. . . . You will learn the motives of *all*[4] of my actions, of all the steps that I have taken, and it is I myself, my dear heart, who will explain all this to you. I am persuaded that you have not always judged me fairly, but it is my hope to convince you that in everything that I have done, there is not one thing that you would not have approved of, or yourself ordered me to do. I leave you to judge how necessary it was for me to have this intimate conviction at least, in the abyss of horrors in which we were plunged and by which we have been separated. . . .

It has seemed to me—and the experience of our three years' imprisonment serves to confirm my opinion—that you ought to have recourse only to what is solely yours and constantly seeks not to be unworthy of you.   /65

[3] Her grandmother, her mother, and her sister have just been guillotined, and she is leaving (by her own choice) to join her husband in his prison cell.
[4] Underlined in the original text. E.S.

There was a time when, on the occasion of one of your arrivals home from America, I felt myself so violently carried away by my emotions that I was almost ill as you entered the room, that I was overcome with fear that you would find my attentions unwelcome, that I would offend your sensibilities. Hence I endeavored to restrain myself. What remained of my ardor doubtless did not displease you. . . . How I thank God that being so violently carried away was but my duty! How happy I have been! What great good fortune to be your wife!   /65

*The age of reason, and of lucidity as well, which caused people to say of
a woman: "Her folly has always been her wish to be reasonable"*

I discovered proofs that the intensity of his feelings had diminished. I
often visited Mademoiselle d'Epinay, and almost always I found him
there too. As she lived close by I usually returned to the convent on
foot, and he would always take my hand as he accompanied me home.
There was a great open square on the way, and when we first knew each
other, he was in the habit of taking a path that led around it. But later
he chose to cut directly through the middle of it: which led me to conclude that his love had diminished by at least the difference between
the diagonal and the sum of the two sides of the square.   /44

So then, pray write to me. You must know that I cannot write you
first. I am dying to answer you. Your letter will be ridiculous, I am
quite certain. I laugh in anticipation, thinking of all the epigrams that I
shall send you in reply. I'm not saying a word; I am simply waiting.
Please note however that I will not be the one to have made advances. . . .   /45

It is my opinion that, in the role of the beloved, however violent the
situation may be, modesty and self-restraint are necessary things; all of
one's passion must be expressed in the accents and inflections of one's
voice. Violent and excessive gestures should be left to men and magi-
cians. . . .   /46

Were you French, I would immediately conclude that you were a
conceited fool. What could have given you the idea, pray tell, that I
have been carried away by the most romantic passion? This infuriates
me and I would willingly tear your eyes from your head; they are said to
be most beautiful, but surely you cannot suspect them of having made
my head swim.[5] I am searching for the proper words to convey my
scorn, but none come to mind. . . .   /47

Let us return to the subject of my supposed romantic excesses of passion. I the sworn enemy of everything that bears the trace of them, I

[5] She is blind.

who have always openly warred against them, I who have declared my foes all those who made fools of themselves by yielding to them—today find that it is I who am accused of indulging in them! And by whom? That is typically English! But I pray you to note and never forget that in no way do I love you excessively, or more than you deserve. . . . I have resolved to behave quite differently henceforward. I shall never again even utter your name. This pains me somewhat, I freely admit. . . . After your departure, everything round about me seems to have become even more ridiculous to me. When we were together, I divined your thoughts, you knew mine, and we immediately shared them. . . . Be Abélard if you like, but pray do not count on my being Héloïse. This combination, or rather this nonsensical farrago of devotion, metaphysics, and physics, is to my mind mad, excessive, disgusting.   /47

Alas, I would love him, were I more lovable.   /44

Spending our days desiring
Without knowing what it is we desire
Laughing one minute, weeping the next
With no real reason for either
Fearing each morning, hoping each night
That we will have rightful cause to complain
Belittling ourselves when self-flattery is in order
Flattering ourselves when self-reproach would be better
Both loving and hating our torment
At once taking fright—and braving all
Taking serious things lightly
And trifles seriously
Showing ourselves by turn devious and candid
Timid and daring, naïve and wary
Hanging back trembling, while at the same time regretting
Not yet having gone far enough
Suspecting friends who are beyond all suspicion
Being a self divided, by night and by day
That is what we complain of feeling when in love
And of not feeling when we cease to love.   /48

And now my charms I coolly weigh
And remind myself each and every day:
I am thirty, and no longer please
Farewell youth, farewell beauty;
When flattering compliments come my way
My reason tells me the contrary. . . .
For a year now, as I gaze in my looking glass
I no longer bother to curl my hair.

A moment of weakness poisons one's life;
Might you envy my serenity?
Let me enjoy the happiness
Offered me by philosophy.   /50

My friend, come back and see me when you are calmer, more self-controlled; let us nourish with zeal, joy and confidence the tastes that can strengthen, that can embellish the sweet and interesting ties that bind us. The fervor of the senses finally dies away through forbidding oneself the enticing preliminaries that arouse it still more, and through the action of sentiment itself; but esteem, knowledge, and the attachment based on them endure forever.

My friend! (I call you by this sweet name in my heart's effusion), you may find less severity elsewhere, but not more tenderness.   /49

Draw up the plan we must follow yourself; I prefer it to be your handiwork; it will thus please me more to follow it. I have no other tastes than yours, and I have found them too like my own to hope to have sacrifices to make. I am pleased to imagine myself near you, occupied by the tasks that fall to my lot to perform, participating in all your affections and ever working to make them agreeable; going out seldom or only in your company, because no tie between us will please me as much as your house and nothing will be more precious than your presence. We shall study a little because the pleasures of the mind never become wearisome and because we must not fail to come to know them; you shall enlighten me, I shall think with your ideas, I shall be more worthy of esteem and love you even more, if such be possible. We shall see very few people, because very few will resemble us and the others will hold few charms for us.   /49

Love is not something earned through one's merits. It cannot be gained even by the most estimable qualities.

In educating women for love, we forbid them to make use of it. We must make up our minds: if we destine them only to please, let us not forbid them the use of their charms.

It is through resistance that feelings are strengthened and acquire greater degrees of delicacy.

Someone reproached Madame de C—— for violating all the rules of propriety. "I wish to enjoy the loss of my reputation," she replied.   /60

Lucidity often borders on cynicism in this society whose end is approaching

I am very well known and will be most candid. My family origins are not lustrous. Virtuous, or knowing how to appear so, I would have remained as obscure as my birth destined me to be. I would have been the object only of humiliation and scorn. The attraction of pleasure and a few useful counsels saved me from the itch to be well-behaved. In offering myself freely to men, I at least learned to know them and to be contemptuous of them. Interesting women, whom they invariably make unhappy in direct proportion to the degree of sensibility they find in them, ought not to hold it against us when we steal such specimens from them, nothing is as vague, as desultory as their mode of existence. Thanks to a last remaining trace of patriotic zeal, I chose to throw myself at the heads of Englishmen and duped them like a good, conscientious citizen. Those accursed islanders are Jack Roastbeefs impossible to amuse! They lead as boring a life as dogs!   /63

On frequenting "roués," women passionately in love get their wings burned

My coming marriage has recently been announced. I am giving you a greater proof of my love than I have ever given you before, since in the present state of my affairs, there is every indication that this will be the greatest misfortune of my life. But as nothing can increase my unhappiness at separating from you, I do not fear others sufficiently for this thought to counterbalance even for a moment that of giving you pleasure. I have done what you wished me to. I will tell you how to go about things this evening. But inasmuch as I am sacrificing myself for you, I pray you not to fail to give me some proof that you have broken with Mademoiselle de Charolais, in such an unmistakable way that the two of you will never be reconciled. I leave it to you to choose what proof you will give me. You can give me one convincing enough to make me as happy as I can possibly be if I am far from you, and it will be a great consolation to me, as I suffer for you, to think that you merit the love that I have for you in view of the proof that you give me of yours.   /43

But what is most characteristic of all of this era is sensibility and the birth of a new sentiment, admittedly based on sexual attraction, but also on complicity, intellectual sharing, mutual trust, sweet self-surrender: in a word, tenderness

I have reason to be pleased with the chevalier; he has the same tenderness and the same fears of losing me. I do not abuse his affection for me. Taking advantage of the weakness of others is a natural human tendency: I would not be able to practice this art. I know only that of making the life of the one I love so pleasant that he finds nothing else more preferable; I wish to keep him mine solely through the pleasure of living with me. This way that I have chosen makes him most agreeable; I see him so happy that his one ambition is to spend his whole life in this fashion.   /46

Once her father has departed, Beauty seated herself in the great hall and began to weep and to place herself in God's care, for she was convinced that the Beast would eat her up that very evening. . . .

"Beauty," the monster said to her, "do you wish me to watch you sup?" "You are the master," Beauty replied, trembling. "No," the Beast replied, "it is you who command as the one mistress of this house." . . .

On the tenth night at her father's she dreamed that she was in the garden of the palace and saw the Beast lying on the grass on the point of death. . . .

Beauty ran through the palace, with great cries. She was in despair.

After having looked everywhere, she remembered her dream and ran through the garden toward the bank of the stream where she had seen him in her dream.

She found the poor Beast lying senseless on the ground, and thought him dead. She threw herself on his body, feeling no horror at his face. "No, my beloved Beast, you will not die, you will live. From this moment, I give you my hand and swear that I will belong only to you." /56

I have no use for illusions. Our love has no need of them. It was born without them it will endure without them, for it is surely not my charms, which no longer existed when you first knew me, which kept you at my side. Nor is it your uncivilized manners, your churlish, inattentive air, your telling, piquant remarks, your great appetite and your deep slumber when one wishes to converse with you that have caused me to love you madly; it is, rather, a certain indefinable something that attunes our two souls, a certain sympathy that makes me think and feel as you do. For beneath this savage envelope you conceal the spirit of an angel and the heart of a woman. You sum up within yourself all possible contrasts and on this entire earth there is no creature more lovable than you, and none more loved. Farewell, my child; farewell, my friend; farewell, my lover.   /54

The chevalier has left for the Périgord, where he expects to remain for five months. You will be most astonished, madame, when I tell you that he offered to marry me: he said as much very clearly yesterday, in the presence of one of my women friends. It is the most singular passion in the world: this man sees me only once every three months; I do nothing particular to please him; I am too scrupulous to take advantage of the ascendancy that I have over his heart; and no matter what great good fortune would come my way by marrying him, I must love the chevalier for himself. You may well imagine, madame, how this step that he wishes to take would be regarded in society, were he to marry an unknown woman whose sole means of livelihood come from the family of Monsieur de Ferriol. No, I have too high a regard for his reputation, and at the same time too much pride, to allow him to do such a foolish thing. How abashed I would be to hear all the things that people would say! Can I flatter myself that the chevalier would continue to think as highly of me? He would surely repent of having followed the dictates of his passion, and I for my part could not survive the pain of having been the cause of his unhappiness and of being no longer loved.   /46

I read your letter over and over again, and the utterly gratuitous phrase "love me" was nonetheless noted with pleasure, and I counted how many times it occurred. And the whole was appreciated in the same manner.

The "yesterday evening" you mention caused me so little pain, and I considered it so contrary to boring, that I would have given a great deal to pass another like it, or several, and I noted with surprise that despite a severe headache I was most happy.

No one loves you as much, understands you as well, appreciates and esteems you as highly and with as good reason as I, and if I die as many years before you as can only rightly be expected you may then take on other habits, but there is no point in changing your ways in advance. . . .

Farewell, Constantinus. /59

Do not hate me, my child, because I love you too much. Have pity on my weakness, laugh at my folly, and may it never trouble your heart's peace. I am overwhelmed with shame and remorse today; I am thinking of all the proofs of interest, friendship, and love that you have given me since I have known you, and that you give me each day, and I find myself an ungrateful monster. I feel that you do not complain enough, and that the names of Shrew, and Alecton, and so on that you called me yesterday in your *wrath*, are still much kinder names than I deserve; but be patient, my child, I wish to love you so much that all my faults will be erased: my jealousy and my ill temper will vanish at the very thought that they might mar your happiness even for a moment. Go then, be as free as the breeze, take unfair advantage of your freedom, and I shall like it much better than making you aware of the weight of a chain that is too heavy. I want it to be your will alone that guides you to me, rather than have you come to me out of politeness or kindness: I cannot be happy at your expense.

Farewell, my darling: love me if you wish, or rather if you can; but remember that no one in the world loves you and cherishes you as I do, and that life is worth nothing to me unless I spend it with you. /54

Yes, my child, I pardon you for your past, present, and future peevishness. I suffer too much when I find it necessary to nurse a grievance against you, and what I really want is to love you and tell you so. Whatever you do, that is how things always end up; hence I am resolving once and for all to do nothing but that. I grant you a plenary indulgence for all your distractions, and I am more aware than ever that the best way to keep you is to give you free rein. A man has a sort of vague restlessness within him that causes him to feel at ease only somewhere else than where he is. You will no sooner be far distant from me than you will want to come back, and I promise you in advance that you will always be well received.

I hope that the affair that was preying on your mind is ended; send me word of it, I beg you: I do not like to see you have other griefs than those I cause you. I would like to be forever the mistress of your destiny, in order to make your lot an enviable one, and apart from a few little teasing worries that often wrongly cause you to despair, you would lead a most pleasant life. I would drive away from you that ugly Morpheus that has such a strong hold over you, and that makes you so dull-witted, for it is no use having a mind if one merely makes of it a place to bed down in; that is a crime of *lèse-spiritualité*.   /54

The compensation for all my pains, the consolation for all my reasons for despair, the nourishment for all my hopes: a big packet of letters from you, even heavier than the last. You laugh at this compliment, I am certain, and can't imagine how sheer weight can contribute to the value of anything but a treasure. But isn't this indeed my treasure? Your words, or rather your thoughts, are golden to me; they are the only fortune I possess, it is through them that I live, and it is for them, that is to say for you, that I wish to live like an old miser. I contemplate my treasure and scarcely dare touch it. I examine the address; I examine each of the *letters* to see if you were pressed for time when you wrote it, what you were thinking of; I then look at the seal, and see that you did not use mine, nor did you use my *emblem*; that makes me a bit anxious; I tremble, not daring to break it; I suddenly fear spoiling the pleasure that I feel by spying some piece of bad news.

My heart pounds and I finally break it, fearing that some bothersome visitor will arrive and thus deprive me for too long of the opportunity of satisfying my curiosity. Once the packet is opened, I begin with the last letter, the most recent date. I think I am reading, but I am not, such is the state that I am in: my eyes brim over, and the packet on my knees is wet with my tears.

Each page is kissed, one by one; but I read them with the same fear and the same precautions as when one touches a razor or some other weapon that one fears might hurt one.

It takes me more than twenty-four hours to realize what they contain, after the first agitation has subsided a bit, and I feel a number of different things in succession, varying with the different situations in which you have found yourself; and when I find you overwhelmed by events and suffering, I turn the page very quickly to see if on the morrow you are still in the same state. But happily for both of us, my child, your trials and tribulations scarcely ever last more than a day, except for that inflammation in your finger, which almost made me die of impatience. Seriously, I read with the greatest pleasure everything that your Monsieur Martin has written about you to the Abbé Gibelin; how astonished he is at everything he sees you say and do, how you have proved equal to every occasion, how you have taken care of everything except yourself. Your minor war caused me to spend a few uncomfortable moments; but on turning the page I saw you shout *Victory! Victory!* and I did likewise, sitting next to my hearth a thousand leagues away, as though you could hear. Farewell, Lord Jupiter; as you prepare your thunderbolts to punish rash kings, look with kindness upon your humble subject, who has never rebelled for a single instant against your supreme power, and who has never known any other will save yours. /54

I arrived here day before yesterday, my child, with no other companion save the chill that lingered on till evening. I would be perfectly happy here if tranquillity sufficed for happiness; but it requires a mixture of pleasure and pain that nothing is capable of causing me to feel. You are the only alchemist who can perform this masterwork, and when you are not with me, I remain in a state of stagnant repose that is very little different from death. Come as soon as you can, so long as you do not do so against your will.

So, then, I wait for you with inexpressible pleasure, for I love you even more here than elsewhere: not that we have quarreled here as much as in Paris, but our quarrels were less bitter and our reconciliations sweeter, and in short I have seen you agreeable to me for such long periods of time here that there is nothing here that does not speak to me favorably of you.

Farewell, my child; think of me if you can; but above all don't go to the Moulin de Javelle[6]; ever since the adventure of the first aeronaut it terrifies me to think of it. . . . Don't try such an adventure again, I beg of you, and don't throw everything I value to the winds. I have only just enough confidence in the element that is natural to us; hence don't trust anything to chance.

Farewell, my friend; farewell, my lover; I love you as though I were only fifteen and the world were in the Golden Age: that is what makes it so difficult to get along well with you, since you are a bit too attached to the iron age. /54

[6] The site of a contemporary attempt to fly. (*Translator's note.*)

*The tragic note, however, begins to sound more and more clearly: ro-
mantic passion precedes Romanticism as a literary movement*

My friend, I love you as one ought to love, to excess, in madness, ecstasy, and despair. . . .   /53

You have left me, abandoned me, and I have nothing left to assuage
my pain. I am alone in the world. I have neglected my friends, broken
off intimate relations, burned the proofs of love that once upon a time
I inspired in my husband. I have burned the shared secrets, confidences,
assurances of tender affection of my childhood friends. Yesterday you
took from me the few words of love that escaped your lips. Farewell,
my dear Vincent: You will nonetheless be the eternal object of my love
if I see you again, of my regrets if nothing brings you back to
me.   /61

I love only for the pleasure of loving. You have already exposed me
to the last degree of misery, I thought that I should die of your outra-
geous eccentricities, I have sacrificed everything in order to put an end
to them, I have done everything in my power to gain your confidence. I
am revolted at not having succeeded, and to see that almost three years
were unable on your return to bring me even four or five days of
tranquillity and happiness. You will find twenty mistresses who will be
more to your liking than I, your reputation is well established; as far as
your glory is concerned, I have not tarnished it, and as far as your tenderness is concerned, I have enhanced it. Many will be tempted by it,
and few will be frightened off by your ill temper; either they will be
strong enough to combat it, or tactless enough to justify it. Farewell, I
am prostrated by the night that I have just spent. I have other things as
well in mind, and am thinking less of reproaching you for them than of
firmly resolving, once and for all, to renounce love and you, my very
dear count, you who have never loved me for myself, and who would
cause me to die without the slightest compunction, even though you
might live to regret it.   /55

I no longer know what I owe you; I no longer know what I give you;
I know that your absence weighs heavily upon me, and yet would be

unable to answer myself that your presence is a comfort to me. But I swear to heaven! what a hideous situation this, where pleasure, consolation, friendship, everything in the end turns to poison!   /53

Could you perhaps fear for your freedom? That would be to impute to me the demands of love. I do not believe I feel any love, because I feel no jealousy at all; go seek your pleasure where you will.

Say that you have sacred rights and claims to me, that no other can have any such, and I shall complain no more.

When I spoke of all that, coldly or in jest, I was deceiving myself, and deceiving you. I am terribly jealous: everything that another woman approaches seems sullied and contemptible to me. That is what I have to say to you.

Do you not know that a man cannot seduce those women whom he has charmed?   /45

Yes, you must love me madly: I demand nothing, I pardon everything, and I am never ill tempered for even a moment; my friend, I am perfect, I love you to perfection.   /57

It pains me to see that when you believe I feel no desire you believe less in my love, and when you know how I feel desire you are troubled, believing that I have arrived at the moment when I shall be unfaithful. I have desires, that is certain. But never such violent ones as when alone, troubled, distressed.   /57

I have every sort of possible feeling toward you: I love you as your mother, your sister, your daughter, your friend, your wife, and even better, your mistress. I love you so much that I think of nothing save that, feeling for everything else so great an indifference that it bears as close a resemblance to death as two peas in a pod.

You are the soul that animates my body; my feelings can be touched only by you; it is your will and pleasure that determine the good and ill that befall me, and I shall henceforth know no happiness unless you choose to make me happy.   /54

I cannot explain to myself the charm that binds me to you. You are not my friend, and you cannot become such: I do not trust you in the slightest; you have dealt me the most profound and painful hurt that

can possibly be inflicted upon an honest soul and rend it asunder: at
this moment, and perhaps forever, you are depriving me of the one consolation that heaven had granted me in these last days I have left to live;
in short—how can I possibly tell you!—you have filled every moment of
my life: the past, the present, and the future hold only pain, regrets,
and remorse for me; in any event, my friend, I ponder, I consider all
this, and I am drawn to you by an attraction, by a sentiment that I
abhor, yet it has the power of a fateful malediction, of destiny itself.
You do well not to take any notice whatsoever of me and of my lot: I
have no right to demand anything of you; for my most passionate wish
is that you come to mean nothing to me. What would you have to say
of the state of mind of a miserable creature who for the first time
would reveal herself to you thus, deeply perturbed, overwhelmed by
feelings so diverse and so at odds with each other? You would pity her:
your kind heart would be immediately touched; you would hasten to
help, to succor such an unfortunate woman. Well, my friend, it is I
who am this hapless creature; it is you who are the cause of this misfortune, and this soul on fire and in mortal pain is your creation. Ah! I still
believe in you as I believe in God; you have every reason to bitterly
repent your handiwork.   /53

All my suspicions with regard to your true nature, all my resolutions
not to fall in love have been powerless to protect me against the love
you inspired in me. . . . I am certain that today you are more joyful and
wittier than ever at Lunéville, and apart from all the cares that weigh
heavily upon me, this thought particularly pains me. . . . I am truly
afraid that a clever remark will make a deeper impression on your mind
than a tender sentiment on your heart; in a word, I am truly afraid of
loving you overmuch. I am well aware that I am contradicting myself;
my reflections, my violent inner struggle, my every thought, are proof to
me that I love you more than I ought.

It is you who will decide everything, and I do not know if your heart
is worthy of so doing.   /66

In worldly circles where you have so many ways of making a success
of yourself, I see you dancing with those women who dance, consoling
those who do not dance, and singling out pretty little faces rather than
proud, haughty beauties, and then finally coming home to our distant
retreat, thinking wistfully of a woman who laughs, who dances, who
likes keeping late hours, yet still truly loving one who does not dance,
who finds it impossible to stay up late, and whose soul can be moved to

joy only when she possesses, as a woman possessed her lover in the golden age, or as a woman tells of possessing her lover in novels (in the space of a single page), after having taken a thousand pages to describe how much she desires him.   /58

Yes, my friend, I love you. I wish this sad truth to haunt you, to trouble your happiness; I wish the poison that has kept me from living my life, that is destroying it, and that will doubtless put an end to it, to spread to every last corner of your soul and bring you this same excruciating sensitivity, which will at least dispose you to regret the person who has loved you with all possible tenderness and passion. Farewell, my friend, do not love me, since that would be contrary to your sense of duty and against your will; but allow me to love you, and to tell you so a hundred times, a thousand times, though never with words that properly express what I feel.   /53

To me you are a word puzzle. I've been given all the definitions, I have all the letters, and yet I cannot quite put the word together.

I once knew a woman who was taxed with not being as polite as she ought to be toward serious-minded persons worthy of the greatest respect. She replied that she was nineteen years old, and at that age one was *past all sense of shame*. I for my part say that at my age[7] one does not offend common decency by allowing oneself to be carried away by passionate professions of friendship.   /47

But I who am spending my days wailing and trembling with fear, I who am growing old and careworn because of you—what will I have left after all your frantic chasing? A heart overburdened by the gratitude that it will believe it owes me and by the infirmities that time will have visited upon me, or the despair of seeing you perish thanks to some treacherous plot or a sudden burst of shrapnel. That is the state of mind I am in, the expectations I have, the fruit of the feelings that I have for you. There are those here who say "She is mad," or others, "She deceives us and is faithless." How can I be certain that you will continue to believe that this is the case? For such a conclusion would make up for all the rest. But there is no one more suspicious and mistrustful than you, and should you find it to your advantage to doubt this, you will not hesitate to do so, and I shall thereupon immediately lose both your heart and the reward for my fidelity.   /55

---

[7] She is sixty-eight years old at the time.

Merciful heaven! how a feeling changes and upsets everything! This *I* of which Fénelon speaks is merely another idle fancy: I am quite persuaded that I am not me. I am you; and to be you costs me no sacrifice whatsoever. . . .

And yet you praise me for loving you! Ah, this is a crime, and even my excess does not justify me. But I shall horrify you: for I am like Pyrrhus, I give myself over to crime as a born criminal. Yes, love you or cease to live—I recognize only this virtue and this law in nature; and this sentiment is so true, so involuntary, and so strong that in all truth you owe me nothing. Ah, how far I am from making any sort of demand, from laying any sort of claim! My friend, be happy, take pleasure in being loved, and any debt you might owe me will thereby be paid in full.   /53

When I am with you, I am most patient with my lot; often I am not even aware of it; but when I am without you, everything looks black to me. I went to my little house today, on foot, and my belly is sagging so, my back aches so, I am so dispirited this evening, that I would not be at all surprised to find myself in labor during the night, but if so I would be very sad, even though I know that that would please you. I wrote you eight pages yesterday, which you will not receive before Monday. You did not make it clear whether you will be back on Tuesday, or whether you will be able to get out of going to Nancy in September. My spirits are so low and I am so melancholic that I would be frightened if I believed in premonitory signs.[8] My letter waiting for you in Nancy will please you more than this one. I didn't love you more then than now, but had more strength then to tell you how I love you.   /66

Never will a reproach, a complaint, trouble your life and Aimée's! I will be a faithful friend to her! All I ask is for her to allow me to kiss your hands, to offer you and her everything I have, all my most loving affections, to hold you close with tender wishes for your happiness that I was unable to make come true.

In the name of the modicum of happiness that I was able to give you, in the name of your many unfulfilled vows, so often repeated, never to abandon me, I implore you not to separate your life from mine and to unite with them the life of the woman who has proved herself more worthy of possessing you than I.

---

[8] Four days later she will give birth to a baby girl fathered by her lover, and die a week later.

O you whom I no longer dare to call mine, though through my excess of love you still belong to me, despite your changing affections, look with pity upon me. Pray consider where I would spend my days should you abandon me. In a house where I have had a tomb erected for Aimée's child, or else in this retreat where you have turned everything topsy-turvy in order to make it beautiful and live there with me. Pray consider whether the torments of hell would be any more painful than that of living in these haunts without you. For me there is no greater horror than that of never seeing you again.

Oh, I beseech you, dear friend, do not abandon me; should your thoughts take you back to one or another of the happy days that you spent with your Sophie, you whose heart is so kind and tender will look with pity on my sad lot, and for me this pity will be the very breath of the only life still left in me.

I await your reply, dear Aimée, here where I am like someone on his deathbed, awaiting the helpful potion which will permit his eyes to linger a few moments longer on the being that he adored.   /58

My friend, I shall not be seeing you, and you will tell me that it is not your fault! But if you had so much as the thousandth part of the desire that I have to see you, you would be here; and I would be happy. No, I am mistaken, I would suffer; but I would still not yearn for the pleasures of heaven. My friend, I love you as one ought to love, to excess, in madness, rapture, and despair. All these past days you have put my soul to torture. I saw you this morning, and forgot everything else immediately; it seemed to me that I was not doing enough for you simply by loving you with all my heart and soul, ready and willing both to live and to die for you. You deserve more than that; yes, if I were capable only of loving you, that would in all truth be nothing: for is there anything more tender and more natural than to love madly that which is perfectly lovable? But, my friend, I am capable of something better than loving: I know how to suffer, and would be able to renounce my pleasure if it would further your happiness.

Do you know why I am writing you? It is because doing so pleases me: you would never have suspected this had I not told you so. But in heaven's name, where are you? If happiness has come your way, that is good enough reason for me to cease complaining that you are robbing me of mine.   /53

Three of these passionate women remain in love and write to their lovers to the very last, knowing that death is close at hand

His many courtesies, his tender thoughts, loving me for myself, his concern for our poor little daughter, whom he wishes to have a decent station in life—all of this has caused me to promise myself to be as considerate of his feelings as I can. . . .

These then, madame, are the resolutions that I have made and shall keep. I do not doubt that by resorting to such extreme measures I am hastening my end. There has never been a passion more violent, and I can safely say that his for me is equally strong. Our concern and agitation are so genuine, so touching, that they bring tears to the eyes of all those who are witness to them. . . .

They say that I am better, yet I find no relief from pain. I spit up hideous things and sleep thanks only to my doctor's arts. I grow thinner and weaker by the day. . . .

Moreover, I am not suffering from some acute malady: I simply find that I am slowly wasting away to nothing. As for the pains of the soul, they are most cruel. I cannot tell you how much the sacrifice that I am making is costing me; it is killing me. But I trust in God's mercy; He will give me strength. One cannot deceive Him; hence, since He knows the sincerity of my will and everything I feel, He will give me rest. My mind is at last made up: As soon as I can be up and about, I shall go confess my sins. I wish in no way to make a show of my conversion, and shall change my outward conduct only slightly. . . .

With regard to my soul, I hope that next Sunday it will be delivered of all its impurities. I shall confess to my every sin. I was a party to a most touching scene yesterday. I am sending you a copy of a letter brought to me in reply to one that I had written, full of expressions of friendship and detachment from the things of this world, and telling of my resolution. . . .

You will be astonished when I tell you that my confidants and the instruments of my conversion are my lover, Madame de Parabère, and Madame du Deffand. . . .

I shall not speak to you of the Chevalier [d'Aydie]; seeing me as ill as I am, he is in despair; no one has ever seen a passion as violent, more delicacy of feeling, more tenderness, more nobility and generosity. I am not at all worried about our poor little daughter: she has a friend and a protector who loves her dearly.

The life that I have led has been a most miserable one: have I ever had a single moment of joy? I could not bear to be by myself; I was afraid my thoughts would overwhelm me; I had known nothing but remorse ever since the moment my eyes were first opened to the ways in which my wild passion had caused me to stray from the path of right-eousness.   /46

Ah, my friend, how my soul aches; I have no words left, only cries. . . .

Alas, as I told you, in my excess of sorrows I know not whether it is you or death that I implore. It is through you or through it that I must be granted surcease from my pain, or cured forever. There is nothing in all of nature that can help me now. . . .

But why did you more or less set your heart on being loved by me? You didn't need my love; you were well aware that you were in no posi-tion to return it. Can you have made a game of plunging me into de-spair? Fill my soul then, or leave off tormenting it: make me love you forever, or make me never to have loved you at all. In a word, do the impossible, calm me or I shall die. . . .

But I no longer need fight against what you inspire in me, I have seen the depths of my soul clearly. Ah! my terrible unhappiness justifies everything that I have done; I am not guilty, and yet in a short time I shall be a woman condemned. . . .

Oh! how many times one dies before dying! Everything brings me pain and does me harm; and the freedom to deliver myself from the burden that is crushing me has been taken from me! I am expected to go on living, in the very depths of misery; my heart is torn asunder by both the despair and the tender feelings inspired in me. Ah, dear God, is it not a good then to love and be loved? . . .

Why pity me then? Ha!—why? Because a sick person doomed to die nonetheless awaits his physician's visit, raising his eyes to his in search of a ray of hope in them, because the ultimate expression of pain is a bitter complaint, because the last utterance of the soul is an outcry. . . .

I received your letter at one o'clock; I was burning with fever. I can-not tell you how much effort and time it required to read it: I did not want to let it wait until today, and doing so came close to plunging me into delirium. I am waiting to hear from you this evening. Farewell, my friend. If I were to be restored to life, I should still wish to devote it to loving you; but there is no time left now.   /53

Do you know any greater boon than that of proving oneself superior to adversity, to death, and finding in one's heart reason to enjoy and embellish life to one's very last breath? Have you ever experienced those feelings more deeply than in the attachment that binds us each to the other, despite the contradictions of society and the horrors of oppression? As I have told you, I owe my pleasure at my imprisonment to this attachment. —Proud of being persecuted in these times when character and probity are proscribed, even without you I would have borne my imprisonment with dignity; but because of you it is sweet and precious to me as well. My evil jailers believe they are breaking my spirit by putting me in chains—stupid creatures!: what does it matter where I spend my days? Do I not journey everywhere with my heart, and is not shutting me up in a prison a chance to surrender myself wholly to this heart of mine? My company is what I love; and my one concern is to ponder it. . . .

You cannot imagine, my friend, the charm of a prison, where one must account only to one's own heart for the way in which one chooses to spend one's every moment! No annoying distractions, no painful sacrifices, no nagging concerns; none of those duties that an honest heart finds all the more rigorous in that they are self-imposed; none of those contradictions of the laws or the prejudices of society with the sweetest inspirations of nature; no jealous gaze watching to catch a glimpse of the signs of one's true feelings or spying on the ways in which one chooses to occupy one's time; no one feels aggrieved by your fits of melancholy or your indolence; no one expects efforts from you or demands feelings of which you are incapable. Left entirely to oneself, to truth, with no obstacles to overcome, no struggles to wage, one is able, without infringing upon the rights or hurting the feelings of anyone, to abandon one's soul to its own rectitude, rediscover one's moral independence in the very depths of an apparent captivity and exercise it to a degree that social relationships almost always set limits to. It was not even permissible for me to seek such independence and thus free myself of the obligation of making another person happy, which I found so difficult and so burdensome; events have procured for me what I would not otherwise have been able to obtain without committing a sort of crime. How I cherish the chains in which I am free to love you wholly and devote my every moment to you! . . .

And you whose name I dare not utter!—You whom others will one day know better as they pity our shared misfortunes; you whom the most terrible of passions did not prevent from respecting the barriers imposed by virtue, will you be overwhelmed with grief at seeing me arrive before you in those precincts where we shall be able to love each other without its being a crime, where nothing shall prevent us from being one? —There in that place fatal prejudices fall silent. . . . I shall wait for you there, and take my rest.   /49

Like life, involuntary
Inevitable as death
Marceline Desbordes-Valmore

·VI·

The Liberation of Feeling

Happy in her prison cell to be able to reconcile at last, without sin, the impulses of her tender heart, her conjugal fidelity, and her lofty thoughts, Manon Phlipon—Madame Roland—left it to her executioners to resolve her profound contradictions through an act of radical violence, and she died on the scaffold, as a *philosophe*, a faithful wife, and a passionate mistress. "O Liberty, what crimes are committed in thy name!"

Three years later, Manon Phlipon would appear to have died in vain. Liberty feeds on minor crimes, little compromises, and a great deal of license. "Frenchmen believe, rightly, that there can be no pleasures and amusements save those that women determine, take charge of, and share. That is the root, my good friend and sister, of the ascendancy that we enjoy, the power that we exercise on people's minds, the influence that women have on affairs," Caroline Wuiet writes that year (Prairial An VII) in *La Correspondance des dames*. Men and women frequent the gaming tables ("All I see are convex men and concave gold coins"). They scrutinize each other, dress and undress extravagantly, caress each other, tumble into bed with each other, try to find a niche for themselves, and no longer talk to each other. "Why would people talk to each other when there is nothing to say to each other? Conversation is a communication, a correspondence of thoughts and feelings, and this commerce falls completely by the wayside when one no longer has thoughts or feelings . . ." (*La Mésangère*, 1797). The sick state of "communication" about which there was such endless talk in the 1960s induces a similar state of paralysis in this hedonist society that has just escaped the toils of virtue and revolutionary terror. Everything is permitted, save idealism, which everyone is sick to death of. A veil of silence is thrown over the recent past: " 'the circumstances' / that is to say the events of the Revolution / that allowed swindlers to swindle, mothers to sell their daughters; the 'circumstances' have become the compass for everyone: the good yet to be done depends on the 'circumstances' to come and the evil that is being done depends on the 'circumstances' of the past" (*Journal des dames et des modes*, 20 Thermidor, An II). A public ball is announced in these words: "On display will be a considerable quantity of languishing gazes, flirtatious glances, affected sighs, whispers, compliments, sententious phrases, witty repartee, and a very small quantity of virtue and decency of which only a very few examples remain. But there will be an abundance of sherbets and other refreshments." The *philosophes*, who are no longer the brilliant men who compiled the great *Encyclopédie*, join the rest: "they have examined the relations between the two sexes with such genius that they have changed all our moral ideas. By their lights modesty was but a prejudice instilled in us by our upbringing, and conjugal fidelity a peril to the freedom of the heart. The stronger sex is constituted by nature to attack, and the weaker sex to surrender. Exclusive claim to a woman violates the rights of society as a whole: it is stealing what belongs to all men. Love and pleasure are the sole ties uniting the two halves of the human race." And as a consequence: "Between the sexes, there is no place for mutual attraction, merely simple habit, a comfortable coming to terms, sensations, physical needs, totally bereft of all the charms of moral uprightness and the magic of imagination."

But thanks to a carefully calculated policy imposed from above, "the charms of moral uprightness and the magic of imagination" were soon to become the order of the day once again, to the point of subjecting an entire nation's aspirations to pleasure to their tyrannical rule. After the revolutionary whirlwind and this collapse of will, an entire weary country enthusiastically allows itself to be taken over by a young general who believes that he can escape the contradictions born of "the circumstances" by exporting to all of Europe his idea of revolution through his Grand Army, like a bloody dream of fraternity and universalism preached to the sound of drums. . . . Domestically, under the aegis of General Bonaparte, who becomes Napoleon, the new society is organized for all eternity. Weights and measures, national manufactories, geographical *départements*, schools, the flow of information, are regulated from above. The Administration brings order to this disordered society, chasing after the dream of a global society of which the Napoleonic Code was to be the more or less definitive expression. Moreover, this system will continue long after Napoleon, for it has great internal consistency. The bourgeoisie, which had won the Revolution, holds the reins of power, according to the somewhat oversimplified analyses of Marxists in search of classes to recognize and oppose. This is partially true, though it ought to be added for our purposes that it was a power elite that was *masculine*.

For Napoleon and his administrators put everything in order and gave each person his function, but at the same time forgot, or kept from power, at least three social groups within the bourgeoisie: women, who are again relegated to the home and childbearing after the libertine excesses of the Directory and the Consulate; young people, who had had easy years in power after the debacle of their elders during the revolutionary whirlwind, and are not consigned by one of their former numbers, Napoleon himself, to the schoolroom, uniforms, and strict discipline; and third, artists, who had been nearly shipwrecked in the storm-tossed waters of revolution and are now reduced to celebrating with their pens, brushes, and sculptor's chisel the antique perfection of this new order.

These three groups, veritable "inner exiles," endure the cold alone in the beginning. But gradually they begin to cast glances at each other, to plot like children, to sigh in concert, and dream of each other. Together with a handful of real exiles such as Chateaubriand or Germaine de Staël, these three groups will create something that Napoleon neither wished nor foresaw: Romanticism.

Women for their part are tired of the revolutionary chaos that had brought the triumph of whores, and the majority of them gladly re-embrace bourgeois morality. Indeed, they make modesty a fashion. Dresses slit at the hems and low necklines revealing part or even all of the breasts are no longer the style, and in the space of just a few years long sleeves and high-buttoned dresses become the height of elegance, while hair styles change from the wild revolutionary exuberance of a "victim" or "Titus" coiffure or Turkish headgear to neat little caps worn over two smooth wings of hair.

For twelve years, women had not gone to church, and now they begin to flock there. "Religion is re-opening its temples today. The prettiest woman in Paris can be found taking a collection for the poor at Saint-Roch Church. The presence of the First Consul, who is to attend the Te Deum mass, the charm of the music, the spectacle offered by the combination of such novel religious ceremonies and parade drills by the military are already arousing the curiosity of the entire capital. Tickets for the gallery and the church square are in great demand. If the church were large enough, all Paris would hasten to attend. It is the fashion today to attend church, and we alert our faithful lady sub-scribers to this fact once and for all."[1]

They hasten to church in droves, leave each other scarcely room enough to breathe, faint, and swoon, as though this were a new form of theater at first, and then very soon thereafter fall under what for them is the novel spell of the subtleties of a religion that is becoming both more sentimental and more dogmatic. Their senses are dizzied by it and mortified by it. Little by little religiosity comes to envelop their en-tire life, and though the utopian visionaries of 1833–38, like the revolu-tionaries of 1848, think along socialist lines, they also speak of God, of sainthood, of sacrifice and charity, a sentimentalism at once vaguely mystical and moralistic.

And above all, by contagion religiosity also completely changes the language of love. As between confessors and women in love, which of them leads the other up this particular garden path? one wonders. In any event, love itself becomes divine by essence. According to the ro-mantic doctrine which soon filters down to every level of society, loving, far from leading away from God, brings one closer to Him. Every person who loves is an Elect, participating in this divine purity, this commun-ion of saints. Love is God on earth, at whose feet one must kneel in adoration. This is the first victory, and an important one, that women in love win over the Church, which had so endlessly rehearsed is abhor-rence of human love. But it is a precarious victory (reactionary French Catholicism will take quite another view of love, fortify its defenses, and mount an even more violent offensive against it), and above all an ambiguous one, for it is a victory won by a sort of invasion by men and women lovers of the domain reserved for religion. And once they have set up camp in the holy of holies, women in love and love poets, like all conquerors, are in turn conquered by the language that they have begun to employ and the dialectic that they have adopted as a tool. As we would say today, they are "co-opted" by the Church. In order to ensure that they will enjoy the divine rights of the *heart,* women boldly use the word as a synonym for *soul*—and disgusted by this deliberate moral confusion, the last great mystics such as Félicité de La Mennais loose their thunderbolts to condemn it. But to their own vast disserv-ice, women consent to this denial of their bodies by ceasing to talk of them: the victory of the heart and its feelings is worth any price. There is, naturally, a tacit understanding that the great Elect among lovers are able to pass from the spiritual-sentimental to the carnal in divine beati-tude, "accidentally," so to speak. But the others, women in particular, will be brought up short by this invisible glass wall, and, obliged to re-

[1] *Journal des dames et des modes,* 1802.

main on this side of it, the side of feeling alone, of timidity and burning remorse, they will begin to be terrified of physical love. And in a word, to be incapable of it. For it is not until the nineteenth century that the suspicion is voiced, and subsequently confirmed, that there is such a thing as a frigid woman. Before then the complaint was, rather, that women suffered from an excess of passionate desire. And now they dare speak of this nonpleasure, and even the horror, they feel at this repugnant act that brings an end to the ethereal period of courtship. The few lines written by Madame Lafarge to her husband, whom she will later be accused of having murdered, speak volumes in this regard. Innocent child that she was, she expected nothing more than friendly hand-holding and affectionate kisses on the brow. But making love and religion synonymous was a vast undertaking, and naturally sex pure and simple could not be dumped all at once into the mixture. For the moment it sufficed to amalgamate religious sentiment and the communion of souls of two persons of a different sex who were attracted to each other. "Léonce, for a moment I was overcome with doubts; I found the unhappiness that had overtaken me more grievous than my sins; but now religious hopes have returned to my heart; heaven has given them back to me, and I shall share them with you," we read at the end of *Delphine* (the fictional name that Germaine de Staël assumes in her autobiographical novel), Love is "by essence divine," George Sand's *Valentine* assures us, seconded by Lamartine, who is of the opinion that profane love is the path to divine love.

There are frequent halts by the wayside along this path, and this entire vocabulary compounded of hypocrisy and confusion (or so it seems to us today) was all the rage in its day. It was not innocent perhaps, but it was doubtless most heartfelt and sincere, and more than we might suppose it represented a liberation—a psychological liberation of imagination and feeling which heretofore had been pitilessly stifled, by coarse ribaldry on the one hand and by a formal, worldly, occasionally mystical, but only very rarely loving and charitable religion on the other.

For far from being, as is often thought, the moralizing of those in power in order to keep the weak in leading strings, this sentimental and religious outpouring, this perfumed opium, was also, and perhaps most important, a protest and even a rebellion against the powers in the ascendancy in the nineteenth century, that is to say, the mechanistic materialism that was then laying the groundwork for its greatest conquests, and the pitiless capitalism that was to bring such rich profits to the most unconscionable scoundrels.

The true history of this period is written in the manufactories, the workshops, the factories, where women of the poor classes begin to labor fourteen long hours a day, in banks, on construction sites, in laboratories. In the eyes of middle-class women, men appear to be totally involved in commercial and scientific conquests from which they are excluded. They immediately ally themselves with those who have been injured and offended by these realities and are creating a wildly sentimental superstructure, a new art of feeling that is closed to noninitiates; they ally themselves with the "young hearts" that Alfred de Musset speaks of, "condemned to repose by the sovereigns of this world, a prey to boorish pedants of every variety, doomed to idleness and ennui. . . ."

Against this somber background of the "romance of industry," the Romantics seek to create another sort of romance: that of the individual, that of the soul, out of a need for vague certainties more gratifying than the purely negative truths of the eighteenth century. In this language that is parallel to reality, that denies it by opposing it, the weak are superior to the strong. To be defeated is to be victorious. Possession comes only with the gift, or the sacrifice, of oneself. Suffering is redemption, and suffering is women's province.

It is women who are the source of good, beauty, tenderness, tactfulness—in a word, love. "It would seem that the name of woman is incompatible with the idea of evil." There is no such thing now as women of loose morals; there are only "unfortunate women." Being weak, women cannot be guilty. They are seen only as victims, expiating the sins of their churlish husbands. When all is said and done, even prostitutes, even "fallen" women, are seen as innocent because they are victims, led astray not by themselves but by society, by men who have dealt ruthlessly with them. And feminists seek not to "rescue them from the mire" so much as to make virtuous wives and mothers realize that both they and their fallen sisters are victims of the same men and must forgive each other, smile at each other, and join forces: "You women whose hearts are charitable, you have doubtless deplored the lot of young and beautiful women who have been plunged into the depths of vice! But how aggrieved you ought to be at the thought that these unfortunate creatures have been led astray by your brothers, your spouses, your sons! It is in God's name that I invite you to contribute to the work that we are undertaking to save our sex from the shame and humiliation that has befallen it through prostitution."

Women were convinced that through passion in every meaning of the word (that is to say, suffering undergone, suffering consented to, suffering patiently endured) they would win respect. And the passionate outcries of women who have given themselves entirely and told of their sacrifice come straight from the heart and reveal extraordinary adven-

tures of the soul. They have tried, truly, to be saints of love and bleed
and weep when the moment of their martyrdom is at hand, in the form
of neglect, denial, abandonment, by the men they love. But they for
their part neither neglect nor deny, and thereby fulfill themselves. A
number of them, in fact, pass through the Strait Gate and attain sanctity: Marceline Desbordes-Valmore and Laure de Berny, and above all
Juliette Drouet. May our heartfelt respect, our amazement, our fervent
admiration be theirs forevermore. Marceline was not at all beautiful,
and so poor that as a child she read only a single book of poetry, but
she found within herself such perfect music that her example alone is
enough to make us believe in inspired genius. Laure de Berny was long
past her youth when at the age of forty-nine and the mother of nine
children she found love, but she nonetheless rediscovered and expressed
the purest spontaneity of soul and the utmost devotion free of the
slightest trace of vapidity in her steadfast attachment to her Honoré de
Balzac, twenty years younger than she. Juliette was beautiful, Juliette
was young, but being fresh out of the convent where she was raised, she
proved a rather spineless courtesan; and then in the space of a single
night she embraced the religion of love and remained faithful to her
vows for fifty years, despite the fact that her God deceived her and betrayed her countless times. They were fifty years full of letters even more
beautiful than those that her lover, Victor Hugo, wrote to her (though
she herself had no idea that this was so, and would not have believed
it), and what is more, fifty years of inventing a whole art of love, of discovering the light within herself at the very bottom of the deep pit in
which she had cast herself; and fifty years as well of what can only be
described as a miracle: true goodness in the midst of the most ardent
passion. Whatever men and women today, who believe that they have
become free by cutting themselves off from genuine feeling, may think
of them, these three prisoners of love passed straight through the wall
surrounding them and explored the infinite.

But countless other women merely mouthed hollow words and
poured out ridiculous floods of tears as they embarked upon their
pseudo-sacrificial search for love—is this not true, Mélanie Waldor, of
the literary suicide you so carefully staged in order to throw a scare into
that great goodhearted giant, Alexandre Dumas (whom you reproached
for "his over-lusty blood and his over-hearty appetites" and whom you
outlived by forty years)?

Whether a genuine or a pretended intensity of feeling, the fervent
disciples of the Romantic movement sincerely believed that it was the
true spirit of the century capable of saving men's hearts and souls. They
also sincerely believed that it was a movement against the ruling forces
of the day, against the machines of the Industrial Revolution, against

the captains of industry, against the police who hounded Republican dreamers and poor people who had fallen hopelessly in debt, against the nouveaux riches and their crude appetites, against vulgar, pitiless bankers. But far from being a true revolutionary movement, it was in large part mere posturing. The enemy was indeed the bourgeoisie, but a bourgeoisie such as Flaubert or Théophile Gautier conceived of it, anonymous straw men invented by artists, and not the bourgeoisie engaged in a very real class struggle against the proletariat.

Romanticism in the last analysis was a sort of smoke screen, serving not to combat the steam-roller progress being made by mechanistic materialism and capitalism but to conceal it. It was a movement based more on a mood and a spirit than on ideas and theories, yet even so Romanticism was more a heterogeneous group of individuals united only by their deliberate wish to be misunderstood than a true communion of kindred spirits. And it soon became simply the ruling fashion of the day.

As the queens of Romanticism, women believed that through art and artists they had at last found their rightful place in the sun. Marie d'Agoult was sincerely persuaded that "the artist owes his genius to the woman." There were veritable legions of female muses, and equal numbers of mediocre artists, all of them fervent believers in their own genius. But while these women who inspire others' verses or write their own celebrate chaste love and unsullied virtue, they were themselves far from chaste or virtuous. We discover to our stupefaction that our image of the century as an age in which "the proprieties" and "moral rectitude" were all-powerful, stifling all open expressions of passion, is a caricature, for in point of fact it brought fame and glory to an amazing number of "loose women." As I drew up the list of names of the nineteenth-century women whose texts will be found at the end of this chapter, I realized that almost all of them had taken no pains to conceal their adultery if they were married, or if they were not, had had notorious love lives: Germaine de Staël was known to be an adultress and the mother of several children not fathered by her husband, and on being left a widow married at the age of forty-eight a young man of twenty-five; George Sand, fleeing home and fireside, leaves behind two children and takes a series of famous lovers whom she flaunts publicly. Despite wagging tongues, both these women were recognized geniuses, vastly honored by their contemporaries, and ended their lives exactly as they had made up their minds they would—respected and celebrated figures, surrounded by grandchildren and young lovers. Hortense Allart, an unmarried mother by her own free choice, was nonetheless received in the salons of the day both during and between her various love affairs. In his celebrated Romantic play *Antony*, Alexandre Dumas caused au-

diences to shed many a tear for the threatened virtue of a heroine modeled on "Mélanie Waldor, his bourgeois mistress who deceived
her officer-husband regularly by taking a whole string of lovers. Flaubert,
Victor Cousin the famous academician, and countless others were lured
into the bed of Louise Colet, a dreadful poetess celebrated for her
graceful arms, and a classic heartless courtesan. In his *Le Lys dans la
vallée* Balzac writes a celebrated paean to the purity of heart of a
mother of nine children who cast her reputation to the four winds by
taking as her lover a young man of twenty. Marceline Desbordes-Valmore writes verses that bring floods of tears to the eyes of her innocent
young female readers, but the lover she adores and celebrates in her
poems is not at all Valmore, her lawfully wedded husband. Lamartine's
angelic Elvira was a married woman in the midst of her third or fourth
serious love affair. Juliette Drouet, a kept woman and an unmarried
mother, was the mistress of Victor Hugo, as Marie Dorval, an actress
and also an unmarried mother, was Vigny's, etc.

It was thus a two-faced century, in both senses of that expression.
These women were often the victims of the hypocrisy that reigned in
their day and age: but at the same time it was responsible for their
fame, whereas the fidelity of virtuous women met with no such rewards
and went unsung. Love excused everything; it had become the fashion,
and been found to have its pleasures.

Love thus flew in the face of the established order; but at the same
time this order too had been found to have its pleasures. And there is no
doubt that women had worked to establish the sort of order in question, thinking it to their advantage to do so. Certain women eschewed
these advantages by defying convention, but the majority of women
were in favor of it and zealously observed it.

The dawn of this century had seen a period when courtesans were
queens of the day and took an active role in politics. Napoleon, who
had married one of them, thought it best to put an end to this state of
affairs. In this he was aided by a powerful army of women who were
eager to restore marriage as a solid and respectable institution. In 1800
Le Phenix mounted a campaign in favor not only of free love but of
the rights of illegitimate children. "What need is there of the sacrament [of marriage] and the bad Latin of a priest? Is it not better for a
child to owe its existence to tender love, to spontaneous sentiment
rather than to the boring want of anything better to do on the part of a
lawfully wedded husband?"[2] Eleven years later, Napoleon's Civil Code
had strengthened marriage and offered the protection of the law and
the recognized rights of inheritance only to legitimate offspring, and
the regional prefects in each of the newly established administrative de-

2 Caroline Wuiet.

partments had been given orders to draw up a list of young women of marriageable age in their district seeking husbands. In one column they were to record their names; in a second column the amount of their dowry; in a third their "hopes" (of an inheritance). The fourth column, no wider than the three others, was reserved for their "pleasing features or deformities," and if possible to determine, their "upbringing and religious sentiments."

It was women who had actively sought the right to divorce one's spouse, and it had been granted in 1792. Subsequently three out of four suits for divorce were initiated by women. But they had not yet forgotten the weapons that would assure them of their economic independence at the same time. And they were terrified to see men use this new right to divorce one's spouse in order to rid themselves of their forty-plus wives and remarry a girl of tender years to lend the warmth of passion to their years of ripeness and old age. Women discovered that they had been duped, wrote about it, and counterattacked by defending marriage and railing against divorce, seeing in it a freedom working primarily in the man's favor, on the principle of the "free fox in the free chicken yard." As a result, when the right to divorce was done away with in 1816, not a single woman's voice was raised in protest.

Women even begin to volunteer their help to further the "marriage industry" represented by the prefects' registers, and poor young women in Bordeaux form a "marriage association." The membership fee is ten francs. Every six months, the name of one of the participants is drawn by lot: the lucky winner's prize is the "kitty" of membership fees. With a sum such as that as a dowry, she should naturally find a husband within the next six months! If at the end of this period she is still a spinster, she must give back this sum awarded her "with the aim of marriage," since she has not succeeded in catching herself a husband with it. . . . And the pitiful lottery begins all over again. . . .

But the much-loathed memory of the mad years of the Thermidor reaction and the license that followed eventually fades. Women gradually lose their passive torpor as parties who are automatically presumed guilty and are less tolerant of the ardent moral preachings of those of their number who had found in bourgeois moral standards a choice terrain for the exercise of their will to power. As they become more and more disgusted at this "policing" of morals, the most courageous among them refuse to bow to these standards and speak out forthrightly against them. George Sand calls marriage legal opprobrium, rape, and prostitution sanctioned by law. *Lélia*, and above all *Jacques*, expressing her indignation in veiled, Romantic terms, will prove much less easy for the public to swallow than her scandalous private life.

After publishing these two works, she comes to know at first hand what is meant by "French nastiness," some hundred years before Simone de Beauvoir finds herself a victim of the same trait on publication of *The Second Sex*.

Even more systematically, and flying even more in the face of violent public attack by reason of their poverty, their naïveté, their lack both of influential contacts and of talent, the revolutionary women supporters of Saint-Simon and Charles Fourier launch their campaign against marriage. There were two quite different sorts of female disciples of Saint-Simon. The first type, the better known of the two at the time, were drawn into the movement by their men: Climbing aboard the baroque barque of Prosper Enfantin, the father of the utopian Saint-Simonians, their husbands had committed to the movement both their lives and their fortunes. "Leftists" before the word had yet been invented, they had promised everything, given everything—including their wives—to this prophet of socialism "to free women and the people." They gave themselves the name *théodemogynophiles*[3] (this was also the title of one of their irregularly published journals), and went off to live in a commune in the Ménilmontant district in Paris—in much the same fashion as the recent "flower children" in California. At first they "renounced" [*sic*] their wives, for no personal possessions of any sort were permitted, and the liberation of women was to begin with that of their own spouses. The latter obediently bowed to their husbands' will, though they were deeply wounded at being thus "renounced," which they translated as meaning "rejected," and found this "liberation" not at all to their liking. It seemed to each of them that her spouse was abandoning her, more or less, in order to devote his attentions to all the rest of the women, and they grew more and more embittered on finding themselves unable or unwilling to express intimate feelings unworthy of the sublime goodness that a faithful Saint-Simonian ought by nature to possess. Angelical goodness is a particularly fearsome variety of terrorism. They lost their minds, or their spouses, or simply the confidence and the love that their husbands had heretofore inspired in them. Many of the Friends of Woman lost the love of their wives. The women tried their best to help and support each other, to militate for the cause together, to love each other: but they had not chosen of their own free will to be sisters. Moreover, all of them were jealous of the favors of the handsome man with the affectionate gaze who called himself Father, and the Saint-Simonian "family" of Prosper Enfantin gradually became a stifling microcosm of repressed hatreds and personal derelictions of duty.

[3] "Friends of God, the people, and women"—from the Greek.

The case of the second sort of female followers of Saint-Simon, those who had freely volunteered their aid in the fight for the liberation of women, was quite different. Unlike the other group, they were not middle-class women, but proletarians, laundresses, seamstresses, midwives, schoolmistresses. Jeanne Deroin, Désirée Gay, Pauline Roland, Claire Demar, and later Flora Tristan confronted together all of the problems of women: that of the exploitation of the proletariat and in particular that subproletariat made up of women workers, that of prostitution, that of maternity ("Maternity is not a duty, since the woman is not free not to be a mother," Jeanne Deroin wrote at this early date, and by giving birth out of her own free choice to children sired by various fathers whose identity she could not be certain of, Pauline Roland bore personal witness to her belief in the dignity of "natural" maternity), and that of marriage, as goes without saying. Suzanne Voilquin publicly announced in the press that she was giving her husband his freedom, since he appeared to have conceived an affection for another woman, for "any intimate relation not based on love is a profanation of the flesh." They were perfectly aware that his freedom—which in their timidity they called "moral freedom"—would not be won in a day, and were also aware, as Suzanne Voilquin added with great clear-sightedness, that "before being morally free, we must be materially free." But unlike her, these women were not all "reasonable and systematic" and quite capable of doing without a lover. The youngest, the most high-spirited, of their number were desperately eager to reconcile their heartfelt belief in "moral" freedom and their most ardent romantic passions. This struggle was very hard on their nerves and led them to desperate impasses. Marie-Reine Flichi committed suicide. Claire Demar wrote a little tract against marriage and in favor of free union, then committed double suicide with her lover, leaving as her farewell message the words "I have been too daring." Marie Talon, who had also tried to do away with herself, was to write twenty years later: "All of these women had embarked in saintly ecstasy upon this mission in which all of them lost their peace and happiness, if not their sense of morality and their lives." "Saintly ecstasy," "sense of morality," "profanation of the flesh": as can be seen by their language, they were scarcely "liberated" women in the sense in which we use that word today. The charms of morality and the glorious heights of imagination had again exacted their just due. . . .

Feminism and love go hand in hand, in a union that is at once passionate and stormy, in the course of this long century of ever-changing female feelings. Delphine, Corinne, Lélia, Indiana—the heroines of Germaine de Staël and George Sand are clearly superior to their male

partners. The reader is conscious of a growing feeling of Romantic disappointment in the man, who ought to be a hero at once long-suffering
and strong, persecuted and a protector, respectful of virtue and scornful
of convention. Then little by little women begin to be mistrustful of
their own sex. This phenomenon, which often occurs in feminism on
the rise, leads to disguised forms of lesbianism. "After 1830 one began
to see among young women a disdain for their sex, a provocative parading of one's eccentricity that created a new type: the 'lioness.' The
lioness affected a disdain of all feminine graces. She sought neither to
please by her beauty nor to charm by her wit, but to shock by her daring. A horsewoman and a huntress, whip upraised, boots with spurs, a
rifle over her shoulder, a cigar in her mouth, a glass in hand, all impu-
dence and rowdiness, the lioness delighted in defying convention, in
disconcerting," Marie d'Agoult wrote, thinking in particular of the impression that George Sand had made on her.

But she shared with Sand and the *lionnes* another trait revealing her
coolness toward women, her relative disdain for them: a male pseudonym. Marie d'Agoult adopts the name of Daniel Stern; Delphine de
Girardin signs her chronicles "Vicomte de Launay," etc. It does not
seem likely that such male pen names were still necessary for a woman
writer at the time that Marie d'Agoult wrote this passage, even though
that had been the case when George Sand first began her career as a
writer. At this date it was more likely simply a fashion, like the men's
spencer jackets and redingotes that had become the vogue for women.
At the same time we find ardent personal friendships between women
all during this century, Madame de Staël and Juliette Récamier, Sand
and Marie Dorval, and a great many others, relationships in which each
woman extols the gifts and charms of the other, at once feminine and
masculine (as defined by the cultural norms of the era), thus paving
the way for the great explosion of sapphic writings in the very last years
of the nineteenth century and the beginning of the twentieth.

These ambiguities are protests, ways of transcending a narrowly cir-
cumscribed fate, as was the earlier tendency to identify love and mysticism. One might coin the word "mystication" to describe this process
whereby love is desexualized by assigning it a divine value. This was a
way of living love as a creature of God, thus escaping the narrow confines of the roles assigned women as women by men. Feeling steps over
the threshold of the domains to which bourgeois mores relegate it,
leaving kitchen, bedroom, and boudoir behind and soaring gloriously
heavenward. It allows women to escape even men, the eternal deter-
miners of their "proper" roles, and offers them an opportunity if not to
totally fulfill themselves at least to refuse to maim themselves, to muti-
late their souls.

The body, however, remains steeped in mystery, in bedchambers with feather beds and strange many-tiered night tables, and beneath tight-laced corsets and long rustling skirts. All during the nineteenth century women's bodies have important duties to perform as signs and symbols. Promoted to the status of a diplomatic language, representing subtle social distinction, hinting at moral ambiguities and enigmas, it is covered up, ornamented with all sorts of ribbons and furbelows, transmitting to its beholder a complicated message as to the wealth, the rank, the virtue, the dreams, and the soul that it incarnates, while at the same time revealing absolutely nothing about itself. "Desirable" is a word that still implies that the woman described is, actually or potentially, a fallen woman, a quality that is all the more exciting in that it is disguised as something else—carelessness, lack of self-discipline, impulsiveness, rashness, exoticism. And meanwhile the woman's body lives its total denial, stifled beneath the social proprieties, swathed in yards and yards of fabric, its most intimate physiological secrets, its heat, its perspiration, its odors, its moist secretions, its humors, its needs, shrouded in silence—an animality made even more shameful and vulgar by the movements and postures required to remove the complicated costume that she has been tricked out in.

Surrounded as it is with such a total sense of shame, secrecy, and guilt, its delights all forbidden pleasures, it is the woman's own body that prevents her from being free and perhaps even from loving. Women in this period look upon their bodies only as a sort of spectacle that must be staged with meticulous care, hiding its true nature and its real drama. This drama may lead them from dull and dreary "vapors" and irritated frustration to the most violent and voracious delirium, but more often still the basic state is that tense numbness of the flesh known today as frigidity, which for several decades to come will continue to be called "virtue."

But there are those who are beginning to study this state in the light of what it appears to them to really be: a frequent symptom in a syndrome that sometimes leads to a major attack of the great malady of the time, which a history of feminine love cannot possibly leave unmentioned: hysteria. The sudden interest in this illness goes hand in hand with the fact that the nineteenth century gives birth to or makes important contributions to all the sciences devoted to the study of human beings: anatomy, physiology, experimental psychology, clinical psychology, psychiatry, and just before the turn of the century psychoanalysis. These researchers have no way of knowing that almost a century will go by before it is realized that this illness, a monstrous deformation of passionate love which they believe to be typically feminine and study as though it were the croup or measles, may perhaps be above all a malady of this particular historical period, the neurotic expression on the part of a few women of tensions that gripped all women of their day. Nor did these researchers have any way of knowing that there would come a time when the classical attack of hysteria as described by Charcot would become an extremely rare phenomenon. Nor that few women would lament, as did Marceline Desbordes-Valmore: "On receiving the gift of life, of all it offered I have known only love."

Romanticism and realism will divide the nineteenth century between them

I now dreamed only of abductors, white chargers, faithful shepherds. Henceforth I was certain that perfect happiness consisted of seeing a handsome knight kneeling at one's feet, swearing eternal love.   /67

> You dream of a lover out of drama or story
> And a nightingale's trill
> Compose tales in your mind: each scene brings bliss
> Or occasion to shine in all of your glory
> From the first secret tryst
> To the grand quadrille:
> Today every young lady's a great novelist.   /68

I spent the day mending my things. I took off the dress I was wearing in order to redo the hem. I was in my petticoat and chemise when I heard a knock at the door. I covered my bare shoulders with a shawl and opened the door a crack. My stepfather[1] came into the room. "You made a conquest just now. There were some nice things said about you at the dinner table. The shortest fellow told me he found you to his liking. I let him know that it wasn't for him that you were heating up your oven, that I was keeping you for myself." . . . I looked and saw that he had double-locked the door and pocketed the key. He hesitated for a moment, reached out his arms to grab me, and said in a low voice: "I want you to love me, I want to have you. And I shall!" He took me by the waist and shoved me toward my mother's bed. "Shut your mouth, stop that, give yourself to me willingly or I'll take you by force."   /69

I didn't lack for chances to relieve myself, you may take my word for that; there were plenty of men around me, younger than you, for whom a single come-hither look would have sufficed. . . . I risked nothing; there were a thousand ways of deceiving you and covering up a moment of animal instinct that Catherine II would scarcely have refused herself.   /70

---

[1] Her mother's lover. (*Translator's note.*)

Neither nature nor society ever pardons those who violate their laws. Out of necessity I found myself rebelling against both. I was obliged to transgress against the latter; I know the punishment it has in store for me.   /78

Narcissism again, in every possible guise

My body is proof of that. Marie Sopogenikoff is quite right when she says that for such a body, I should have a prettier face, even though I'm far from having an ugly one. When I think of what I'll look like when I'm twenty, I clack my tongue approvingly. . . . I compare myself to all the statues and find no back as gracefully curved and no hips as ample as mine.   /71

Your letters from Rouen are not as passionate as the others, you didn't talk about me as much, you don't fill up the whole page.   /72

. . . take care
Make me radiant with joy! And when I look at you
Return my gaze. Never let your hand touch mine
Without clasping it.   /73

Love, that is the eternal subject! To allow oneself to be loved by a man who is so much your inferior that he considers you a goddess descended from heaven would have a certain charm. Someone who would recognize his humble estate. Knowing that with a single glance one bestows on its recipient a happiness worth thousands! There is a certain charity in that which makes the generous impulses that one may have all the more gratifying.   /71

But above all love, love, love . . . love as a cult, as a vocation, love as a
way of life, as life itself, and above all love as one's very soul

Love is not only a regeneration
It is a bounden duty.   /67

My love is my life. Take it from me and you will take from me all
the worth you profess to see in me. I would be no more than an ordinary woman whom you would no longer even deign to look at, and you
would be right in so doing. It has become the essence of my life, and
when I depart from this earth I shall take it with me.   /74

Before ever I saw you I was yours, it may be,
My life pledged to yours, as it quickened in me;
Your name was the proof; my surprised heart divined
That your soul hid therein to awaken mine.
I heard it one day, and was stricken dumb;
I listened enraptured, but no words would come:
My being with yours seemed blended as one
And my own name pronounced for the very first time. . . .
Cherished name that so charms me! Name predicting my fate!
Alas how you please me! How I'm touched by your grace!
You announced life to me; and mingled with death,
Like a kiss shall my lips form you, with my very last breath.   /73

As one hearkens to God, I gave ear to my love. . . .
You were my devotion! My heaven, my poetry!
I dare not speak out yet my heart calls you each day
My brother in God, my soul, or my child. . . .

If death were to snatch you away from me
My soul's eyes would blaze with such fire,
It would so plead, pray, and weep
That death would be forced to open your eyes again.
I know the shiver of fear your mother surely knew
As she watched over your slumbers when you were a child:
I too have seen you asleep.   /73

I love you with more than all my strength, I love you with my soul, I love you with the love of the life beyond the grave that for me is a part of this life. I adore you.

. . . Look into my heart: you will find me there, kneeling at the feet of my love.

. . . I love you, with all my spirit.

. . . Thank you and love to you whom I love with my heart full to overflowing.

. . . My candle is not yet lighted and I write to you by the light of my soul, without the slightest difficulty, for my love has neither obverse nor reverse.   /75

How true what you say: I'm but a woman; my one art
Lies in feigning, to please you
Surprise at seeing your wonder-filled heart. . . .
Wait: I should like to know if on so seeking me
You said to yourself: "I shall share this soul's destiny
And be wed in death as in life—for eternity.
I should like to know. Ah? You've already said so? Pray pardon
     me.   /73

What does it matter that in a day one spends an entire lifetime
If in loving the heart is drained to its very last drop?   /76

Oh love! who can say what it is? . . .
Whence does it come? Where does it go?
Might it a fallen angel be
Paying the price of its sins in this world below?
A breath of heaven sent to mankind
To reveal to our hearts, by doubt rendered blind
Another life's hell, or the mystery
Of its paradise that as yet we cannot see?   /77

If I were persuaded that people might thereby understand the love I have for you, I would proclaim it from the rooftops, from the crests of mountains, no matter where, certain that it would cover me with glory, surround me with a halo.   /78

Everything in your letters radiates love, including that most cherished turn of phrase that you have invented. Am I not entirely persuaded that you feel "a filial passion" for me? My dear Alphonse! I shall try to let that be enough for me. The ardor of my soul and my feelings might wish it were accompanied by yet another passion, or that at least it were granted unto me to love you with true love and every other sort of passion. But if it behooves me to hide this fact from you, O my angel, if you so dwell in heaven that you reject the passions of this earth, I shall say no more, Alphonse!   /74

He loved me. It was then that his beloved voice
Awakened my entire being, announcing love. . . .
 . . . I was no longer myself, I was you. I listened, I imitated what
   I loved;
Long after parting, my speech still kept the accents of yours
And your voice in my voice still stirred my senses.   /73

I should like to bare my innermost heart to you so that you might see how much your presence delights me, my dearly beloved; can you know how much I love you and the ways I love you? Very often I tell you only the half of it, out of fear that you would think me mad were I to tell you precisely how I feel. My adored one, I could die for joy when you merely speak to me. There are other moments when I should like to kneel before you and kiss your feet. And there are still others when I feel the need to share my happiness with any passer-by, I speak aloud, I call you my spouse, call you my lover in my heart of hearts. Yes, my dearly beloved, I have accesses of joy and rapture that I am obliged to repress because of our way of life and our manners and morals, which do not permit a poor woman to show in public how happy she is.   /75

Save for her love, a woman has nothing, her life becomes dreary and meaningless; if she is no longer loved, she feels dead, and if she herself is no longer in love, life is not worth living

I believe that a person who works all the time and whose mind is occupied with the thought of fame does not love in the same way as those who have nothing else to do save that.   /71

Women have no existence apart from love; the story of their life begins and ends with love.   /80

There are pains within my bosom that I shall never express, not even in my writing. Love alone can fathom these abysses. How fortunate men are to go to war, to risk their lives, to be carried away by their quest for honor and bravery in the face of death! Women have nothing outside themselves to relieve their heart's sorrows.   /80

A woman who has not seen her lover during the day regards that day as lost for her. Even the most affectionate man regards that same day only as lost for love.   /79

Having fallen from the great heights of love, I have also fallen from the heights of myself; I am once again following the low road. I am nothing more than an ordinary woman now.   /79

A true love seeks sole possession of everything, mind, heart, soul, and all the rest, but the rest first and foremost. And if this latter is the only thing that remains intact, it turns ghastly pale, suffering a shame as great as that occasioned by an all-consuming, evil passion.   /78

Ah! Ought women not be forgiven the heart-rending nostalgia they feel for the days when they were loved, when their existence was so necessary to the existence of another, when at every moment they felt themselves sustained and protected? What loneliness must follow these delightful days! And how happy those women are who, thanks to the holy bonds of matrimony, have been serenely led from love to friendship without ever experiencing the cruel moment that tears a life asunder!   /80

"Didn't you tell me however that you were once deeply in love? But love means living together as a couple, sharing everything."

"Not knowing what I might devote my soul's strength to, I laid it as an offering at the feet of an idol that my own worshipful faith had created: for he was but a man like many another, and once I grew weary of prostrating myself before him, I smashed the pedestal to bits and saw him at last for what he was. But in my ridiculous adoration I had assigned him so lofty a place that he had seemed to me as great as God himself. That was the deplorable error I committed, and the moment my illusion was shattered, I could do naught but bitterly regret its loss. The fact was, alas, that I had nothing left to put in its place. . . . I had been as happy with this chimerical fantasy of mine as any person with a temperament such as mine may expect to be. I enjoyed a luxuriant flowering of my faculties; intoxicated by my error, I found myself plunged into truly divine states of rapture. . . . My naturally stormy soul delighted in this frightful agitation that drained it of all strength, to no point or purpose. . . . It required obstacles, raging jealousies to brood upon, cruel acts of ingratitude to pardon, great undertakings to pursue, vast misfortunes to endure. All this was a career unto itself, glory to conquer. Had I been born a man, I would have loved encounters on the field of battle, the smell of blood, danger's thrilling embraces, and perhaps the ambition to impose my will through sheer intelligence; to dominate other men by the power of words would have brightened the days of my youth. But having been born a woman, I had but one noble destiny on this earth: to love. And I loved *valiantly*."

"Yet you are no longer in love," Pulchérie remarked.

"And hence I am dead now," Lélia replied.   /70

A man can begin anew, come what may
His dawn is followed by radiant day
His youth, then his glory are splendid attire
Even crowned with white hair, he holds kingly sway.
While women are merely creatures desired:
The one thing we have is our love.   /81

What! it is summer still?
What! the meadows are in flower? There are people in this world?
Yesterday I lacked only him, then, in order to be?
Dear God, summer, light, heaven—all that is only he!   /73

Oh, how unhappy I am, I am not loved, I am not in love! I am incapable of a feeling then, a useless, barren, accursed creature! —And *you* have come to me to speak of transports of ecstasy, of desires. . . . I doomed myself to suicide the day I persuaded myself that offering you friendship would save your life.   /70

I had no idea of the loathing that follows ecstasy
Nor of the weight of a chain hanging by its last link.   /76

Why have so many women loved kings? Because a king is a symbol
of power and a woman loves to dominate . . . I love A you see. . . .
Continually crushed beneath the weight of my wounded pride, humiliated by this ignoble dependence. . . . All that remains is a sort of torment that makes me say yes one moment and no the next, that makes
me hesitant, indecisive, mercenary, miserable.   /71

*Sacrificial fervor: the burning desire to give oneself, dedicate oneself,
deny oneself in order to feel more alive*

I should be capable of abandoning everything in this world, of coming
to throw myself at your feet, of saying to you: "Do what you will with
me, I am your slave. I am ruining my life, but I am happy. I have
sacrificed everything for you: reputation, honor, station—but what do I
care!"   /74

You have killed all my gifts: but there is no harm done, since it is
you who have taken their place.   /82

You have enormous gifts, but your gentle mistress is able to appreciate, to understand each and every one of them—oh why am I not a
thousand selves in order to give you everything I should like, in the way
that I should like! But if my entire being, enhanced by everything that
the most perfect love can add thereunto, is enough for you, I shall be
content, for nothing of myself belongs to me. I want to see you one day
happy, powerful, highly regarded—that for me will be like a dream
come true.   /78

I want what you want, my angel
I give back the flowers forbidden me.

What strange creatures we are: we wish what we give
   to be fair exchange.
And hence to repay you for the look you gave me
I should like to be a world and say to you: Take me!   /73

You are my life, my joy, my soul, my religion, I adore you, I should like to kiss your feet, I should like to die for you, in your service, at your whim.   /75

One sees in this book, clearly described and frankly confessed, the cravings to dominate that are characteristic of the woman. One is also struck by woman's sense of *self*-possession, which constitutes her strength amid weakness and her victory amid defeat.   /70

But when I am far from him, what am I? What can a woman be when she is left by herself to lead her aimless existence, her secondary existence, which heaven has created only in order to give it to the man as one last gift?   /80

Love comes along, to spoil, all by itself, all other pleasures. It turns one's life into a lonely desert. To be loved is to be isolated, stripped bare, dispossessed, robbed of everything. It means losing overnight one's affections, one's talents, one's merit, one's personality, one's will, one's past, one's future, in a word: everything.   /83

If it were your pleasure to spend the rest of your days in some remote corner of Scotland, I should be happy to live and die there with you; but far from renouncing my powers of imagination, I should put them to good use, the better to enjoy nature, and the vaster the realms of my spirit should become, the more pride and happiness I should take in declaring you the master of it.   /80

Romanticism is, of course, a "complaint" that is all the fashion, as are pallid cheeks and floods of tears. But perhaps it is also the very special moment when the woman, casting decorum to the winds and refusing to repress her true feelings, finds herself able to give voice to her suffering and her passion

In today's novels, passions excuse everything. A woman does not give proof of her sensibility by loving her husband and children. She must "have a grand passion," allow herself to be carried away by melancholy, go mad, or kill herself.

This gloomy genre has many charms. It pleases those sensitive souls for whom strong emotions are frankly enjoyable and weeping a necessity. Léonora will make you shed many a tear. You will approve of the excessive love that devours her, for without excess there is no true love.   /84

But when one loves as I do, when one loves as Elvire and I do, to the point of death—does that make one merely a woman with a tender and generous heart?   /74

I abhor the pain of being apart; it is barren and calm, all-consuming and monotonous.   /80

Love is the bitter struggle of the highest faculties of two souls seeking to become one with each other through shared feelings. When they do not succeed in so doing, the desire of each to at least prove as worthy of esteem as the other becomes a torment to the wounded pride of both. Each would have the other suffer the bitterest regrets, and that soul persuaded that it alone is possessed by such feelings becomes the victim of genuine torture.   /70

What could I do? I loved him. He alone pleased me.
His features, his voice, his vows brought him mine
Tender as love, awesome in his fury . . .
I loved him, I adored my tormented life
My heart melted the more at his blind jealousy
As he tortured me I said: I confess I am wrong . . .
My doubt of myself had made a slave of me.   /73

Oh, pray believe me, my angel, if you were to take your love from me, I should best be advised to kill myself forthwith. *But think, I beg you, think of how much you have loved me!* You are not capable of deceiving me, I feel it when there is something that you are hiding from me. . . . I am falling prey to the most heart-rending thoughts. You might choose to put a stop to my life as one stops the pendulum of a clock, by simply reaching out a hand to arrest it. . . . I am no more deceived by your letters than by the expression on your face, and now that I have reassured myself that you are not ill, I am left with the fear that you love me less, that *your thoughts are less occupied with me* when your letters are not the same as they have always been, your letters, that *you* forget you've even written, but that I keep reading again and again, they are so adorable, so full of a *devoted* love! You write me as tenderly as you have spoken to me these past four years! *What if you didn't love me any more!* What if you didn't say all those *cherished* words to me! The shock would kill me.   /72

Once upon a time your letters called forth letters from me, your love sought mine, and that was as it should be, for as you so often said to me, "the man must always lay siege to the woman." It is always awkward when one or the other shifts roles, and I know full well that a caress that I offer first gives me more happiness and security than a thousand caresses that I might tease you into giving me. I do not believe that there is any torture in this world greater than loving and being a constant prey to fear.   /75

Farewell, farewell, I do not want to leave you, I do not want to take you back, I do not want anything, my knees are bent and my back bowed; I do not want to hear another word from anyone. I want only to clutch the earth and weep. I no longer love you, but I still adore you. I want nothing more to do with you, but I cannot do without you. . . . Stay or go, as you please, only I beg you not to say that I am not suffering. That is the one thing that could make me suffer more than I am, my one love, my life, my very vitals, my brother, my blood, go away, but kill me as you leave.   /70

He'll not return! Tell me, is that truly a certainty?
Say it's merely a test—not meant cruelly
Say he'll come back, that he's on his way:
Deceive me—and somehow induce him to
Deceive me in turn, in the same words as you
Go ask him, implore him, beseech him: stay.   /73

He is killing me, and I love him! What bitter tears I weep!
Resting on your bosom, then could I never sleep
That profound slumber that leaves life refreshed?
But it's heaven I yearn for, if it is there I seek my rest!
Yet this distance between us is decreed from above:
Those who speak in the name of a heaven incensed
Have told me it wills the end of our love
My Lord! at Thy feet alone dare I worship then?

But what have I said? Our love is heaven on earth.
And my heart tells me it was simply traversed
By a pang of regret
Like life, involuntary;
Inevitable as death.
I tasted this love: I weep for its delights
Dear lover! When beneath yours my heart beat wildly
Our two souls were fellow-thieves, stealing through the night
And you kept mine, pleased at this larceny
Oh never, never give it back to me!   /73

All that, don't you see, is a game that we are playing, but it is our
hearts and our lives that are the wagers on the table, and it is not quite
as amusing as it appears to be. Shall we go blow our brains out together
at Franchart? No sooner said than done.   /70

Pride stands between us. A mortal chill seizes my limbs.
Does he not flee me, does he not deal with me cruelly?
Never reproach him. I adore him, remember.   /73

I spare his pride the cruel pleasure
Of seeing tears prove my excessive love
What would I owe to my cries? His flight? His return?
What is given to live is lost forever! . . .   /73

And what if I ran out in the streets when love overcomes me? What
if I yanked on his bell cord till he opened the door and let me in?
What if I lay across his path till he passed by? . . . What if I said to
him: You still love me, your love is making you suffer, you're ashamed
that you love me, yet you pity me too much not to go on loving me.

You can see that I love you, that I can love only you. Embrace me, do not say a word; let us not argue; whisper a few sweet words to me; caress me, since you still find me pretty . . . And so when you feel yourself growing tired me of again and cross and irritated at me once more, send me away, abuse me, but may it never be with the terrible words: *this is the very last time!* I shall suffer as much as you like, but I pray you to permit me every so often, if only once a week, to come to you seeking a tear, a kiss that will allow me to go on living and give me courage. But you are not able to do so. Ah! how weary of me you are, and how quickly you too have recovered. . . .   /70

Love can endure only if there is pain; it ceases once one is happy, for happy love is perfection, and every perfect thing eventually comes to an end. Oh! Love itself knows instinctively how long it will last. It knows that it must feed upon torment, that torment is the guarantee of its lasting, and it invents a thousand heartaches in order to assure itself of a longer life; it inflicts upon itself make-believe torments of its own devising, in order to conjure away the real misfortunes that it so fears; it feels jealousy for no reason, out of fear of being jealous for good reason; often, alas, lovers go so far as to betray their love in order to safeguard it by profaning it. The truth of the matter is: love is the precise contrary of all the things that one invents.   /83

The one affection that might have made me happy at that time would have been a passionate and exclusive love for one of those men whose great devotion brings them vast woes, who suffer terribly from such misfortunes, which become ever more terrible and ennoble the victim who falls prey to them. He grew afraid of my love. He feared that I might love him too much.   /86

Last will and testament:[2]
I wish, before his departure, to obtain: my letters, in order to re-read them, and my portrait. Our chains and our rings. His watch, which I shall purchase from him. His bronze medal. La Prière, Le Lac, La Jalousie. The rings with the lock of poor Jacques's hair. His Ecce labia signet ring. If I die, I wish that all these items (save the portrait) be buried with me in the cemetery of Ivry, near Jacques's tomb. I wish only a white marble tombstone, with the date of my death inscribed on it, and my age, and then below: Sara di te o di morte[3] and at the four

[2] Written before a projected suicide which was never committed (see Biography number 77). The notes in parentheses in the text above added by André Maurois; see his *Les Trois Dumas* (Paris: Hachette, 1957), p. 102. (*Author's note.*)
[3] She shall belong either to you—or to death. (*Translator's note.*)

corners of the tombstone these four dates: September 12, 1827 [*the date of the first avowal of love*]. September 23, 1827 [*the date of her fall from virtue*]. September 18, 1830 [*the date of leaving La Jarrie*]. November 22, 1830 [*the date of the projected suicide*]. These four dates are the sole and only ones that sealed my fate and determined the course of my life. . . . rather than being buried in a shroud, I wish to be interred in my blue dress and my yellow scarf. I wish our black chain to be placed around my neck. . . . I wish his watch and our ring, along with our crushed geranium, to be placed over my heart. His poems and our letters at my feet.   /77

Self-pride and tenderness, the drive to dominate, the wish for independence, the desire to understand one's love partner in order to keep him, put a keener edge on the psychology of love; with the aid of hollow clichés, and also flying in the face of them, an important question is confronted: What sort of fundamental relations ought to exist between a man and a woman? What form does the war between the sexes take, and the peace that may eventually be arrived at?

Will you be an ever-present help to me, or a master? Will you console me for the hurts I suffered before I met you? Will you understand why I am sad? Are you capable of compassion, patience, friendship? You have perhaps been brought up to believe that women have no soul. Are you aware that they indeed have one? . . . Will I be your companion or your slave? Do you desire me or do you love me? When your passion is satisfied, will you be able to thank me? When I make you happy, will you be able to tell me so? . . . Do you know what a soul's desire that is neither assuaged nor fulfilled by any human caress is like? When your mistress falls asleep in your arms, do you remain awake to gaze at her, to pray to God, to weep? Do the pleasures of love leave you panting like an animal, or do they plunge you into a divine rapture? Does your soul survive your body when you leave the bosom of the woman you love? . . . I shall be able to interpret your reveries and make your silence speak most eloquently. I shall attribute to your actions whatever intention I desire. When you gaze at me tenderly, I shall believe that your soul is calling out to mine. . . . Let us remain that way; do not seek to learn my language, and I shall not seek in yours the words to tell you of my doubts and fears. I wish to know nothing of the life you lead and the role you play among men. I should like not to know your name. Hide your soul from me, so that I may always believe it a beautiful one.   /70

A dauntless courage conjoined with the most circumspect concern for the person one loves. I know not what combination of strength and gentleness, that makes the same man the unfailing protector and the submissive friend of the woman he has chosen.   /80

You forbid me to be jealous; that is to bid me to love you less. Yes, I am only too well aware that a concession in love is not made with impunity. In order that love may remain entire, no part of it must be surrendered; if such a thing is forced upon it, it is thereby diminished. In order for it to remain pure, it must in no way be divided, for to divide it is to adulter it. I know that I possess your heart, my friend, but the breath of other women spoils it for me. I see other women flocking round about you, and when I tell you that this no longer causes me pain, I am lying to you because I am trying my best to lie to myself. But this continual pretense is frightfully tiring. In order to profit from a woman's counsels, is it necessary that this woman belong to you? Does this female Genius cease to exist when she is no longer within the purview of your senses? I cannot help but tremble in my very soul when I think of the moment when I shall no longer be permitted to banish with a kiss every care that afflicts your heart.   /78

O heaven! How could I have been the one to have given the first kiss on the mouth? Mad girl! Loathsome creature! It makes me weep and tremble with rage! Turpis execrabilis! Vatican and Kremlin! I am choking with fury and shame.   /71

"So it would appear then that it was I who caused those lovely flights of fancy to which I have owed the most intoxicating joys of my life to wither and die?" Oswald said.

"It is not you who should be held responsible, but a deep-felt passion," Corinne replied. "Talent has need of an inner independence that true love never permits."

"Ah, if that is the case, may your genius fall silent and your heart belong entirely to me!" Lord Nevil exclaimed. . . .

Corinne dared say nothing in reply for fear of clouding in some way the sweet bliss these words brought her. She felt loved.   /80

The longer I live, you see, the more persuaded I am that one is capable of truly loving only a man whom one does not respect.   /72

"My son has often, in fact, said to me: 'Women's affections are gained through suffering.' Might it not be, that he has inflicted upon you the pain that he has—a bit too much of it, I grant you—simply to test your love?"

"Ah! Madame! You are so right; women's affections are gained through suffering . . . but through the suffering they cause, not that which they are made to endure!"   /83

Assure your mother again and again that you love her! She is sometimes so unhappy at the terrible thought that you might cease to do so! Even though you've told her endlessly that that could never be! Do not take this, I pray you, to mean that I fear such a thing, a mother does not mistrust her son, she is ever and always his mother, she can be told everything. Ah! my child! how I love you! how I love you! . . . Sleep, dearest heart! my angel, my love, my child, your mother blesses you and blesses your return!   /74

The man kneels at the feet of innocence, at the feet of a virgin. The woman reverently bows her head before the strength, the omniscience of the man whom she has chosen. Both delude themselves, both worship an idol with feet of clay, but what they really love is precisely this self-delusion. They do not understand each other in the slightest, fail to see each other as each of them truly is, yet love thrives upon this mystery, this unknown quantity. If you would have the man and the woman share precisely the same tastes and the same defects, the same thoughts and aspiration, and come to know each other perfectly, you will then have two excellent comrades, but they will no longer be lovers; if you do away with the reserve, the reticence, and the lies between the two sexes, you do away with love. Moreover, these illusions also vanish one day, and then everything falls to pieces.   /87

It matters little whether I have been your mistress or your mother. Whether it is feeling of love or friendship that I have inspired in you; whether I have been happy or unhappy with you—all that has no bearing upon my present state of mind. The one thing I know is that I love you.   /70

He has no need of my strength; he has his own serenity and courage. He loves me with quiet self-assurance; he is happy without my suffering, without my struggling to make him happy. But I on the other hand need to suffer for someone. I need to find a use for this boundless energy and sensibility I feel within myself. I need to indulge this sense of maternal solicitude that has long since been in the habit of watching over someone who is weak and sickly and suffering. Oh, why could I not have lived with the two of you and made both of you happy without belonging to either one of you! I could have spent ten happy years in this fashion. I readily grant that I needed a father; why could I not have kept my child with me too? . . .

By renouncing the relations that had become impossible, we would remain bound to each other for all eternity. You are right: Our embrace was an act of incest, though we did not know it. We threw ourselves, innocently and sincerely, into each other's arms. Tell me, do we have a single memory of these intimate embraces that is not chaste and holy? One day, when you had a fever and were delirious, you reproached me for never having been able to bring you love's ultimate pleasures. I wept at the time, but now I am pleased at the thought that there is some truth in this reproach. I am glad that these pleasures were more austere, more obscure than those that you will find elsewhere. At least you will not be reminded of me when you are in other women's arms.   /70

How does it happen that two creatures who have shared their most intimate thoughts with each other, who have spoken to each other of God, of the immortality of the soul, of pain, suddenly become strangers to each other once again? What a staggering mystery love is! As deeply religious as the spirit that moved the Christian martyrs, or more indifferent than the most superficial friendship.   /70

I love a man who does not love me. I love him submissively, docilely. He takes unfair advantage of me, and toys with my heart. He shall love me some day; I so will it. When I shall have used up all this love, I know full well that I shall detest the man who inspired it. I shall then love only my fixed idea: to be in the first rank of fallen women who are admired, who are loved! I have neither heart nor soul left, only a machine, and this machine is covered with cashmere shawls, lace, and diamonds.   /69

Marriage continues to be a goal eagerly sought; an ideology comes to surround it; its true nature is further explored. Yet married life rarely inspires masterpieces (perhaps because the husband and wife see each other constantly, and are seldom separated by circumstances). Nonetheless, the traditional situation is beginning to be reversed: it is now the mistress who envies the wife

The continuity of a perfect friendship, the mutual striving for virtue on the part of two persons who like each other, an affection that knows no bounds save those of duty, the mind's progress, the sharing of each other's thoughts—all these goods accumulated in the course of a long and legitimate union make the hours of one's old age as lively and absorbing as those of youth, provided that one never allows oneself to yield to any sort of discouragement.   /88

> I am here to watch over your sleep, if you take your rest
> And to make for the oars of your barque a lake on which to glide
> I am here to love you, lying at your side.   /89

> How it pleased me to guide your slow, feeble steps
> To feel your arm clinging tightly to mine . . .
> Leaning on your strength, with my hand in yours
> I've walked without fear, for some six years now.
> May my arm link yours, and sustain you in turn
> Should the path for a moment seem steep and wearisome!   /90

> You suffer! I feel how you do!
> Your chills and your fevers
> Break my heart too!
> Yet a wife sits watching there by your bed
> Has this thought, I wonder, entered your head?
> If my prayers were answered, my heart understood
> I would fall at her knees, and ask if I could
> Take care of you a short while in her stead
> The potion that calms. . . . My trembling hand would then place
> The soft cushions next to your feet I adore
> Oh to cradle your forehead for one moment more
> As I smooth out the wrinkles in your pillowcase.   /91

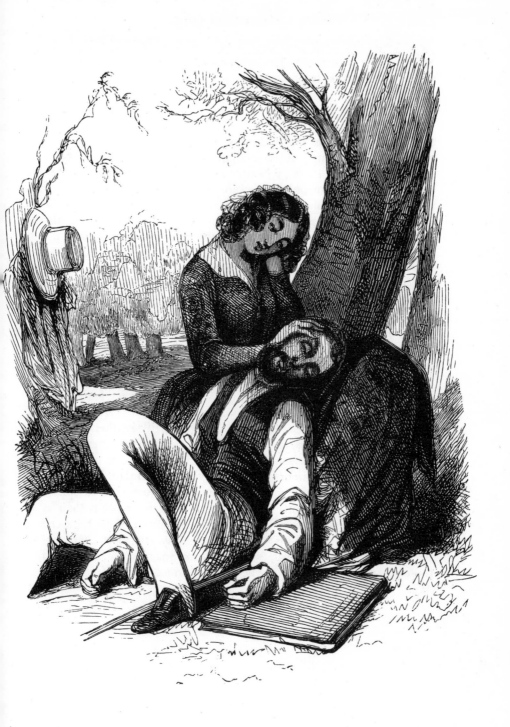

*Such a thing as marriage for love now exists, and sets the "liberated"
woman of the time to dreaming*

I am beginning this letter to you sitting in the room next to my
mother's, not having yet secured permission to see her, but heartbroken, terrified by these preparations for her death, all the details and
stages of which I am only too aware of. Every evening my father has
musicians come to play the same pieces we heard when we went boat-
ing on the lake. These sounds make me feel sadder still. In the silence
between one melody and the next, my poor father weeps and my
mother says the most truly touching things to him. Yesterday I heard
her say: *"Think of the horrible tortures others are suffering these days.
You see how much sweeter my fate is. I have your arms about me as I
die.* Her words broke my heart, and the second moment of my
overwhelming grief took the form of a painful reminder of my own
fate: I shall not have a legitimate nuptial tie, a pure bond, a solemn
link that I may treasure. I shall die all alone, cared for by distant rela-
tives and separated and perhaps forgotten by the one who is so close to
my heart. By what right, really, might I merit your eternal love? When
your initial enthusiasm has waned, you will remember my faults, and all
my feeling, and even its every expression will merely serve to remind
you of them. Ah! I love you, I love you, but I risk neither the danger
nor know the happiness of illusion. No, I shall have set eyes on you
only to have seen in person what I have dreamed of, to personify my
fondest fancy, and to mourn the loss of you forevermore. Postpone this
moment yet a little; give me this summer, the weather is so splendid,
the trees round about my house are just right for casting their cool
shadow on your sweet head! Ah, come, do come soon! What a sacrifice
I agreed to when I gave up this month of May, the most charming of
all the months of the year, which will be spent sadly remembering
those pleasant winter days when you warmed yourself at my fireside.   /80

But marriage nonetheless continues to be a market place as well, where uneducated young girls are sold, and women revolutionaries, from every class of society, attack the institution of marriage

I was ignorant of the mysteries of marriage. I trembled with happiness as I clasped your hand. Poor creature that I was! I sincerely believed that all that would be due you was a kiss on the forehead, that you would be like a father to me. . . . can you possibly understand what I suffered those three days?   /92

What steps are you taking in order that the woman may free herself from the weakness with which you tax her? In the boarding schools for rich girls, every effort is made to keep her ignorant even of the way a man's body is formed. . . . And the working-class girl, for her part, is taught prayers and hymns by the Sisters of Charity, and then, having been put to work at the age of twelve, she earns fifteen sous a day . . . laboring from seven in the morning till nine at night.   /93

In marriage, there is a material principle involved that is not sufficiently taken into account. Even if it were freely granted that an intimate rapport existed between them, even if they were persuaded that there obtained between them a perfect unity of feelings, thoughts, and wills, all that might still not withstand a last decisive, and at the same time necessary and indispensable, test: the test of matter by matter, the trial of flesh by flesh. An engaged couple who adore each other may well make an unhappy wedded couple, and hence it is to be recommended that before entering upon marriage the future spouses embark upon a wholly physical test of the flesh by the flesh.   /93

Any and every intimate relation that is not based on love is a profanation of the flesh.   /94

Marriage is legalized prostitution.   /93

A woman of the usual sort would have dominated this vulgar-souled man; she would have agreed with whatever he said, and reserved for herself the pleasure of thinking otherwise; she would have pretended in public to bow to his prejudices and trampled them underfoot in secret; she would have embraced him tenderly and cuckolded him. Indiana saw many women behave in this fashion, but she felt so above them that she would have blushed for shame had she followed suit. She did not want his affection, because she was unable to return it. She would have regarded herself as much more worthy of blame for offering proofs of love to this husband whom she did not love than for offering such proofs to the lover who inspired them.   /70

We wish to have no more to do with the formula: "Women, bow to thy spouse's will." We wish marriages between equals. Sooner spinsterhood than marriage.   /94

And in the first place, it is not true that the one purpose of love is reproduction. The purpose of love is love itself, that is to say, the happiness it promises and the happiness it gives. One loves for love's sake and not to have children. To love is to enlarge the scope of one's life. To procreate is to limit it by merely perpetuating it.

Monsieur Prudhon,[4] who refuses to grant that a woman is a representative of the human species, is unable to accept the idea that she is the man's equal in a relationship. Monsieur Prudhon, who limits love to a purely physical union, refuses to recognize that there can exist between two creatures of different but absolutely equal sexes such a fusion, such an intermingling of their intellectual and moral natures through the exchange of their rational and artistic elements, of their qualities of heart and mind.   /95

So I am unhappy, am I? And why should I be? I have left behind me the tortures of love between two partners who are not equals and have rediscovered the riches of the universe. Often I thank heaven for independence.   /96

Before the mayor and the priest, before the eyes of the social order and the religious world, a man and a woman have brought a long procession of witnesses, and the priest with the gold stole and the mayor

---

[4] The socialist theoretician.

with the tricolor sash, in the name of God and the Code, have blessed
and sanctioned the union. The union that allows a woman to say without blushing for shame: On such and such a day, at such and such an
hour, I shall allow a man TO SLEEP IN MY WOMAN'S BED
WITH ME.[5] The union that slowly wends its way amid an orgy of
wine and dancing to the nuptial bed, becomes a bed of debauchery and
prostitution, allows the delirious imagination of the wedding guests to
follow and conjure up, down to the last detail, all the incidents in the
lustful drame played out beneath the title "Wedding Day."   /93

The passionate love that you did your very best to feel for him is an
unnatural sentiment, and one doomed to die away as quickly as a straw
fire. But before it does, your husband will cause you to suffer cruelly,
and however patient he is, he will make himself intolerable in your
eyes. It seems to me that passion is wholly at odds with the dignity and
sanctity of marriage. You probably fancied that it was you who aroused
such passion in your spouse: I doubt that very much. I am persuaded
that what you took to be enthusiasm was merely the violent caresses
that a newly wedded husband forces upon his wife from the very first,
when like you she is very young and very pretty.   /70

"Yesterday I was offered a wife for a hundred thousand francs," a notary who had just begun his practice remarked to a young solicitor
friend of his who had recently finished a clerkship, "but it has cost me
too much to set myself up in business and I can't afford that much, so
the thought occurred to me that you might be interested in such a
match."—"I need twenty thousand more than that," the latter replied.
"But I'll pass the word on to one of my colleagues; a hundred thousand
francs would see him through nicely—he's already gone through all of
his inheritance and his tailors refuse to give him any more credit." The
colleague in question was madly in love, but the beauty he had his eye
on would bring him only fifty thousand francs as a dowry. The offer of
double that amount made him think twice, and these reflections re-
vived the flames of his passion, once he had icily broken off with his
sweetheart and was thus free to give his heart to the young lady worth a
hundred thousand francs. The wedding plans were all made when
bang! the July Revolution came along! Everything was turned topsy-
turvy: the ones on top found themselves on the bottom, and vice versa.
The man aiming at a hundred thousand francs thinks he can aim even
higher: it is his friends who are top dogs now. . . . To make a long

[5] Author's emphasis. E.S.

story short, he asked for a 5 per cent commission for himself and cleverly contrived to hand over his intended to the son of a wealthy manufacturer about to go bankrupt.

As the saying goes nowadays, down with preachers of patriotic sentiments, down with the generous-hearted defenders of the emancipation of women whose real loyalties and devotion lie only with the elite that has come out on top. I call upon you, mesdames, to rebel, to abolish the marriage industry.   /97

The great hymn to the joys of the body and the senses is now voiced less freely, and is often hidden beneath lyrical flights celebrating the soul's raptures; nonetheless it can still be heard—throbbing with life, intense, passionate, and never merely lewd and licentious

O my blue eyes, you will never again gaze upon me! O lovely head, I shall never again see you bending over me and envelop you in my gentle languor! My little warm supple body, you will never again lie atop mine, as Elijah lay down atop the body of the dead child to bring him back to life! You will never again touch my hand, as Jesus touched that of Jairus's daughter, saying to her: "Damsel, I say unto thee, arise." Farewell, my blond hair; farewell, my white shoulders; farewell, everything that was mine! I shall now embrace, in my nights of burning passion, the trunks of pine trees and boulders in the forests, crying your name, and when I have experienced pleasure in my dream, fall in a faint upon the cool, damp forest floor. . . .   70

Oh, how I love such tenderness! I feel it welling up from my very vitals. A thousand kisses on your mouth that I cherish, *your* mouth, that you know how I adore. May it touch nothing in this world! I allow it to kiss only your mother's forehead.   /72

I love you, my body that was his desire
His field of reaped pleasure, his garden of ecstasy
I love you, my flesh that made for his flesh
A burning tabernacle of passion fulfilled.   /98

Oh, how I thank you for having made me a woman! Feeling alive from head to foot! Feeling surrounded on every hand by loving hopes, grafted upon a root-stock of delightful memories, feeling my entire soul melt and dissolve: a love pure enough, sublime enough, to cause all petty social conventions to disappear, to see it alone soar proudly, majestically, above all the worthless shards of this world, turned into a mere whirl of dust round about it. Oh! My beloved! My beloved adored one, glory unto you! Tell me: how can one feel what I feel at this moment and continue to live a common mortal's life?

Hail to my sweet master, the fountain of my life, everything that comes to me from you is my delight and my happiness . . . I confess that I am babbling to no point or purpose, and it is as though I were asking you to turn your beloved dark brown eyes into blue ones. Do I not have another most pleasing way of occupying my time: contemplating your beloved face? On his deathbed Rousseau asked to be carried to the window, in order to enjoy nature, the sunlight, one last time. When my last hour has come, I shall imitate him, except that I am richer than he: My sun and my nature are mine alone.   /78

> His neck, his arms—nothing fingers can touch
> Or eyes see of him is as voluptuous
> As his ravishing mouth and its ravenous bite
> His mouth fresh and sweet—and a burning coal
> A voracious flower of lust and delight
> Draining your heart, drinking in your soul.   /98

> Ah, what bliss to flee
> The world's prying eyes
> For the forest's peace
> To be loved, to feel the senses' surprise
> To be him, to be me!
> A man and a woman!
> I've not yet told enough
> How my joys never cease
> O my splendid loves!
> O nature! O nature!
> As I worship you: In everything
> In shadow or sun
> In all creation as one
> And in us your creatures.   /99

My chastity has caused me great suffering, a fact that I do not hide from you; I have had dreams that greatly sapped my strength; my blood has rushed to my head a hundred times. In the hot sunlight, in the heart of a lovely mountain country, hearing birds sing and breathing in the softest perfumes of forests and valleys, I have often sat alone, far from everything and everyone, with my soul full of love and knees trembling with sheer sensual pleasure. I am young still. Though I tell other men that I possess the calm of one ripe with age, my blood seethes. . . . I walk ten leagues more, and as I tumble into bed in a simple country inn, I think to myself still that the breast of a man that I adore is the one pillow on which both my soul and my body will find rest. . . .   /70

Other women live the dream of socialist utopias in which their sisters are free at last, but as they live out this dream they struggle desperately, searching for the meaning of their own lives, seeking their own hard-won personal truths

Thus far the woman has not answered the summons to free herself addressed to her, save by humbly following in the footsteps of her emancipators. The day has now come when she will answer their call for freedom by emancipating herself. . . . A thousand sufferings are involved in achieving all this, I know full well, but has not pain always been the price that must be paid for the progress of humanity? I shall endeavor to marshal every strength I possess to confront the moment when I shall hear you renounce me as your wife, and your little Amélie as your daughter. Such a thing requires an enormous effort of will! I shall be able to summon it, I hope. A tender farewell from the woman who soon will no longer be able to call herself "your Cécile."   /100

Dear Aglaé, I shall not tell you that when I next set eyes upon him, it will be with no suffering in my heart, no grief. I have given him too much and received from him too little for me not to feel a sort of heartbreak mingled with my pleasure at seeing him again after such a long separation.   /100

Today marks a year since I gave myself to you with all the abandon and all the lack of foresight of the most heartfelt sense of utter loyalty. . . . How could I have been expected to reconcile your most tender, affectionate behavior in days gone by with the distant manner you display toward me today? In the long run, what does the birth of one child amount to? Nothing but a mere grain of sand! But this grain of sand is part of you and part of me. . . . If your heart has not embraced her, my idol is totally shattered.[6]   /101

Mark my word, my daughter, the love that one feels for one's superior is the same love that causes you to accept with joy the counsel offered you, and *your* happiness is the one that matters most to the man who guides every step of your life.   /102

You first appeared to me on the rue Monsigny—to the young woman who resembled a timid, dreamy, affectionate young girl, married only a few months before to Rogé, whom I worshiped with a profound, exclusive love, in which I lovingly allowed my life to be cradled—paying little heed to your mission and your doctrine. In the goodness of his heart and soul, Rogé could not help but be moved by your eloquence and immediately converted on hearing you champion the cause of freedom for women of the poorest class. You asked him for his heart and his life. He gave you his all. After many a quarrel, he said to me one day: "My child, don't be so aggrieved, do not weep like that in desperation because I am a man. They are good, they want everyone to be happy, should we not help them work for the emancipation of women?" I answered with a sigh: "Go then where your conscience calls you!" Alas! one must be a woman to understand the pain that racked my heart, despite its being quite prepared to receive the teachings of a new faith. I loved him; I went with him. Then the day that all of you retired to Ménilmontant, Rogé said to me, "Be patient a while longer, my dear Clorinda, Father tells us that in six months the two of us will be together again and will never again be parted." I shook my head and replied: "Enfantin has no way of knowing what is going to happen. . . ."[7]   /103

He came to see me every day. I had time to sound this man's mind and realized that he was perhaps the only one, in Peru, who might be able to further my ambitions. . . . The desire to contribute to men's common good had been the constant passion of my soul, and an active, adventurous career had always been my fancy. It seemed to me quite

[6] Letter to Prosper Enfantin, "father" of the utopian Saint-Simonians.
[7] Letter to Prosper Enfantin.

likely that if I aroused Escudero's love, I would come to have great influence over him. . . . My inner struggles began again, the idea of associating myself with this witty, bold, debonaire man intrigued me. . . . But I feared I might fall victim to that moral depravity that generally results from the exercise of power. I was afraid I might become hard, despotic, criminal even—the equal of those who were lords and masters of the world. . . . The sacrifice was all the greater in that Escudero pleased me. He was an ugly man in the eyes of many people, but not mine. He was about thirty to thirty-three years old, of average height, dark-skinned, with very black hair, gleaming, languorous eyes, and teeth like pearls. . . . I am intimately persuaded that had I become his wife, I should have been most happy. . . . It required all my strength of will not to succumb to the temptation that such a prospect offered. I was suddenly afraid of myself, and departed forthwith to Lima.   /86

Love? What book has not been embroidered with its mawkish compliments, its fine phrases? Did I not meet it at the latest Salon, a poor plump-cheeked toothless child in its thick blond wig, at the side of its eternal darling mama Venus? Of all the definitions of love that have fleshed out so many thick volumes, only one seems beautiful to me in its truth, conciseness, and forcefulness, that of Madame de Staël. . . . Yes, a strange and illustrious woman, as you so rightly say: love to her was merely mutual self-interest. The moment you looked upon a man with pleasure, the moment that he seemed to you more handsome, more witty than your lover or your spouse . . . an act of prostitution took place, adultery was committed, at least in intention. Only convention or fear held you back, and you compounded adultery with guile and prevarication. That is where we inevitably end up as a result of the "law of fidelity" bolstered by "publicity."[8]   /93

And the time has come when the flesh must be rehabilitated, when matter will be the equal and not the slave of the spirit. . . . For very often, on the threshold of the bedchamber, a devouring flame is suddenly extinguished. Very often, for more than one great passion, the scented bed sheets have become shrouds. For more than one female reader of these lines, perhaps, will have entered the marriage bed palpitating with desire and emotion on the wedding night and risen next morning cold as ice.

[8] Around 1830 "publicity" meant "the act of making public." What the author is referring to here is the posting of nuptial banns and the bonds of matrimony, as against the secrecy and the freedom of illicit liaisons. (*Author's note.*)

And I who address these words to you *through my own choice* remained but an hour in a man's arms, and this hour sufficed to raise a barrier of satiety between him and me, this hour was long enough to cause me to relegate him to his proper place, so far as I was concerned, amid the monotonous crowd of indifferent men who leave no trace in our lives save a vulgar, cold, banal memory, as valueless as it is pleasure-less.   /93

DETAILS CONCERNING A DOUBLE SUICIDE

Committed by two disciples of Saint-Simon, one male and one female, each of whom put pistols to their hearts and shot themselves to death Saturday evening, at number 9, rue Folie-Mercourt, Paris. Other details on their fatal resolve, on the funeral and graveside ceremony which will take place tomorrow at the Père-Lachaise cemetery. Last words to be spoken over the tomb of these two unfortunate victims of love and jealousy by Father Enfantin. Funeral hymns by Saint-Simonians, etc. Interesting conversation between the two of them. Extraordinary letters that were found on the night table next to their bed.

In the limitless desert of love, sensual pleasure has an ardent but very small place, so incandescent that at first one sees nothing else.

Colette

· VII ·

TWENTIETH CENTURY

Sexuality as an Intellectual Exercise

Since I have lived my entire life in the twentieth century, I cannot hope to sift through the mountain of twentieth-century documents before me and pass judgments that will be entirely fair and objective. One cannot really *analyze* a language when one's life is lived inside, as ethnologists realize and hence journey far afield in order to acquire the detachment necessary for proper observation.

And how can I hope to put that same distance between myself and my material? There now appear before me words, songs, laments, that date from my mother's time. Each line evokes a memory, calls forth a smile, for when I was twelve years old, she seemed so terribly "old-fashioned"! Can children ever really accept the reality of their parents' feelings of love? The fearful, adorable, fascinating mystery that surrounded my mother's femininity, and its pitiful, painful, delightful secrets—is not all that forever taboo, and have I ever been able to use the words that I found in her love letters after her death? My mother's time is like a room that one forbids oneself to ever enter, out of a sense of awed devotion, and also out of fear of finding oneself face to face with the books lined up on the shelves, so out of date, so touching, so naïve. And yet these were the books that she read as a woman in love, and the books that she freely allowed me to read after I was nine or ten: one always learns love in the language of one's parents, so as later to create one's very own.

There then appear before me texts from the years of my adolescence, the years of my first loves. These are texts I know by heart, and there could be no apter expression: I know them by heart, and by the perfume of the mock-orange flowers when I read this passage, all by myself, or by the smell of the rumpled bed when I read that one to *him*. How can one judge the cries that pierce one's life, that express and arouse one's inner turmoil? The young girl who buys *The Story of O* in a bookstore cannot know what it was like to be given it as a gift by a lover in the days when it was a forbidden book. And here come the faces of living authors who are friends and acquaintances of mine, and the gap that I am aware of between the person I know and what she writes. And then comes the time of one's own children's first love experiences, which we modestly pretend not to be able to understand because age and experience have made us all too clear-sighted, because puppy love by nature is a phenomenon that does not lend itself to systematic study. . . .

Yet despite all this, we must make an attempt at some sort of intellectual analysis of love in this century of ours—this twentieth century in which the problem is further complicated by the fact that the realm of love evolves as rapidly and as dramatically as countless other domains: economics, production, consumption, scientific discovery.

Pasteur gives the world the keys of asepsis. Marvelous progress is made in the fields of biology, physiology, medicine. Techniques are perfected that win many a battle in mankind's fight against death. In order to have three children who will live to adulthood, it is no longer necessary for a woman to bring six of them into the world. She is gradually freed of the obligation of being scarcely more than a bearer of children. She has more time and strength to devote to her children and their upbringing—and also more time and strength for herself, her own flowering, her love-life. Scientists discover female hormones, the rhythms of ovulation, methods that enable the woman to control her own fertility. Maternity and sexuality become functions further and further divorced from each other as time goes by. Age-old "eternal laws" are overturned, age-old fears are allayed, and the ritual dances centered on these fears gradually slow down and wind to a halt, like a clock running down. From the seventeenth century on in France, it was the man who was more or less (in the literal sense!) responsible for "birth control," through the practice of coitus interruptus; the risk of pregnancy thus depended upon his good will and his ability to control his own body. He was thus able to use coitus interruptus as a weapon or a mark of respect, a threat or a responsibility. The woman's one recourse was trust in him. Now suddenly it is she who is in control of her own fecundity, and the roles are diametrically reversed. The gift of herself is no longer a matter of helpless self-surrender, a sort of double-or-nothing bet which is won or lost merely due to the laws of sheer chance or to the self-mastery or tenderness of the male. With this reversal of roles, the precarious balance between love partners is upset, and the moral codes founded thereupon collapse. The woman discovers the vastness—and the anguish—of complete freedom. What George Sand or Claire Demar, each in her own personal language and style, rebelled against— the rites, the taboos, the eternal second-sex status that determined the woman's entire love-life—begins to crumble to dust. The woman who for century after century was obliged to accept her lot, to take risks, or to rebel (to precious little avail), the woman who had been obliged to build her entire life around, or in spite of, the fear of the proofs of her carnal passions that her body might produce, is now free to opt for ex-periences that will leave no trace. . . . What is left is the heart, and the other profound meaning of fidelity, which she may now espouse as freely as the man: "If you really love me . . ." The ending of that age-old phrase has also changed. And virginity, its preservation, its price, its meaning, have changed too. And "the fall from virtue," "the gift of self," "abandon" as well: none of these key figures in the dance of love has the same meaning now that it once did. They are now only figures of speech, both within marriage and without, whatever sentimental or ideological content the two lovers may attribute to them out of habit or pious respect.

And yet I have merely mentioned in passing a few of the conse-quences of a single dramatic change among countless others. . . . Even listing all of them would take much more space than I have at my dis-posal, and I must perforce pick and choose. It would be tempting, and helpful, I suppose, were I to hazard a guess as to which phenomena, amid this abundance of material, simply constituted a fashion of the moment and which added up to a really irreversible revolution with in-calculable consequences for love and for women. Seen from this per-spective, surrealism would seem to be merely a passing thundershower, and psychoanalysis a relatively durable vogue with a high "fall-out effect," though reversible in the foreseeable future. The fact that girls and boys receive more or less the same education would appear to be an even more dramatic evolution than those brought about by the two great world wars, the effects of which have been institutionalized rela-tively rapidly.

This extremely brief diagnosis would doubtless hold true until around the turn of this century. But it would not even begin to explain the qualitative variations in the expressions of feminine love. For on closely studying women's writings on love, one is much more aware of fashionable trends than of deep-seated changes. These writings follow sinuous, meandering paths, echo prevailing manners and morals or oc-casionally rebel against them, run counter to history, give it the touch of color of traditions stubbornly clung to, of nostalgic returns to the past, and then head straight for domains hitherto unexplored.

One must therefore modestly confine oneself to simply following them without trying to explain, and to sift through them with no illusions as to one's own infallibility. There are so many women who write in the twentieth century! There is no need now to prove that authentic women writers exist, to dig up forgotten manuscripts in the National Library, to sort through volumes of their letters. (What is more, "people don't write each other love letters nowadays," I was assured by a taxi driver who deposited me at the National Library as I was doing research on the eighteenth century, "and when you get as far as our time, you'd be better off going through the wastebaskets in telephone booths. . . .")

From the dawn of our century on, there is an abundance of material. Women write by the hundreds. The great feminist movements of the end of the nineteenth century continue, centering their attention on education, with the vast ambition of making women's talents the equal of men's. Films, radio, television, do not yet exist. Women read and write. The telephone does not yet exist either. Women write and read.

During the age of Romanticism, in order to free feeling, the gradual manifestation of the body, that fact so imprudently denied, begins as a hymn of pantheistic adoration. Nature. Women seize their pens and describe landscapes, flowers, and fruits—or rather, they describe their own sensuality by writing of landscapes, flowers, and fruits. A heady, sensuous *joie de vivre*, an amazing, all absorbing need to experience life, consumes them. They are so vibrant that they love, they are so in love that they vibrate, they yearn to experience, to drink in all of life, their sensitive nostrils flaring, their palms open to embrace, their eyes dazzled.

"I write, so that when I shall no longer be / It will be known how much free air and pleasure pleased me," Anna de Noailles writes, and adds: "I was a star, green leaves, wing, perfume, cloud."

It is no longer a question of lyrically romantic or realistically precise descriptions à la George Sand, or of set pieces as a backdrop for sentimental affairs of the heart. It is, rather, a straining to live fully, to be one with life, ardor, the fever of communion. "The jasmines tonight are intoxicated with love's ecstasy / And with my mouth to the wind I drank in the universe," Hélène Vacaresco writes. And "I shall fling myself upon you, O nature fair! / And pray to ever a woman remain / So that your gaze will ever linger in the depths of mine," Marie de Sormieu echoes. Gérard d'Houville, Valentine de Saint-Point, Marcelle Tinayre, Colette, Camille Marbo—all these women writers raise their voices in chorus to the intoxication of the senses that calls forth within them the pagan conjoining of the love of nature and the love of their own bodies, or rather, of the fusion of the love of their nature and their beauty and the beauty of nature.

The unusual narcissism of this celebration is what lends it its distinctive nuances as an expression of love. Leafy greenery moves me, for my long locks sweep across my bare shoulders, the sun is my very skin, the moon my white breasts, the fruits—because they are my female parts, even if I dare not mention them outright. I must therefore "grow languid, seized by every imaginable ecstasy," "bite into ripe fruits," offer my "pure flanks," my womb, my "erect breasts," trample the grass underfoot with my "slender feet," offer to the wind my hair, the locks that Colette's Claudine calls her four seasons, "for their color changes with the calendar," a world of fragrances that are one's very own and "offered" when a man passes by. . . .

Women *are* nature. Who would have suspected such a thing, contemplating the costumes they were obliged to imprison themselves in from 1900 to 1920! And yet a veritable outpouring of forthright autoeroticism on the part of these tightly corseted ladies makes its appearance, the celebration of a pact with a nature that was not yet "set up" for leisure-time activities—bathing beaches swarming with vacationers, forest paths complete with litter baskets, fields of wheat covered with pesticides on either side of expressways teeming with cars that did not exist as yet. Our young ladies of 1910 perform the first act of the love drama of the twentieth century in the flower garden of the parish priest, bare their naked bodies to the moonlight of a summer evening behind the venetian blinds of drowsy little country towns, and pedal down paths just wide enough for their bicycle to pass, as loutish peasants along the wayside leer at them.

Because it is addressed to the sun, to forest glades, to greenery and to the wind, this great love hymn in celebration of warm skin and the shivers of pleasure beneath it finds a place in schoolroom texts. Oddly enough, our teachers seem to have been unaware of the secret meaning that these sensuous texts exuded. For a schoolgirl, as I can personally testify, Anna de Noailles's verses about a garden were far more exciting than Baudelaire's funereal works, which were admittedly superb but "strange." Whereas when one reads these ladies who wrote so movingly of roses, one feels a secret stirring within one's bosom that seeks its release in ecstasy and tears. . . .

But the verses that follow in this hymn to love penned by women at the beginning of the twentieth century are not "suitable" reading for a twelve-year-old schoolgirl. These ladies passionately break the chains in which men with pince-nez and stiff collars seek to imprison them. One wonders, indeed, how women could have possibly fallen in love with such creatures. Men of this period are so unappealing—so unbendingly bourgeois, so pretentious, their minds so dulled by positivism, scientism, nationalism, clericalism, or priapism that, as a sort of heart-felt aesthetic protest, vast numbers of young women choose each other's company instead, and spend their days contemplating and caressing each other. And the century rolls on, with an unparalleled explosion of lesbian literature. The word for it at the time was "sapphic," which admittedly has a more pleasant ring to it, perhaps because of its associations with the words "sapphire" or "sophism."

And a sophism it was, ending as it did in a blind alley. A sensuality that prides itself in no longer being exploited, taken advantage of, imprisoned, done violence to. What it seeks at any cost is to find expression as a desire, without running the risk of confronting the unknown in the form of a desire totally different from itself, and is persuaded that its powers are multiplied twofold by being reflected by a diffuse, parallel sensuality on the part of its object. Though pleasure may have been thereby liberated, it nonetheless ends in loneliness and jealousy, never reaching that most mysterious resolution of all for the woman: becoming herself a man, while at the same time allowing the man to become a woman, not in order to find some vague missing half that is lacking, but rather in order for both the man and the woman to fulfill themselves and become as one.

The sapphism, whether latent or acted out, of the women of the first quarter of the twentieth century is a quite natural result of their reaction against the dreary post-Romantic period. It is a means, first of all, of compensating for the deadly silences of the corseted society of the end of the nineteenth century through the narcissistic celebration of the self as mirrored in another woman. And a means, secondly, of expressing a profound hostility against man the stranger, a man whose sensuality is more infantile than ever, divided as it is between an undying affection for his first beloved mechanical toys (his trains, his automobiles, his airplanes, that he builds models of with the enthusiasm of an adolescent), his virtuous wives-and-mothers, on whom he fathers the smallest number of children possible, not out of respect for them, but out of a fear of how much it costs to raise them, and his favorite-prostitutes-in-their-undies in some bordello. The man has ceased to be a poetic creature. He refuses the role of androgyne that will make love between man and woman a perfect thing. He is no longer a knight in the service of his lady, courting danger and keeping his desire in check the better to glorify her; no woman passionately in love would dream of writing him, as the most touching of all possible compliments, the words that Éléanore de Sabran penned in the eighteenth century: "You have a woman's heart!" And he has also ceased to be a poet inspired by womanliness. He dissects and classifies and in horror tags with the epithet "hominists" or "Amazons" those women who merely wish to share his way of life, to educate themselves, to drive a car, to smoke, to come out of the kitchen and read the newspapers. Forced to share their lives with these potbellied men in pince-nez, how could these women have helped but dream of "sapphic embraces"?

In any event, even though the style is somewhat out of date, this lesbian literature is nonetheless very good writing. Its authors enjoyed the freedom to write, a certain recognition, and in some cases even fame. And those who did so were not the most scandalous, but the most talented—all of which reduces to its proper proportions the absurd statement of the lesbians of the early seventies that they were an "oppressed class." With their eyes riveted on New York and Berkeley, the majority of the latter were totally ignorant of the fact that in France there has never existed, and still does not exist, any sort of law against feminine homosexuality—and the majority of them have no knowledge of either the names or the works of their illustrious predecessors.

The third characteristic of this first part of the twentieth century, up to the beginning of World War II: It likewise gave to French literature (and I underline the word *literature*) the most profound and most subtle psychologists of love of this century—in no way comparable to the crude brickbats cast by sexologists, erotologists, psychologists, pedagogues, and analysts who followed, crushing love beneath the weight of their pedantry and obscurantism. The penetrating, lucid passages penned by these women are well worth reading. I have deliberately chosen to present them without the names of their authors—it was in fact these texts that made me decide to present the writings found at the end of each chapter with only a number to indicate their author, thus forcing the reader to confront an "anonymous" text and be obliged to look up in the numbered index the name of the author whose words have proven particularly striking. I was well aware of the "purgatory" in which these analysts, equipped with no "dictionary of complexes" and belonging to no "accredited school," had come to languish in. Colette alone would appear to have escaped this fate. I know another, however, whose works lie undeservedly slumbering beneath tons of oblivion—to the point that I can unfailingly predict what will happen if I read a passage of hers to my friends. Deeply impressed, intrigued, dazzled by this veritable revelation, they invariably ask me: "Who in the world wrote that? It's marvelous!" And when I reveal the author's name, they exclaim: "I can't believe it! It's true though that nobody reads her any more. . . . I don't know her works at all. . . ." A woman author who said that she wrote for "the unknown young man of tomorrow"![1]

But the great victory of the twentieth century, which refuses to recognize it, and of women, who do not yet realize that it is their living monument, their precious handiwork, is marriage. For the first time in

[1] I am speaking, of course, of Anna de Noailles. (*Author's note.*)

their long history, for the first time since time began, for the first time in France, women marry for love. They marry the man of their choice —the man they love. Moreover, a proportionally greater number of them marry than in past centuries, when many women remained spinsters. (There was, however, one sad exception to this trend: the countless "fiancées" of 1914–18, left without anyone to marry after the monstrous bloodletting in the trenches of World War I.) They marry younger and younger, and young women of the seventies, who claim that marriage is an institution that is dead and buried, troop to the altar in great numbers than any generation of women before them, and marry at the age of twenty or twenty-one, whereas their mothers waited several years longer before pronouncing the wedding vows, and their grandmothers tended to be around twenty-six when they married.

Marriage has indeed changed, and it might also be said that marriage has changed everything: The woman's love-life tends to be lived entirely within marriage. Women now choose "to live with someone." Since 1945 and the end of World War II, they have chosen to do away with all the trappings of a Catholic, bourgeois marriage, complete with a formal contract signed before a notary and vows exchanged in public, and as they have changed the institution they have changed the words to describe it. They no longer speak of "matrimony" or of their "husband"—or even of being a "couple." They refer to the man as their "partner" or "companion" and "live with him," night and day—an irreplaceable, difficult way of sharing one's life with another. They enter into a lasting relationship, without absence from each other or exterior obstacles to pique their interest in each other. And they come to know both the joys and the sorrows of such a relationship, its daily sense of communion, and its pitfalls and shortcomings: satiety, indifference, lies, the dull daily tasks, slamming doors, beds to be made, the tyranny of the clock, and the children, and the office, and the dishes, and the Sunday afternoons with friends. To live through all that, infatuation and even deep affection no longer suffice. Another common source of ecstasy is needed, something else to enrich a thousand and one nights spent together: "a good sex life." "I get along just fine with my husband" is a statement that has changed meaning entirely. Today it is a frank confession that all is well, in bed and out. To "get along well together," to understand each other body and soul, is also to listen to each other attentively. Never before have women so thoroughly studied, listened to, looked at, their men. This is a relationship fraught with danger, which vast numbers of women willingly embark upon in the twenties, in the thirties, but above all in the forties, fifties, and sixties. A word seldom heard before now appears, and soon becomes a banal cliché: the word *couple*. It is no longer for love, through love, that most women now live, but for "the couple," for "the couple that the

two of us make." "A couple that really go together," "a great couple," "a perfect couple," have become, in the dream heaven of women of the second half of the twentieth century, the stars that guide them—not "grand passions."

The writings of women bear witness to this, as women at last attempt to give expression not only to their own eroticism but also the eroticism of another: the man. The man finally exists in the words that women in love speak and write: as a spectacle to be contemplated, as an object to be celebrated. In 1908 there appear verses to a lover that the great critic Émile Faguet compared favorably to the *Letters of a Portuguese Nun*, Marguerite Burnat-Provins's *Le Livre pour toi* (The Book for You). Born and raised in the north of France, married in Switzerland, she was to other women (along with the Belgian Marie Nizet, who preceded her in the nineteenth century), a lyrical expression of the most heady feminine myth of antiquity: the sleep of Endymion. One understands why Robert de Montesquiou, the model of Proust's famous homosexual Baron de Charlus, was so fond of these "sentimental and sensual variations on the sculptural beauty of this wonderfully mysterious young man." "I shall tell of the bright gleam of your eyes, the sensuousness of your mouth, the strength of your arms, the burning heat of your powerful haunches, and the warm softness of your skin. . . . Like an idol my adoration will cover your superb nakedness with perfumed lilies and phlox gathered in my garden." And this quite some time before Lawrence and the effusions of his Lady Chatterley, before d'Annunzio and his smothering of his mistresses in rose petals. . . . Woman seemed at last on the point of giving expression to what she had always felt and always hidden: her intoxication with male beauty, and Marguerite Burnat-Provins's *Poèmes pour toi* (Poems for You) went through countless editions. But they were followed by a work entitled *Poèmes troubles* (Confused Poems), whose dedication on the first page speaks volumes: It reads "For myself." And the collection begins with the words "Dolly, my Dolly. In your man's hands my flesh took shape. Since when do dolls play with grownups?" Once past these surprising first pages, matters grow even more confusing. Constant subtle shifts in gender convey Dolly and her lover back and forth across a sexual borderline never clearly defined: "My male pleasure, imperious and self-assured, kneads your male form, and when you cry out 'my Dolly,' it is a madwoman's cry that will give answer to my woman's cry."

But in the very same year, or thereabouts, a voice rings out in a hymn of adoration so unambiguous that no aesthete can mistake its intent: "You grow erect and hard: the vigor of the forest . . . I kissed you, like a robin in my hand / I love the warmth of your body in my palm. . . . You are handsome as a wolf / You spurt forth like a beech / Whose sap swells beneath the bark. . . . Desire tinges your lashes purple. The axis of the world lies in your flesh / You are its compass-rose of delights." At long last, after all these centuries! At long last, the unmistakable expression of a love for someone who is clearly *other*, for someone not one's self! At long last, the appeal to nature to symbolize beauty, the desire for another, for the man, heretofore so scantly praised, an orphan bereft of poems celebrating his glory. At long last, the lover accepted, awaited in all of his pantheistic fullness of meaning and received in per-fect tenderness. Was all this so hard to say? Was it so unexpected that no one even remembers today the name of the author of these words? It was Marie Dauguet—happily in love and happily married, celebrating her love in innocence, not lust.

A hymn such as this, with no reference to the self, remains unique. Granted: People today speak openly of a phallus, a penis, of male sex-ual pleasure—men especially, but women too are no longer ashamed to call up concrete images of this creature who is other than themselves. But only rarely do they do so to celebrate the man. It is *themselves* that they glorify, and the pleasure the man gives them, *their* intimate feelings of him, the man as *they* live him. And even the miraculous Mireille Sorgue, whose first name in French is mindful of the sun and whose family name is that of a river, who tells us she "has, for the man as grave as a child, feelings of tenderness," listens to him laboring inside her body, and describes the self-revelation that he brings her, even if "When I know from the vague look in his eyes that he is going out of his mind, I arch my back and fell him. I crush his strength between my legs, and see him fall on top of me with the grace of a musical tree." The other, the stranger. "Lying there he quivers still, in brief spasms that resound beneath his forehead and break the seal of his eyelids. It pains me to see his skin fade as the color drains from it." Dead-silent, she contemplates him. "It is after the moments when the battle is joined / And we've united in combat, loin against loin / As my head leans back, though our bodies still touch / That I feel the full force of what separates us. . . . What can there be, O my incomparable love, / That is common to the two of us?" Anna de Noailles asks.

It is, rather, *her* pleasure that the woman explores as she follows love's meanders. To achieve this end, she invents a poetics that is at the same time gentle and tense, rich in symbiotic discoveries. From the depths of time sea images well up. Was not Aphrodite born of Chronos's sperm falling into the sea, from seething foam? The woman writer constantly returns to these tropes, which she perhaps under-stands even better after a seaside holiday that brings these age-old leg-ends to vivid life. The sea is a woman, the woman is a beach, a sea cave, and pleasure successive waves, breaking gently or crashing upon the strand. Tides lick the shore or beat upon the rocks. Algae have the odor of love. The man is a shipwrecked hulk. Primal waters are a true image of every feminine truth: liquid, salty, sustaining, engulfing, eternal. "Lovely land visited and lost / The lapping of water surrendered to itself / Shore-woman, beach, a stretch of sand / Your sole destiny: being here as you are," Thérèse Aubray says for all of womankind.

And in this sea cave of her pleasure her powers of imagination unfold and project the most fantastic shadows. In order to feel more fully alive, as though in reply to the very wise but very foolish Héloïse, she dreams, eight centuries later, of self-annihilation. "I am the Door. / Before you enter, I must have withdrawn from myself, and no longer be / My neck is bowed beneath an age-old yoke. / I know the pain of being an object," Mireille Sorgue writes. "My powers, turned inward, have imprisoned me." And Pauline Réage deliriously rehearses delights that have no limit save death: ". . . At the very first word or sign from one of your masters, you will abandon your tasks in order to perform your real service, which is to make yourselves available. Your hands do not belong to you, nor your breasts, nor any of the orifices of your body in particular, for we have the right to explore them and penetrate them at will." Everything within you will be sexual in order that everything within you may become spiritual. And as Saint Theresa of Avila put it, you will die of not dying. "We are all jailers, and all of us are in prison," Pauline Réage explained several years later when she had come to know the tenderness and confidence that shared love can bring: "By a curious irony, it is prison that opens the doors to freedom." And more important, to a sort of intoxication at having won out, a fervent passivity that basks in the incandescent heat of the imaginary, "triumphant in their bonds," as she somewhere writes of such women.

In this period, from around 1950 to 1965, eroticism takes the form of philosophical meditation and a lyrical celebration of sexuality. It is at once a metaphysics and a poetics, a word with the taste of sap, iodine, and death, exchanged between lovers who are intellectuals.

But all of this changed almost immediately. The mystique of the couple was taken over by women's magazines and became part of everyday manners and morals. Lyrical eroticism, for its part, was born of the necessity of transcending incredible collective experiences. We were still dazed and terrified at having discovered, after the fact, the extent of Nazi atrocities. Many of us could remember having been deeply in love during these same years of night and silence, perhaps without knowing it. Out poets (and we read a great deal during this time of hunger and curfews, of tremendous material discomfort during the long years that followed Liberation) were Louis Aragon or Paul Éluard. Both had dedicated verses not only to France but to their wives, and sung of love as well as of the epic heroism of the Resistance. Among us there were many who believed in eternity, and those who did not nonetheless reread Saint John of the Cross and Saint Theresa of Avila. And saw Alain Resnais's film *Night and Fog*. And all of us searched for the meaning of the dramatic events taking place round about us.

And then little by little the pedantic practitioners of lay analysis crammed their explanations down our throats, burying us beneath their descriptions couched in terms of phalli, penis envy, vaginas and clitorises, sadism and masochism. What can poetry say in answer to such an onslaught, especially when it has been robbed of all its symbols in order to catalogue them and strip them of their richest ambiguities? There were also the "committed" writers, whom we were fond of, who needed our help in denouncing every form of oppression, not in order to transform them into poetic love situations, but in order to temper the spirit of resistance in the heart of every man and every woman once the Resistance was over, to make up for the cowardliness of the mob that had gripped so many during the war. Then there were American films, full of oedipal situations that stuck out like sore thumbs as they set out, with naïve self-confidence, to combat the Anglo-Saxon evil of the moment: puritanism—even though this latter was already a stinking corpse. America was strong, and we bowed to its culture even as we fought its imperialist ambitions. This game is still going on, as a matter of fact, and the ordinary Frenchman accepts the scientific lessons of sexual liberation preached on the other side of the Atlantic, forgetting that the French, however hypocritical and tradition-minded, have nonetheless never been puritans. But it was such a pleasant pastime to translate such works and play at being backward pupils. . . .

Then came the time when children born during the war reached adolescence—children begotten by young couples in days of famine and privation. They were now thirteen, fourteen, fifteen years old. There were countless numbers of them, and they were spoiled. They became consumers courted *en bloc* by hawkers of consumer products. Special boutiques catered to adolescents with cash in their jeans. There were teen-age records, teen-age excursions, and these youngsters learned of sexuality by way of teen-age magazines printed on glossy paper. They sang the *yé-yé*, and Lolita, with her miniskirt and her teddy bear and her head nodding in time to a rock tune, became queen of the day.

And suddenly women in love who were thirty or forty, or even a mere twenty-five, found themselves old hat. Remembering Suzanne Voilquin's teachings that moral freedom begins with economic freedom, they took jobs and went to work with a will. And meanwhile young women who had ceased to be virgins at the age of twelve or thirteen became the queens of the world of advertising, and frequently the heroines of this period's fiction. They were all victims of the vogue for "scientific sexuality" and sincerely convinced that the "biddies" older than they were conditioned victims of bourgeois repression. After shocking the public when it first appeared in print, Simone de Beauvoir's *The Second Sex* became a classic, a manual, rather than a painful outcry against woman's condition. It no longer occurred to anyone to analyze the other works of this same woman author, to trace the long path taken by this woman whose "extramarital" adventures, so to speak, take place only because her lover leaves her free, being himself totally absorbed in his own work. A strange *oeuvre* which sums up perfectly the experience of women in the twentieth century, being as it is the clear-minded hymn in celebration of an exemplary couple whose relations are founded on the permanence of a free woman's love, and at the same time a collective cry of feminine revolt.

Supported by psychoanalysis and Marxism and fascinated by youth, which must reveal everything, bring everything in its wake, as though it were intrinsically revolutionary, certain young women begin to write erotically, following the taste of the time. They are all capable of looking at their genitals in a mirror and talking of them. It is quite true that before them this was seldom done in women's writings. They also speak of the man, like brave little female Célines of the fashionable sixth arrondissement of Paris, their eyes riveted on the fly of his blue jeans. They dream of assuming every possible position, though they nonetheless are capable of laughing at their own ridiculousness. They prefer their clitorises and their "jewels" nestling amid fur. They love each other and are impatient. They write well, being talented young people, and are too "up to date" not to date very quickly. Their "indiscreet jewels," to us Diderot's phrase for female genitals, speak of their liberation. They tell how it is to have their periods, and for the first time tell the story both often and well. A handful of them, such as Monique Wittig, write better than well, inventing a new language in which to celebrate the respected vulva of victorious Amazons: a new, mythological celebration of a revolution that heretofore had been inexpressible.

And the "indiscreet jewels" also speak of love, that great fiesta. And suddenly love is no longer love. The man is no longer the beloved. Become a pitiable creature, his one role is to bow before the vagina, which women writers celebrate in such universal terms that it becomes anonymous. They have invented anonymous intimacy—which men, poor things, may well have invented before them. It is only voyeurs who find such empty, lonely literature interesting. What has been lost? Eroticism has changed meaning. It has become mere trading in obscenity, in a cosmopolitan French, relieved here and there by a touch of humor, rather than heaven, but for how long? Eroticism, an iridescent and terrifying word, a high note that is bloody and beautiful and difficult to reach, like the heights of every secret cult, has become as dreary as a line in front of a porno movie. Courses in sex education, however necessary, will never give it back its lost nobility. Claiming to be liberated, women display their nakedness on walls, in bus placards, advertising a pure fruit juice of a pair of synthetic panties. Young girls weep over *Love Story* and other such sentimental claptrap, having failed to find any expression of true feeling elsewhere. Men, secretly jealous perhaps of having no clothes of their own that are not worn by women, disguise themselves beneath flowing mustaches, beards, and long locks, in order perhaps to proclaim that their hormones are different.

André Breton's sun has set. Men no longer adore women, who no longer adore men. One does not adore a "partner," much less "partners."

The soul's violence is a taboo subject, hidden as it is by the shameful images of physical violence that fill the television screen—to disgust us or to secretly delight us?

In this baring of intimacies, a necessary stage perhaps, women in love hide from others' sight to write letters, as their adolescent sons and daughters speak laconically of their love feelings over the phone. Or else they hide to reread Anne Philipe, who seems to date from another era. Conjugal life, curiously enough, remains the refuge of love amid a thousand fumbling searches for love—a fact which would have come as a surprise to our medieval women writers.

Unless today's young women with powerful imaginations reinvent gods in order to adore them, and fear, and recompense, and the legend of the great lover who will again clothe them in order to again teach them the soul's prayer. The time is now at hand once more for prophets.

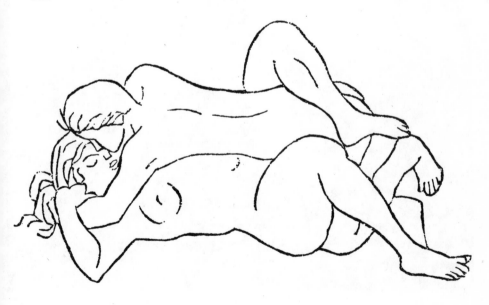

The twentieth century opens with an explosion of feminine writings that are sensual, pantheist hymns to nature and to woman, a beautiful creature amid nature—passionate, carnal hymns to life

I would bite into ripe fruits, grow drunk on sun and sheer light
Know the languid intoxication of every possible pleasure. . . .
My body shivers and trembles with desire
Arches upward toward the unknown, burns with its fever. . . .
And drunk with love, panting for breath,
With my breasts straining toward you, I shall cry out to you: More!

Sometimes my being by sunset is blinded
As a tide rushes toward me, so life in me mounts.
"I love you, I sob, overwhelmed and delighted
At the sound of these words for the first time pronounced.

I am joyous, tender, weary—and light as a bird!
A rose its secrets confides to me
I love my sweet white breasts, by desire stirred
And in this light I cry out suddenly. . . .

I weep, all too aware of the grace I possess
But innocent still as a stalk of wheat
Life rests its beautiful head on my breast
I kiss it, laughing, and fall asleep.   /105

My love is a tree and my heart a fruit
You may savor or bite—whichever you choose
I give with myself the sun and the night
Heaven and nature passionately fused.   /106

Nature, you did make the world for me
To serve my joy and my despair
The sun to steal into my embrace
And pure blue air in which to drown.

O animal earth, in love with day!
O sun proud of your handsome face!
You know my one pride, my one serious love
Is the sweet honor of my age.   /107

My dream is so vivid and burning a bush
That if I open my arms clasped about such tenderness
Love, despite me, will fall on the world.   /107

Sweetness of the world! How your music mounts and descends in my heart! Your magic holds for all eternity. An hour at the heart of your beauty, a real terrestrial hour, beatitude beyond memory, a present without a future, in its impersonal love. . . . A frail carnal vessel, a secret and open universe, wherein the sweetness of the world surges with the blood.   /108

Out of the depths of my heart a love like sand is born
Higher than love there are clouds
Higher than glory love finds its place
But the heart in pain is the axis of the poem.   /109

I walked in my joy and at the first light of day
I carried the happy morning in my flower basket
And in my voice was the honeyed buzz of bees
I said to the dawn: Are you ready, my sister
The glance of my eyes was tender and soft
The wave parted before the advancing prows
Less willingly than my shadowy locks upon my two cheeks.   /111

I was a star, green leaves, wing, perfume, cloud. . . .   /107

I shall fling myself upon you, fair nature!
And ask to remain a woman
So as to have you gleam in the depth of my eyes.   /113

Amid my subtle fingers I possess the meaning of the world
For touch, like a voice, penetrates. . . .   /114

Tell them how beautiful they seem:
My hair as dark as a prune
My feet glistening with a mirror's gleam
And my eyes the color of the moon.   /107

Lovers came to adore me
And I thought each was to be my dream. . . .
But alas! lovers did not understand my soul
And I saw their charms fall away one by one
They knew not how to love me, they knew not love,
They knew not their beloved, they knew woman not.   /112

It is not you I love. I love to love as I love you. I am not counting on anything from you, my beloved. I expect nothing of you save my love for you.   /107

The other, the Man, exists more clearly. Once more he has a body, sometimes an active one, sometimes a passive one, that the woman at times describes in detail, at times merely senses. The man finally has sex organs, virility. At last he is desired for himself, overtly, and for his male mystery

I shall one day taste your eyes, your brow, your hand
More than I have partaken of water and of bread
Your mouth shall one day forever quench my thirst,
I shall have dreamed your soul entire,
I have coveted you as gold is coveted,
I have possessed you as one embraces death,
I have traversed you like a road new to me,
You have rippled like a river in my arms. . . .

I shall one day drink from your life's living source
You were eternal amid fleeting time. . . .

I have made of you my couch and my laden table,
I have taken you everywhere, enfolded in my shadow
You were my house and I have planted you
Forever, like a tree, in the center of my life. . . .   /105

I ask not if you good or evil be.
I know that you are You, and that is quite enough for me.
Why should I fret if others find you fair
I know that you are You, and that is quite enough for me.   /116

This is a wound, a scar, lips, certainly, that open every month, breathing in the will and the light of reason of those hapless creatures, men.

The lighthouse loomed up, enormous, rising toward the heavens like a threat, colossal, in the direction of this gaping shadow, of this black slit in the brightness of the sky, fatally attracted by the supreme duty of being as great as God. . . .

How beautiful this pure moon was, a fallen pearl, a severed head, gleaming with the pleasure of another, but forever saying nothing of it. . . . O tower of love, put out your light. It is dawn!   /118

What tie can there be between the poor man, driven by nature to a rapid exchange, and women's solitary incubation of their creative dreams?

Beloved marionette, through whom I have smiled, blushed, and wept, paled and suffered for two years, I bear you no ill will for having subsequently shown me the strings that made you move, since it was to you that I owed the fact that at last I understood the mystery of the heart, half tender and half violent, without which one's entire life would be lived in vain, to the end of one's days. And what does it matter that you were only the reflection of my dream, and what does it matter that you possessed none of the marvelous traits I believed I saw in you, since in the space of two times twelve months, thanks to the false image concealing your soul, double but nonetheless meager, I knew the purest and the maddest joys, and those pains that only joys can pay for, and these knees of mine bending at times in adoration, at times in despair.   /116

Léa smiled and savored the pleasure of being warm, of remaining motionless, and being a witness to the bouts of the two naked young men, whom she compared in silence: "How beautiful the Boss is! He's as solid as a house. The little guy is shaping up nicely. You don't see knees like that every day—and I know what I'm talking about. His hips too are . . . no, will be . . . marvelous. Where the devil did Mama Peloux find him . . . And the curve of his throat! a real statue! How wicked he is!

He's laughing, you'd swear he was a greyhound about to bite. . . ." She felt happy and maternal, bathed in calm virtue. "I wouldn't mind exchanging him for someone else," she said to herself on seeing Chéri naked in the afternoon beneath the lime trees, or Chéri naked in the morning on the ermine coverlet, or Chéri naked in the evening at the edge of the tepid pond. "Yes, as handsome as he is, I'd be quite willing to exchange him, if only I could do so with a clear conscience." She told the Boss of her indifference.

"But he's got a good build," the Boss objected. "You can see—he's got muscles like guys who don't come from around here, like colored guys, even though he's as white as can be. Little muscles that aren't the least bit sensational. You'll never see biceps as big as cantaloupes on him."

"I do hope not, Boss! But I didn't hire him to box!"

"Obviously," the Boss agreed, lowering his long lashes. "You've got to make allowances for sentiment."   /119

I shall tell of the bright gleam of your eyes, the sensuousness of your mouth, the strength of your arms, the burning heat of your powerful loins, and the warm softness of your skin.

I shall tell of the touch of your slender hands that form a trembling sash at my waist. I shall tell of your penetrating gaze that turns my thought to nothingness, your palpitating breast cleaving to mine, and your limbs solid as a maple, around which mine twine like clinging tendrils of hops.   / 117

I saw all of you chase after girls
When spring sap rises and flows
And come back, your hearts in tatters
After plucking the wild rose.

I saw you at Sunday dances
Parading your charms under the lanterns' heat
But who was it held your arm
When you lowered your flags in defeat?

I saw you weep, my good sirs
As I cradled your heads in my lap
It was my confidence showed you
That brought your smiles back.

On Sundays and during the week
You served as my calendar
I loved you, I didn't make scenes
And you knew my door was ajar.

I saw you go, one by one
In your new-bought suits down the aisle
But I'm still entirely yours
My one way of forgetting a while
My life lived apart, my suffering
Many a cruelty
Your wives despise, reject, persecute me
And you . . . all treat me highhandedly.   /120

O reserve of good blood lines
Buck, gander, bull, cock
You have all of the future in stock
In your double sacks, your garlands of grapes. . . .
Battering rams crowned with a capital
Jupiters nourished on round loaves of bread. . . .
Stallions, cousins of Pomona
Displaying your grapes, your melons, your prunes. . . .
Tell me, you males by profession
Champions of love come by wholesale
What do you feel in those nuts of yours
When your cries of the busy season
Swell to a tidal wave?   /126

Can love be born only through resemblance?! How to go about
furthering the comprehension, the fellow-feeling for the humanity of
one different from ourselves? I grant that I love bodies, but do I not still
have a repugnance toward a certain part (against nature, as my mother
would say) of the body of the other, even that of my beloved? The fact
that I can offer the entire surface of my body to the caress of my lover,
reserving nothing, does not mean anything if there remains the slightest
reticence at offering him the same thing that he gives me.   /154

You are the power of the sun
And your sap perfumes the air
A May rivulet beneath the hawthorn
Sweeter than the elderberry in flower
You grow erect and hard: the vigor of the forest
Its movement in the light
Your chest is rough beneath my cheek
Your loins hurt my clenched hands
You are rugged as an oak
I kissed you, like a robin in my hand
I love the warmth of your body in my palm
I drink in your wild scent
Of woods and marshes
You are handsome as a wolf
You spurt forth like a beech
Whose sap swells beneath the bark . . .
Your head gorged with instinct is a leaden thing,
And your fists are heavy weights
Desire tinges your lashes purple
The axis of the world lies in your flesh
You are its compass-rose of delights. . . .
And I laughed, for you have no more idea of what you are
Than a bull in the meadow, or a cornflower in the field. . . .
I shall praise your brutishness
And the hoarse sob of your flesh
I shall praise your immense flood of sap
Containing the potential universe
I shall praise your fists and the way
They suddenly unclench, as you fall back
Upon the hollow of a shoulder:
Softer, more gentle than a babe in arms.   /122

            The earth cherishes your true man's weight
            The wind envies my shoulders' thrusts
            Neither memory or aught else added to
            My quiet acceptance of the load.   /127

        To die of your flesh in me
        To sleep and dream that I dream of you. . . .
        To have you as my master
        O this great good fortune, this miracle
        This fit of you at my side.

To await
So as to reinvent you
The sudden appearance of your face
To know your face
To know your kiss
To know your love,
To die of it, to die of it. /123

The sweetness of being mingled
With this love of ending that possesses all men
That impels them into the dark womb
Just as there appears
The great sun of God
The splasher. . . .
He is heavy, impelled by unknown forces
Toward resurrected bodies
To take them, penetrate them.
Make them truly women
Spouses of flesh and smoke
For boiling invisible eddies
That overturn the established order of things. /124

I listen within me to the man straining. He is as serious as a child, and I feel tenderness toward him. When I know, by the vague look in his eye, that he is losing his senses, I move my hips and fell him. I crush his strength between my legs and see him fall atop me with the grace of a musical tree. Lying there, his body is once again traversed by brief shudders that echo beneath his forehead and force his eyelids open. It hurts me to see his skin pale as the color drains from it. /125

This place at table is that of a friend who comes and goes, not that of a master of the house who treads across the creaking floor of a bedroom, there upstairs in the dark of night. . . . The days when the plate, the glass, the lyre are not there across the table opposite me, I am complete by myself, not abandoned . . .

It seems to me that between the man and me, a long recess is beginning . . . Man, my friend, come breathe with me . . . I have always liked your company. You look at me so tenderly now. You are watching the emergence, from a heap of cast-off feminine garments, still weighted down, like a shipwreck victim weighted down with seaweed—though her head is safe, the rest still struggles, her fate still hangs in the balance—you are watching the emergence of your sister, your pal: a woman who is making her way free of the age of being a woman. . . .

Let us stay together: You have no reason now to leave me forever.   /119

From the beginning of the century on, however, another parallel theme will be celebrated: sapphic love, the love of a woman for another self, woman in the paroxysms of narcissism, the torments of uncertain possession—and the tender joys of complicity

Through heaven knows what mystery, the first day I saw her I became her slave and through heaven knows what instinct I hid my love so well that my behavior toward her was nothing less than that of a monster.

Like all creatures, I was a monster and an angel.

I am convinced that the angel would not have pleased her as much.

This cold, implacable woman needed a distraction and a battle. She had both for several years, and my absolute love.

She was tall and dark-haired . . .

Her hands were the most beautiful in the whole world and could tame me when I rebelled.

What rages I had against her for not loving me as I loved her.

When the day had been a bad one, she would treacherously wait till evening, and at twilight, she would begin her songs, with their passionate words, to torture and delight me.

What was her charm? Her eyes, her voice, her languorous movements? I was unable to explain to myself what it was.

I almost always saw her reclining in a chaise longue, her soothsayer's eyes fixed upon me.

Cats were fond of her and there was always one with her . . .

. . . Madame wished to banish every trace of sensuousness in me. It was most difficult with her robes with a long train, her silence, and this house where everything was silken and unknown.

For years she showed only disdain for me, and then a link was forged between us, a subtle link that lasted her whole life long, which flatters me still. The proud one, the disdainful one changed her ways with me and rewarded me with a tenderness of the rarest sort . . .

I imagined that I was brilliant. I dared to express my desires. They were fulfilled.

A divine period, and one of extreme freedom.

It was now I who intrigued Madame, and if my eyes met her dark ones, they no longer had an arrogant expression.

Anxiety made its appearance. An anguish that I caused to linger on this proud face, and our relations grew even more subtle.

I lied. She divined my lies each time. She also divined that I ought to be allowed to act as I pleased, and thereupon died.   /133

And I for my part
Have pinned on your breast
Ten stars in the form of nail marks
So that you not forget me.   /138

As between your lashes your half-closed eyes gleam
Able to call up images of love with neither form nor face,
Have passing lovers no place now in your dreams?
—What joy do they offer to equal your distaste?—
They prowl about, wolves seeking prey to capture
Knowing for your body only the desire that leaves a dirty mark
But they are far away now, and the one master of your bed,
Your own desire, is the creator of your nights of rapture.
And when desire causes you to lose your head
Surrendering all, become more ardent and more supple still,
When your double being, lover and mistress side by side,
Skillfully possesses you, more than any couple will
You find ecstasy, and your gestures a surpassing grace
Loving yourself alone, you pity that woman who
Enslaves herself to facile loves; for you, eyes filled with pride,
Serve only your beauty, there in the dark.   /134

My eyes are ringed with a warm shadow, reddish brown and blue, like the one that sleeps in the water's depths . . .

There passes across them the phantom of your rearing body, the sleeping vision of your vanquished head, still more beautiful in its abandon, leaving in my hands the softness of silk.

Oh, come put your lips that possess me on the velvety orb of this beloved shadow . . .   /117

During the day I left the night's abandon
I left the rumpled pillows, the trailing sheets
The furrow that your form hollowed out.
It is there, atop your shadow, that I shall lay me down.   /117

O Lady, behold these sophisticates
Those who flee men's kisses
To join with fond caresses
Their feminine flesh, turned away from men. . . .   /112

My eyes follow you: wanton little minx
Giddy as a balloon without ballast
Your hesitant soul of a Sphinx
Is forever betwixt and between.
And I pant after the bait:
Of the live torso with quivering breasts
Where strength and grace mate
And a pair of eyes green as the west.   /114

"Sweet and terrible desire," a phoenix that nothing will ever consume because of its diversity and the power of its wings; that finds, beyond joy, a strange miraculous joy, so rare that men have not given it a
name: a heavenly ecstasy, the immaterialization of the sensuality that
hovers within us, above us, around us, like unto our souls. Hearing the
voice that it bestows on our voices, the gaze that it bestows on our
gaze, being present as pale witnesses to ourselves, absent at times from
ourselves, creators, in the impalpable air, of this chimerical and miraculous birth of dreams more permanent, more like ourselves than earthly
progeny.   /134

It is not from passion that fidelity of two women is born, but from a
sort of kinship. I have written kinship when I should perhaps write likeness.
Close resemblance even furthers erotic pleasure. The beloved friend is
reassured when she caresses a body whose secrets she already knows,
whose own body indicates her preferences. . . . Two women passionately in love do not forgo sensual pleasure, nor a sensuality less intense
than spasm, and warmer. It is this sensuality, which is without resolution and makes no demands, happy at a look exchanged, an arm across

the shoulder, moved by the smell of warm wheat in the beloved's locks and similar delights of being constantly in the beloved's presence that engender and justify fidelity. Perhaps this love which is said to be an outrage to love escapes the round of the seasons, the dying of love, providing that one holds it in check with an invisible severity, that one feeds it on little, that it lives feeling its way along haltingly, and that its one flower is a consciousness such that the other love can neither ponder it nor comprehend it, but merely envy it.   /119

The beauty of other women, which with constant generosity she was inclined to find superior to her own, nonetheless reassured her as to her own beauty, which she saw, on looking into other mirrors than the habitual ones, as being a reflection of theirs. The power over her that she granted to her women lovers served her at the same time as a guarantee of her power over men. It made her happy, and she found it natural that men who were passionately fond of her should ask of her the same thing that she demanded of women (and rarely if ever gave them in return). Thus she was constantly involved with both men and women and gained on both scores.   /135

> Oh, your beauty!
> The balm of my weary limbs
> Take me in your arms, my beloved friend
> I want to be beautiful
> So that you may be . . .
> Enfolded in each other's arms
> We suffer as we wait
> The embrace of our stiff limbs is painful
> Our lips have lost their taste
> God is passing this way . . .   /136

In your house, all by myself between you and the high flame of a lamp, you said to me: "Dance!" and I did not dance.

But naked in your arms, bound to your bed by the ribbon of fire of pleasure, you nonetheless called me a dancer when you saw my inevitable pleasure leap from beneath my skin, from my arching neck to my curled toes . . .

Weary at last, I put my hair up again, and you watched my docile locks coil on my forehead like a serpent charmed by the flute . . . I left your house as you murmured: "The most beautiful of your dances is not when you run to me, full of eager desire, already fingering the catch

of your robe. . . . It is when you leave me, your fervor calmed and your knees trembling, and look back at me, with your chin on your shoulder. . . . Your body remembers me, sways and hesitates, your loins regret me and your breasts thank me. . . . You turn your head and look at me, as your divining feet feel their way along and choose their path. . . . You go off, ever smaller, your cheeks reddened by the setting sun, until you in your orange gown are no more than a flame dancing imperceptibly at the top of the hill." /136

I lift with light fingers the black trains of your eyelids. /134

I love you for being weak and affectionate in my arms. . . .
I love you for walking slowly and silently. . . .
And I love you most of all for being pale and dying
In the cruel pleasure that torments and consumes. /114

I thought again about Tamara's attitude during this quarrel, about the way I had allowed myself to be humiliated and mistreated by her, with her taking her pleasure in dealing thus with me. At times, when I again saw on her face the expression that she had had at the moment when I finally yielded to her will, when I had kneeled in the middle of the bedchamber, I trembled once again with shame and anger. And yet I had found in her more brutal caresses that day, still marked by a will to humble, to subdue, almost to hurt, a more vivid pleasure than I usually experienced . . . She made me pay for each moment of abandon, of tenderness, by acting most capriciously, refusing to see me for several days, subjecting me to bizarre tests, and when I had obeyed, instead of receiving me at her residence, she chose as the meeting place some tea room, or her hairdresser's, where I waited for hours as she had an impeccable manicure or pedicure. /137

I am the one you sought to charm last night with your naked breast
The one who could neither love nor hate you sufficiently,

The one you devoured as voraciously
As your escort: crabs that feed on dead flesh. . . . /114

But what lies at the end, Narcissus, is hell
The sheer hell of the creature ever charmed by the chase
Of a self that endlessly flees its embrace.   /138

*Sensual pleasure, orgasm become major themes: meditations on the
meaning of erotic pleasure, but also descriptions of feminine pleasure,
if poetry may be called "description"*

Sensual pleasure is not the only thing. . . . In the boundless desert of
love such pleasure has an ardent but very small place, so incandescent
that at first that is all that one sees: I am no longer an innocent young
girl blinded by its incandescence. Round about this flaming focal point
is the unknown, danger. . . . What do I know of the man I love, who
wants me? When we get up from a brief embrace, or even a long night,
we must begin to love, one beside another, one through another. He will
manfully hide his first disappointments in me, and I will say nothing of
mine, out of pride, out of shame, out of pity, and above all because I
will have expected them, feared them, *because I already know what
they are.*

I have met you before and I recognize you. You think you are giving,
but aren't you taking, rather? You came along to share my life, yes, to
share it: to take your share of it, that is!   /119

My breast smothers me. My breast suckles me
I am hungry for my own lips, oh my mouth I cannot bite!!
The ringing in my ears deafens me. The sea surges into their folds.
May I be seized by the waist and my two mouths wrenched apart
and each one be cured.

How sweet it is to lose one's senses to the point of thinking: Here I
am, freed of the need to think. Kiss me, mouth for whom I am only a
mouth.

It is wicked of your hand to pretend it does not know where I am
hiding, where I am waiting for you; wicked to come to the place where
I reveal myself, your thighs thrust forward, your groin leaning over me,

and then to my regret going away. It is wicked to hunt me down, to force me from hiding so that I will part my legs like a thirsty sea shell, visible to the depths of me, so that I will spread wide open.   /125

Pleasure: of all words the saddest, the most profound
Embracing all hope, all oblivion,
As we rejoice, or find ourselves drowned
In the awed ecstasy where tears abound.
Pleasure: of all things the end and the goal
The meeting of life and eternity
Fulfillment and void, vast pause, quiet shoal
Pleasure: Blindness, then revelation
Once the bar of death passed, illumination:
Become as gods. The perfect light of awareness
And then: the fall to mere human tenderness.   /107

It is after the moments when the battle is joined
And we have united in combat, loin against loin
As my head leans back, though our bodies still touch
That I feel the full force of what separates us.

When this fury we've so willingly shared has abated
We fall silent, each pondering, sated
The mystery of how, so simply, so suddenly
We are again each ourselves: can this be?

And yet you are happy, it seems! My self's loneliness
Spies in you no trace of that disarray
That marks and mars my own sad ecstasy
What can there be, O my incomparable love,
That is common to the two of us?   /107

By the mere desire to live our two lives as one
We are become the image one of the other;
By the mere leaping of our hearts flaming as one
We are what the fire has kindled.

By all that our souls fail to share
We are strangers one to the other;
By the night that bears within itself both twilight and dawn
We are that love from which there is no deliverance.   /127

Divine tears of the moment that follows the carnal embrace. Hours of grace and repose.

Why, oh why this awakening? Oh why these carnal eyes that destroy oblivion?

I think of flames setting each other on fire, of this anguish at being undressed for a dream-resurrection.   /142

When satiated, carnal pleasure brings with it coldness and indifference. When starved, it yearns only for what sustains it.   /119

I am the well and thirst, you will not traverse me without danger, my friend, my friend.   /141

Passion leaves its lingering marks on bound beings.   /142

Our honest bodies have trembled, have yielded together, and will remember on the next contact, whereas our souls will shut themselves up once again in the same dishonest silence.   /119

This sensual pleasure is at the same time the revelation of the woman's femininity, by way of images. Oddly enough, sea images occur again and again. The woman is a sea. The sea is a woman. As are beaches, sea caves, ocean shores

The sea skirts you. It is thirsty for you! Yet you would set it on fire, I know. It is too much like you, my wild one. Merely to see you, to breathe you consoles it, reassures it. Like yourself, attracted by the moon, it moves far in the distance in waves, in swells, moaning, toward the motionless beach.   /128

I love sea water, that multiple sorceress,
That mistress the lover fights or yields to in vain
The heart at once of hope and of darkness, of fire and of indolence
Whereof love and death united are the leavening.   /106

And the writhings of a siren allied
With the great swelling, surging tide
Wriggling in the net that is spread for me
My cry within you deep and raging as the sea!

A beach, a breaking wave
A woman lying in repose
Marvel at their mutual caresses
And their secret shared tendernesses.

In this woman in her quiet loneliness
Quenching its thirst for happiness
Full of love and gentle indolence
The sea chooses its rest.   /129

The sea, like beds that one loves to lie in. . . . This sweat this bitter
seaweed this crowd fingers on a ripening face.   /130

Lovely land visited and lost
The lapping of water surrendered to itself
Shore-woman, beach, a stretch of sand
Your sole destiny: being here as you are.   /124

Shores and rocks, curl on curl, terse temporary pacts
Embracing swirling tides,
Beautiful triangle full of acts
Fostering love that abides.
O penetrating, penetrated
Soft female of the world.   /129

Swimmer drifting across me
As you dive for promises
All the sea will answer you
All paths lie open before you.   /124

Femininity explored is also the offer of oneself to the other, the dependence of desire on the other, on the love of the other, the poignant sweetness of "celebrating defeat"

I gave in, I confess I gave in, by permitting this man to come back again tomorrow, by yielding to the desire to keep him not as a lover, not as a friend, but as an avid spectator of my life and my person.

Freedom is really splendid only at the beginning of love, of one's first love; the day when one can say on offering it to the person one loves: "Here, take it. I should like to give you more. . . ."   /119

> I fear that I shall live no more
> The moment you cease to love me   /107

Look at the dead woman you are when you are no longer loved.   /107

> And now I am a woman come to you. . . .

> I am one who, never having had a lover
> Cannot yet know herself,
> And seeks in your arms to discover
> What she means by love.   /112

Sylvie forbade herself to love, fearing to lose in this ecstasy what is known as freedom, which consists of experiencing the fact that one is dependent on everything, but not that everything depends on a single face, a single being, who may suddenly announce to us that he is leaving on a trip, that he is about to marry, that he has stopped loving us, that he is taking his vows as a priest, that he has resolved not to lie to his fellows, or to grow old—thus taking away with him all of our thoughts, our house with its windows and its horizon, our bed and our midday meal. For it is an absolute disaster, that leaves us utterly bereft, to feel oneself suddenly a total stranger to oneself and all these great necessities out of reach because a man has left the room while he was talking with us, in a different mood that has come over him all at once, or without leaving us his address.   /107

          And I fall back across many a bed
          Worn out with celebrating defeat.   /139

          When I had given up all hope of his coming
          He opened the door and came in.
          And I didn't even say to him
          How late you are getting here!
          I just held my hands out to him
          They were trembling because they were empty,
          And he gave me everything
          My heart was hungering and thirsting for.   /116

   The strength of the woman in love lies in the weakness, in the
smallness, in the instability of the share that she has won as her due.
She learns everything through passion and fear. Obliged to be sagacious
in order to create the monument of her perfidious and sublime hope,
on a tiny shifting bit of ground with no written proof of ownership, she
collects, with all the prudence of a bird, the most subtle the most solid,
and the most tangled materials. . . .   /107

   And scorn steals inside me to attempt to destroy you.
   For you are nothing save the mystery of revealing all to me.   /142

You come into my life. No one finds it a miracle
That I was waiting for you, and only you
I from the shadowy retreat where my love lay in wait
Like a wild rabbit in its warren
Aware of you drawing near before I hear your footsteps. . . .
The air stirring round you
Coming to rest on my back. . . .
And everything about you
Taking on the firm stance
Of soldiers tried in battle standing at attention. . . .
As meanwhile, unmindful of these proud birth-pangs
You free your knee imprisoned by the stiff fabric
Taking care not to spoil the creases in your pants. . . .
With the dreary indifference of someone who has never been in love
With in your heart the certainty
That you will in no way change the air that I breathe

That my eyes will ever continue to see things just as they have always
   been
Drowsing in their reality. . . .
When your gaze that falls upon me like a stone
Will no longer knot together all the magic spells that I have fallen
   under
I shall be dead.   /140

Unfaithful to the pact of silence that all women observe together toward the man, I shall reveal their secret to you. You may be sure that
however haughty they may appear to be, however smart, from their
gleaming dark slippers to the tops of their heads crowned with feathers
and flowers, they possess nothing without you, they await everything
from you.

   The secret that I have promised you and that betrays women, is this,
my love: If it pleases you to make sure of their passion, their attachment, deprive them of your heart for a moment, torment them, make
them jealous, instill doubt in them, make them suffer, if only a little,
and these proud, happy foreheads will easily bow beneath the terrible
yoke of lost confidence and calm and stupefied tears will flow down
these beautiful faces, and you will see before you nothing more than
the pitiable Eve who was humbly born of the generous body of Adam.

   Do not take advantage of the secret that I have revealed to you; be
kind. Love as best you can, poor man, you who are so ardent but so
poor in love, and allow me to live in the light of women's wisdom,
whose "instinct for power is a protective instinct," as Pascal might have
put it, and remember that they would give their lives with a joyous violence in order never to see on your proud face, even when you are
wrong, the disconcerted expression of confusion, of sadness—and the
tears—of the little boy you once were. . . .   /107

   If it is necessary, without my knowing why, to have lost your tenderness that brought me to life,
   I shall not weary you with my pale cheeks or endless complaints.
   I shall simply go away, and like a lamp that has not been supplied
with the necessary oil,
   I shall perhaps go out quietly, without a vain struggle and without
flaring up one last time.
   Ah, tell me why love feeds on little nothings in order not to lose
hope?   /116

You have taken everything from me,
The extraordinary, the simple
The complex, the commonplace
Dreams and understanding.

This blotting out of the world upon awakening
These eyes half-closed to my soul,
My last chance to experience winter
My last sky reflected on snow
You have taken them from me
You have taken even my last second of forgetfulness.   /123

To catch him, to tremble lest he escape my grasp, to see him escape, and patiently approach him again in order to catch him again—that shall henceforth be my task, my mission. Everything I lived before him will then be given back to me—light, music, the murmur of the trees, the timid and fervent call of household pets, the proud silence of men who suffer—all that will be given back to me, but it will be through him, and provided that I possess him. . . . He has been so close to me, so frequently in my company since the first meeting that I believed I possessed him. I foolishly tried to get over him, taking the limit of my universe for an obstacle. . . . I imagine that many women make the same mistake as I at first, before taking their proper place once more, which is below the man. . . .   /119

Belonging totally to a man is not only dangerous but also a difficult relationship to begin. And yet the will to submit to the will of the man drives women to a dangerous, ecstatic flirtation with masochism: "It is necessary that I cease to exist"

Feeling herself loved, Christine had that immediate sense of recognition, that bowing of the will in the face of men's desire that is the sign of women's respect for love. Is it their veneration of this sole sign, which they readily identify with the man who bears its ephemeral mark, that causes there to be something fatal about this spiritual acceptance, as well as something fortuitous? Seeing herself loved with greater and greater tenacity, she feels that she has been conquered with a passion. Whatever people may say, the woman's struggle against the

man is not for the sake of escaping from him, but for the sake of belonging to him in larger measure than the poor male ever seeks. A woman who has no doubts about the desire that she inspires does not seek to flee the man, but rather to besiege, invade, penetrate so to speak the man who loves her.   /107

Woman: subtle flesh offered to virility,
Gently curving amphora in whose depths joy slumbers
White prey, bruised by love and torn asunder,
Painful womb wherein lies our eternity.   /112

In the bite of your fierce teeth
And my dizzying light-headedness
You have felt your mouth's power
Allied to the seed of the seasons.
A thousand deaths make you ever-fecund
Attuned to all the earth's stirring
Obedient to the sign
Set before your eyes that love seals shut
As it orders all to continue on its appointed rounds. . . .
Forever, forever, driven by desire.   /124

I must venture forth against the wave
Curving back on itself from beginning to end
As it traces the path of what I become
Freed of its joy, giving in to its tears
Carried away, obeyed, more a woman,
Nothing now save the will to love.   /129

Before being left alone with your hand that always precedes you.
Let it come. You must come. I fear it. I wish it. If you wanted to you could join me, and it is cruelty on your part. . . .

I for my part
Can wait for you no longer.

Ah, I shall praise your hand, which first opened an unsuspected body to me! My night was pierced with light. I made my way within myself.   / 125

I have no name and no clear image; a welcoming place and a shadowy bedroom, a road of dreams and a place of origin, my friend, my friend.   /141

> The blind gropings of your hands
> On my shivering breasts
> The snail-slow movements of your tongue
> In the folds of my pathetic ears
> All my beauty drowned in your pupil-less eyes
> My brain sucked dry by the death in your belly.   /144

There remains a likeness of our intimacy in the joy of opening my arms wide and the pride I take in my breasts. . . .

I bear my belly like a living star in the heart of its extinguished bark. And I am warm in my dress, where the coolness of day does not touch me. . . .   /125

> Terrible strength and power in another's hands . . .
> Surrender,
> Defeat is more searing than the heat of combat,
> Female in whom the divine assumes a mask of flesh
> And consents to death—
> Which do you yield to—a male or necessity? . . .
> Surrender—woman is land seized, booty,
> Crouching over your love like a she-wolf
> You concede victory—brought beneath the other's yoke
> By a power greater than he: the seeds of the beginning and end
> As between the two an island appears: the life of a man.   /124

Did I even have breasts before your hands told me of them? For a long time I was duller than a sheet of fresh water, colder than a dead look. I was somewhat irritated by this reticent body, and you pretended to scold me and we finished in a chorus of laughter, as one disdains the person who stays out of a game after being invited to play. Yet as though you had no doubt of your powers, you constantly made me the subject of the same tireless invocation, and little by little I ceased to laugh beneath your hand, so occupied was I, so delighted by this awakening like a double star catching fire. . . .   /125

A new reign is about to begin!
Among the powerless
New signs are being born
They will be carved one day in your very flesh—
For you are both problem and solution
The voice saying yes, and the voice saying no. . . .

But on your brow no sign of power yet
Only a woman's face a little more nakedly bared
A little closer to the fountainhead
A little more soundly asleep . . .

You have always been but an instrument
A life-machine
Love of a man has wrought
What your living hell could not:
Made you deaf, a stranger to
The changes in the wind . . .   /124

I have no idea where these repeated long reveries came to me from—
just before falling asleep, always the same ones, in which the purest and
most ferocious love permitted, or rather demanded, the most atrocious
abandon, where childish images of chains and whips added to constraint the symbols of constraint. I know only that they were good for
me, and in some mysterious way protected me. . . .   /135

We are all jailers, and all of us in prison, in the sense that there is always within us someone whom we ourselves bind in chains, whom we
shut up in a cell, whom we cause to be silent.
    By some curious reversal, it happens that this prison itself leads to
freedom. The stone walls of a cell, the solitude, but also the night,
more solitude, the warmth of bedcovers, silence deliver from bondage
this unknown person to whom we refuse the light of day. It eludes and
escapes us over and over again, making its way through walls, through
ages, through taboos.   /135

My flesh that desired, somewhat, that it be killed.   /105

Here you are in the service of your masters. During the day you will
do whatever task is assigned you about the house, such as sweeping, or
putting books away, or arranging flowers, or serving at table. There are

none more difficult than these. But at the very first word or sign from one of your masters, you will abandon these tasks in order to perform your real service, which is to make yourselves available. Your hands do not belong to you, nor your breasts, nor any of the orifices of your body in particular, for we have the right to explore them and penetrate them at will.

As a sign that you have no right to attempt to escape our attentions, in order that this may be ever-present to your memory, or as present as possible, you will never close your lips completely in our presence, nor cross your legs, nor press your knees together, which will signify in your eyes and ours the fact that your mouth, your private parts, and your behind are open to us.   /135

Thus in this way, as by way of the chain fixed to the ring around your neck that will tie you to your bed for several hours a day, far from causing you to experience pain, to cry, or to shed tears, will make you feel, through pain, that you are constrained, and teach you that you are entirely bound over to something that lies outside yourself.   /135

I am the Door.
Before you enter, I must have withdrawn from myself,
and no longer be.

My neck is bowed beneath an age-old yoke.
I know the pain of being an object.
I have felt my hands losing the strength to grasp, my
legs the will to move, my tongue the privilege of naming.
My powers, turned inward, have imprisoned me. . . .   /125

Love is not just physical pleasure and its strange metaphysical prolongations. Love is also burning fire in the heart, white-hot jealousy, the fear of losing the partner, strategies for outwitting happiness

To conjugate we love: I love you
In every tense and mood:
The present that's already dead
The future, as it pants for breath
The past, imprisoned in its doublet.   /143

Take me away
Where I may be you
Love
Take me away
Love
Thy sandal will I tie
And it will still be night
Yet the day's first light
Will find me gone
Like a garden round a well
Like a well at the center of a garden
Like a row of trees at one with my bare feet
Like gestures at one with their joy
Love
Take me away.   /145

Love nothing for its tears: they last but a day
Love nothing for its song: hymns last but an hour.
O my soul that would have your love endure!
Love every fleeting thing for the pure love of love . . .   /147

Most exalted love, if I should die
Without discovering whence you came to me. . . .

When the mirror of self shatters one day
And over the formless abyss I am scattered
Infinitely, in infinite shards
When the present I am clothed in falls away

You will form again my name and my image
Of a thousand bodies gone with the wind
A living unity, without name or face
Heart of the spirit, oh center of the mirage
Most exalted love.   /146

I had the occasion to descend to the depths of jealousy, to install myself there and dream at length. To remain there is not intolerable, and
if in my writing I once compared it to hell just as everyone else does, I
pray that the word will be considered as merely lyricism on my part. It
is, rather, a sort of gymnastic purgatory where the senses are trained,
one by one, and as dreary as a gym. I am speaking of course of jealousy
that has a well-founded reason for being, and not a monomania.

Cultivation of the sense of hearing, optical virtuosity, a swift and silent footstep, a sense of smell attuned to the perfume that lingers in the lover's locks, the scent of talc, the passage of an indiscreetly joyful creature—all these things are mindful of the soldier's field training and the art of poachers. . . .   /119

She watched over this happiness as no mother has ever watched over her smiling child who has suddenly been taken ill. She watched herself act, astonished by her energy, grateful to herself, silent and calculating, a martyr and triumphant, dazzled at what a woman can accomplish against herself, for herself, in the name of the man she loves. . . .

And then she remembered, thinking of the ever-anxious heart of two women in the company of a tranquil man, the infallible maxim of antiquity: "In all things Athena favors the male."   /107

In this century dominated by the image of the happy couple and the cult of sexual pleasure, of pleasure as a value, solitary women, lonely women, women whom love has passed by, weep at their loneliness and the impossibility of "embracing oneself" to warm one's heart

Sad in sleep, my palms that had forgotten
Caresses, suddenly remembered all of them again
You come if I call your name, and I feel beneath my hands
The tautness of your arms or the fire of your cheeks
I no longer exist if your eyes no longer look on me. . . .
You said: spring—like a new country
That we would visit together
One I have wandered through without you, summoning your image
Searching sadly for your hand to put a flower in
Blood is flowing. Farewell. The sweet earth is mad. . . .   /149

Let us forget our dream and its fierce metamorphoses:
Graceful youths as light as the breeze,
The incubus wreathed in roses' death
That mute Vampire with softest breath . . .
The hard brass Satan . . . and your closed eyelids,
Celestial sailors in a port without ships . . .

But oh, the pangs of the heart are treacherous!
Bitterness, the prime ferment, lies deep within us . . .
To serve my rancor with its cruel piercing eyes
You'll stubbornly cling to those glorious shames
My old carnal demon invented last night in my dreams.   /105

Since he is dead now and far away
And his blood no longer speaks like leaves rustling
In answer to the rustling of my own
Or to its humming like a swarm of bees
Or its insect-clouds of soft whispering
Bury in the grave with him
The gleaming iris of my desire
Since his hands shall never again
Brush from my breasts the snow
And make them proudly blossom amid rose-tinged curves
And waves that make my body open round its center like
      flowering suns
Since his eyes, his love will no longer be
What pierces me and bears witness to my innocence
Take him! I abandon all claim to him!   /145

They conjoined our two lives
Thus wedding winter and summer,
Sun and rain.
And to make the tie more secure
They bound our hands together with nettles. . . .

The April cuckoo belongs to the soldier
I write to you there where the cannons roar
Troops belong to the king
But the sky belongs to each and every one
And my heart beats only for you.   /149

Ah, may we have peace again.
Your hands, dreaming and sleeping
You must be home before the hawthorn has finished blossoming
Along the paths where your shadow strides
In this tired spring ending without you.   /149

I am left today with nothing for my own to keep
Save a widow's weeds, a poem edged in black
And my single bed, a tomb wherein the right I lack
To embrace myself in fraternal sleep.   /150

Loneliness slips through my fingers, bead by bead
My shadow lying at my side
Plays hide-and-seek with sleep
Dawn throws my night's dreams in my face.   /109

You wither away in the company
Of desireless women in the toils of ennui:
With dull leaden pupils, hearts choosing monotony
And souls like the soul of a long-dead mummy. . . .

The ennui of belladonna and aconite
As voices rehearse in the dying light
Betrayals long past: the refrain lingers on
Like the cold, sickly taste of a deadly poison!

The ennui of belladonna and aconite!   /148

Here I am: come round to the age of chastity
I'm a hundred thousand years old in my woman's body
Weary of the pull of ageless moon-tides
Of female blood so weary of loving
Yet a beautiful body in ripest maturity
Look at yourself at night when no one is looking
Your soul rejoices, spitting in scorn at the body's birthday candles

Why worry about dying when it's not yet time?   /121

⚡︎⚡︎⚡︎⚡︎⚡︎⚡︎⚡︎⚡︎⚡︎⚡︎⚡︎⚡︎⚡︎⚡︎⚡︎⚡︎⚡︎⚡︎

The couple triumphs. To marry or not to marry? Marriage is put on trial, especially after 1945, but this institution nonetheless remains unscathed. And there are still marriages for love, bringing the security and the mystery of living many years together

The label "conjugal love" leads to all sorts of repressions and all sorts of lies. First of all, it makes it impossible for the husband and wife to really know each other. Daily intimacy creates neither understanding nor sympathy. The husband respects his wife too much to interest himself in the metamorphoses of her inner life; this would be to recognize her secret autonomy, which might prove to be both bothersome and dangerous; does she really experience pleasure in bed? Does she really love her husband? Is she really happy to obey him?   /151

> I maintain that we were two
> Bodies joined as one
> Mine and yours, and others' too
> Numbering almost a million.   /130

The advocates of conjugal love readily plead that it is not love, and that by that very fact it becomes something miraculous. For the bourgeoisie has created an epic style in the past few years: routine takes on an aura of adventure, fidelity of a sublime folly, boredom becomes wisdom, and family hatreds the most profound form of love. In all truth, the fact that two individuals detest each other without being able to get along without each other is not the truest, the most moving of all human relations but rather the most pitiful.   /151

Knowing each other too well kills love, mystery is as indispensable to it as sun is to wheat, certain people tell me. But mystery has no need to be cultivated; to foster it is to recognize its fragility. It must be attacked, we must do our best to dissolve it. The farther our knowledge goes, the more we will realize that the mystery remains.

I look at you lying asleep, and the world where you are, the smile at the corner of your lips, the nearly imperceptible quivering of your eyelashes, your naked and abandoned body are mysteries. . . . We speak: your voice, your thoughts, the words you use to express them are

the most familiar in the world to me. Each of us can end the phrase begun by the other. And you are, we are, a mystery.   /153

"We could stay together for a little while," he said after a pause. He then fell silent once again. "It's strange that both of us are alone. I had thought . . ." This man who has the courage to want to be happy: in the most straightforward fashion. Who demands no proofs. Who never demands his rights. How can she ever deserve this simple, subtle man?   /152

For years we had the feeling that we could make something of our love. From it we could build a profession, friendships, houses, children, and perhaps even help to build a new world. The time for accomplishment had come.

To our vast surprise we are architects. During the night, perhaps because being away from home gives us a heightened sensitivity and because the night is so beautiful, we discover that our plans have become a reality.

The children will be able to find themselves only if they pass your way. I see in them resemblances that delight me and upset me. They are often fleeting ones, that go and come from one to the other. It is a matter of a gesture, a way of lacing up a shoe, of liking the same hours, of waking up in the morning, a look that I have never seen, which already existed perhaps but which I seem to see aborning. I listen and I contemplate. I go back along the path of your life, and discover you at an age when I didn't yet know you. I endeavor to put together the images that the children give me and those of your twentieth year, and thus perfect my knowledge of you.   /153

And women now explore their freedom to exist in and through sexuality. Not sensual pleasure, but sexuality: Does it lead to resembling the man? to using the man? to thwarting the man? They seek answers. But their genitals no longer experience love; they are, rather, something to be explored

A god appeared very often in Marie's dreams while the assassin was absent or asleep; the presence of the latter in a waking state seemed to keep the god away.

Lying on her back on her bed, her cone of ecstasy inverted, the hairs of her pubis standing on end, Marie invoked her god, and the god came. . . .   /144

Soldiers bivouacking in the desert found in the succulent flesh of cactus leaves, the "legionnaire's mistress," a rather tender outlet for their sexual hunger.

I too will have recourse to a vegetable lover. I shall go look for some very figurative root, pull it up, wash it, and remove the little root hairs, but I shall not remove its satiny skin as I usually do; rather, I shall warm it between my two clasped hands, and taste it, and caress it, and be mistress of it as never of a male member. I shall fill my sex with amazing simulacra.

At times I consume myself in the dark and violent fire of imaginary orgies, sometimes I wallow in dreary self-denials. Sometimes I try to rediscover excitement of the past, but the only thing that remains beneath the ashes is embers that turn to dust the moment one blows on them. Till the next time they flame up.

I love these heights of my freedom. Is it not in love, as a means and as an end, that it will finally take refuge, in its full ardor, for we see it more and more whittled away, attacked, stifled during this century of ours that is ruled by civil servants and concentration camps. It cannot be hunted down in the bedroom, and far less in this marvelous inner theater that each of us has within himself.   /154

When the assassin was not there, however, Marie lay down on the bed and rang for the parrot. "Come, do not scoff at my arms. Follow me, winged spirit, into the ecstasy of masturbation, come, my organs call unto you." The parrot took off its apron and plunged into the woman as she offered herself. After hours of fixed smiles and sly strokings, Marie thrust her nipple into the parrot's beak, turned yellow by boasting, and engaged the desperate, inhuman language of its eyes. The parrot still did not resist. It was becoming pink and plump, its feathers were beginning to disappear, and its beak as well. Milk welled up in the offered breast and Marie felt a sense of relief flood over her at last. . . .

Marie never knew how the miracle of the parrot-child ended. Suddenly an eloquent silence filled the room, a strong taste of liqueur paralyzed her tongue, and the parrot became a parrot once again. "This is happiness," she said to herself, and lowered her legs. . . .   /144

Every time I meet Morgana at the crossroads of life, she says to me: "Why wait to live? Humble yourself in the presence of love, but never in the presence of men!"   /109

[The women warriors] say that it has been written that vulvas are traps, vises, pincers. They say that the penis has been compared to the prow of a boat to its bow to a combshell. They say that vulvas have been compared to apricots to pomegranates to figs to roses to carnations to peonies to marguerites. . . .   /155

They have made of my desire the flattered, grateful acquiescence to their desire. They have made of my enjoyment, of my orgasm, a sort of sacred trance brought on by penetration of the vastly superior supreme virility.

In the final analysis they are not far from saying, and in fact do sometimes say, that if I climax it is with the illusion of *having*, at last, in a brief and miraculous instance what elsewhere I am tragically and painfully *lacking*: a penis.

What I would like is to *give* myself? But which of us gives something of himself or herself? You or me?

What I would like is for you to *take* me? But isn't it I who take *you?*

It is you who abandon yourself, is it not?

And it is also you who are supposedly sad after making love.

Not me.

I came back again and again. It was like an everday approach to my ignominy. To naked men shining with crusted dirt and sweat. The hair on their heads was stuck together in thick curls. In this moist greenness Jim was only a vague shadow. . . . He was not extremely attractive, with a rather weak mouth, not even remarkable when all was said and done, a nonchalance that was more like a lack of vivacity and intelligence, many of the young men round about must be his equal, a stinking arrogance, but he was nonetheless *mine*. He was me. My dreams. My fondness for men, and my entire youth.

Putting a pine needle between my legs and letting it slide in, acutely painful: that was a sort of morphine and what I should have done instead of watching him, a clever but not a conscientious worker, guiding the saw as though unaware of its keen edge. . . . I wish to speak also of the blinds where hunters wait for a duck to fly by, where modestly, and doubly hidden since they were erected in the depths of the lonely forest, I gave myself over, again and again, to a natural inquisition of my crimson vagina, endlessly inspecting its secrets without the least excitement (the contrary in fact would be more true) ever coming to interrupt me for it was important to know that I had this thing even when I was dressed and walking between my father and my mother and that in that regard I was incurable. . . . I could not manage to catch Jim's eye, he did not see me as I really was. He himself wasn't important, but he was a test and I had chosen him.   /158

There are also the legends where young women, having stolen fire, carry it about with them in their vulvas. There was the story of the one who had been put to sleep for a hundred years because she pricked her finger on her spindle, the spindle being taken for the symbol of the clitoris. A propos of this story, they engage in many a pleasantry regarding the clumsiness of the woman whose precious indications of femalarity were missing. They said laughing that she must have been the phenomenon mentioned elsewhere, the one who had a poison dart instead of a little tongue all ready for pleasure. They say that they do not understand why she was called sleeping beauty.   /155

I could easily demonstrate to you, taking as my point of departure terms that are your own, that your pretension has no equal save your blindness, and that it is I who win and you who lose, I who possess. That it is I to whom victory definitely belongs.   /156

So perhaps some day I shall tell you how impossible it is to reduce my orgasm to a defeat, to the "little death" of which doctors speak. I do not answer the ecstasy of your orgasm with a corresponding ecstasy. We are not mirrors reflecting each other in that manner. You lose yourself and I lose myself also, but it is life that I win. What I call death is my limit, my desertion, my solitude. If the other possesses me, then I am no longer myself, I am the other also. I am no more. The other, the world, life is, and I am no more than the total carnal enjoyment of them.   /156

Lovely hair, I have stroked you long enough. Sitting tailor-fashion, I make myself young again. A little cutting now and again doesn't do any harm. Here I am then, with the hairless sex of a little girl, with great swollen lips. A plump cunt. It is good enough to eat! That's the only thing I'm unable to do myself: taste myself. . . . When I think that I carry *that* around everywhere with me! And no one, no one suspects as much, no one! Not the slightest telltale odor!

It's true that dogs are the right height to find out about it. We're higher and don't have the same sense of smell. In the street I have legs, arms, a head, breasts, a behind, but they are provocative enough.

That's all I lack though! By the looks of him sitting there, *that* counts. His eyes are slightly crossed. One of his hands is hanging down, and the other is resting flat on his thigh. With curious pauses his robot-hand begins to move slowly to where it wants to get: simply because *that* attracts him, he'll make room between the taut folds of his pants, and will push his stiff sex from one row of folds to the next, as his mouth twists sideways.   /157

Prudery is as nonexistent as indecency and all that is left is the sad caresses of this strong hand on her legs bared by fashion, not by him. By her own self with scissors and a needle that the cat has threaded, making it shorter and shorter how little and shrunken life is. The Man was a vague cousin of her last lover (a laugh, lover) for something like one day

She did not know what he thought, but knew what he was aiming at because it's always the same thing.   / 158

A sex organ lives, exists only because it is different from that of the other sex.

I agree. But that sexuality concerns only a search for sex organs, or their meeting, no, no, a thousand times no.

What should I call my periods, my big belly, my confinement to childbed, my milk other than facts of my sex organ, how should I call everything that I experience from and through them except sexuality?[1]

[1] For a long time it was called simply femininity. (*Author's note.*)

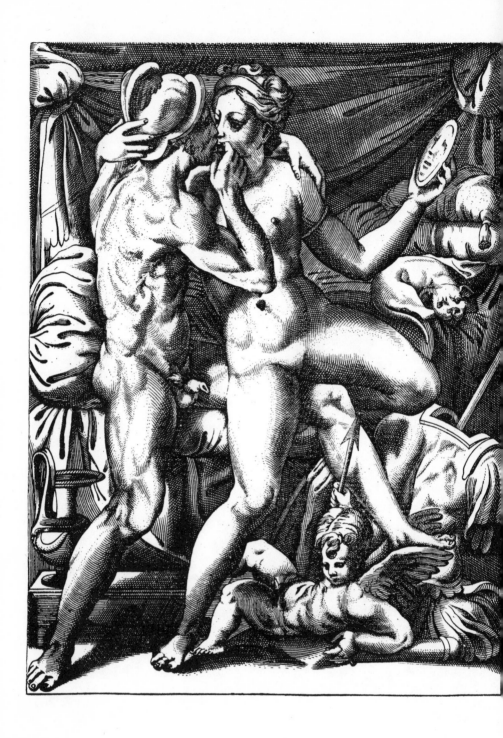

Biographies and Works of All the Authors Cited

Each quotation is followed by a number that refers to the following list. Each entry identifies the author, provides a short biography, and gives the date of the woman's chief works if she is a writer, the title of the volume in the case of collected letters not originally intended for publication, and the date and number of the periodical in the case of articles that appeared in the press.

Many unknown, surprising, or revealing lives are presented here, illuminating an era or a personality and serving as an indispensable complement to the texts cited. These pitiful or extraordinary women, these adventuresses, these sufferers, these independent souls, these passionate lovers, really existed.

We have merely cited the names of twentieth-century authors since the majority of them are still alive.

1

MARIE DE FRANCE, also known as Marie de Compiègne. She herself said that she was "from France." Part of her life was spent in England. The author of 103 fables and 12 known lais (she doubtless composed more) of which she herself stated that the point of departure was often a Breton legend. Her principal lais, which appeared around 1170–80, are those of *Guigemar, Eliduc, Luastic, Lanval, Yonec* (The Blue Bird), *The Honeysuckle* ("Sweet friend, so will it with us be: / Neither me without you nor you without me"), inspired by the legend of *Tristan and Isolde, The Two Lovers, The Ash-Tree, Milon,* etc. Certain of them have Normandy as the setting. "One can recognize in them remains of an ancient mythology that has usually been misunderstood or represented in almost unrecognizable form; in them a tone at once tender and sad predominates, as well as a passion unknown in the epics of the time. Moreover, the characters of the Celtic tales are transformed into knights and ladies" (Gaston Paris).

2

Cour d'amour des dames de Gascogne (Court of Love of the Ladies of Gascony). After André le Chaplain (Andreas Capellanus), 1186.

3

An anonymous Occitan woman troubadour of the twelfth century.

4

Another anonymous woman troubadour of the twelfth century.

5

ERMENGARDE DE NARBONNE, twelfth century.

6

MARIE DE CHAMPAGNE, daughter of Éléanore of Aquitaine and patroness of the poet Chrétien de Troyes, author of *Lancelot*, etc.

7

BEATRIX DE DIE, or the Comtesse de Die, wife of William of Poitiers, mistress of the troubadour Rambaud d'Orange. Herself a Provençal poetess, twelfth century.

8

CHRISTINE DE PISAN (1364–1434). Married at the age of fifteen to Étienne de Castel, who became royal notary, a widow at the age of twenty-five after ten years of conjugal happiness, and the mother of three children. The first "woman of letters" who makes a living from her writings for herself and her children, composing songs, ballads, virelays, rondeaux, and love laments. Also the author of *La Cité des dames* (The City of Ladies), *L'Épître au dieu d'amour* (Epistle to the God of Love), *Le Dit de la rose* (The Story of the Rose), *Le Débat des deux amants* (The Debate of the Two Lovers), etc., and of historical works. A passionate woman who was faithful to the memory of her husband, Christine de Pisan was also a feminist, and the first of her contemporaries to celebrate Joan of Arc. Her life was full of trials and tribulations, among them financial difficulties and lawsuits. "Alas, where will poor widows find comfort for the goods they have been stripped of!" The translation here is based on the admirable adaptation of her poems in modern French by Jeanine Moulin.

9

THE LADY OF CASTELLOZA, thirteenth century, a poetess from the Auvergne, "most fair and well-schooled."

10

An anonymous poetess of southern France, twelfth century.

11

HÉLOÏSE, the "most wise Héloïse," whose story is too well known to bear repeating in detail here. The niece of Canon Fulbert of Paris, pretty and well educated, she met at the age of seventeen the famous Abélard, professor of theology at the Cloister school near Notre-Dame in Paris, a celebrated philosopher whose lectures were attended by the brightest students of the day. He was engaged by Fulbert as Héloïse's tutor and soon won her heart. "Under the pretext of studying, we devoted all of our time to love," Abélard writes. Fulbert discovered what was happening. Abélard then ran off with Héloïse to Britanny, where she gave birth to a child, which the couple named Astrolabe. To pacify Fulbert, Abélard secretly married Héloïse, but Fulbert bruited about the news of the theologian's marriage. Abélard then handed Héloïse over to the nuns of Argenteuil. But Fulbert took his revenge by having Abélard castrated by his servants: "They cut off the parts of my body with which I had committed what they complained of, and they then took flight." Before cloistering himself, Abélard demanded that Héloïse enter a convent. Some two years later they saw each other one last time, for administrative reasons. After this meeting, Héloïse wrote to him first, and the two began corresponding. She became Abbess of Paraclete, but one can judge by her writings how badly she bore up under this forced retirement from the world.

12

Provençal poetess of the twelfth century.

13

"The Anonymous Beguine," also known as "The French Beguine," thirteenth century. She lived near Lille and wrote three *Dits de l'âme* (Stories of the Soul), the manuscript of which is to be found in Berlin.

14

PERNETTE DU GUILLET, born and died in Lyons, at the early age of twenty-five. Shared love and friendship with the poet Maurice Scève. Spoke Italian and Spanish and was acquainted with Latin and Greek. A musician, she accompanied herself when she recited her works. Odes, songs, epigrams, elegies of many sorts, published after her death by her husband and the printer Antoine du Moulin in 1545.

15

CATHERINE DE FRADONNET, Lady Desroches, the daughter of Madeleine des Roches; mother and daughter both interested in belles-lettres, receiving at their house in Poitiers the magistrates who came to the sessions of the Court of Assizes. They died on the same day in 1587, of the plague that ravaged Poitiers. They published together a translation of Claudius' *Abduction of Proserpina*, two plays, *Panthée* (Panthea) and *Tobie Tobias* (1570), and a number of poems.

16

MARIE DE ROMIEU lived in the Vivarais. Her brother, Jacques de Romieu, a gentleman and secretary of the King, had written a satire against women. Marie decided to answer him and prove "the pre-eminence of the female sex," "in candor and good faith." Numerous poetic works, published in 1581.

17

LOUISE LABÉ, "Lyonnais lady," the daughter and wife of ropemakers, married in 1550 Ennemond Perrin, who was much older than she. Brilliant and extremely beautiful, she knew Italian (she wrote a sonnet in that language), Latin, and music, and was a fine horsewoman; she even took part in the siege of Perpignan in 1542. She was the center of the Lyons school and is widely recognized as the greatest lyric love poet of the sixteenth century. Certain of her sonnets foreshadow the metaphysical poets in England. She herself would appear to have been influenced by Petrarch. The passion she writes of, full of a much more striking lyricism than that of the poets of the

Pléiade school to which she belongs, earned her a reputation (most likely false) as a "courtesan." In point of fact, she was a woman passionately in love, and like many such, she was also a feminist. Her work was published in 1555; it consists of twenty-four sonnets, three elegies, and the *Débat de Folie et d'Amour* (Debate of Folly and Love). In Louise Labé the two outstanding characteristics of the woman passionately in love are notable: masochism and independence, traits that men frequently take to be precise opposites of each other.

18

MARGUERITE DE NAVARRE, Marguerite of Angoulême (1492–1549), daughter of Louise of Savoy, sister of Francis I, whom she adored; first Duchess of Alençon, then queen of Navarre and mother of Jeanne d'Albret, herself a poetess. Great patroness of the arts and writers (Clément Marot, Rabelais, Dolet, Des Périers, etc.). With a consuming interest in the life of the spirit, she entered into correspondence with the great minds of her time (Erasmus, the humanists Lefebre d'Étaples and Briçonnet) and interested herself in the doctrine of the Reformation and in the dissidents of the time. Played an important role in diplomacy, particularly at the time of Francis I's imprisonment by Charles V. Said to have "a female body, a man's heart, and an angel's head." Proving herself a mystic in her *Le Miroir de l'ame pécheresse* (Mirror of the Sinner's Soul) (1531), *Le Triomphe de l'agneau* (The Triumph of the Lamb), etc., the queen of Navarre shows herself to be a most realistic and indulgent observer of human passions in her *Heptameron*, a collection of tales modeled on Boccaccio's *Decameron*. In 1547 *Les Marguerites de la marguerite des princesses* (Pearls of the Pearl of Princesses) appeared. The *Heptameron* was published anonymously after her death. Marguerite de Navarre remains an extremely complex woman, scarcely known today. If she expressed the victory of love over all things, and mystic self-discipline through love, it is out of love of God; in her "Bergère ravie de l'amour de Dieu" ("The Shepherdess Enraptured by the Love of God"), on the other hand, she speaks of God in the terms of a woman in love.

19

ANNE DE GRAVILLE. Her poetic works were discovered in an attic. Though she composed panegyrics to the female sex, her poetry is marked both by the idealistic tradition of *fin amor* and a more "Gallic" tradition which is somewhat uncomplimentary to the woman.

20

HÉLISENNE DE CRENNE, née Marguerite Briet. A bourgeoise of Abbeville. In 1538 published the first French psychological novel: *Les Angoysses qui procèdent d'amour, contenant trois parties composées par dame Hélisenne de Crenne laquelle exhorte toutes personnes à ne pas suivre folle amour* (Painful Tribulations Occasioned by Love, comprised of three parts composed by Milady Hélisenne de Crenne, who exhorts one and all not to follow mad love). The work gives proof of Italian influences (Boccaccio's *Fiammetta*) and Spanish (Juan de Flores). Her style is intended to be learned, but remains heavy and often pedantic. The great interest of the novel is its autobiographical nature and the psychological analysis it presents of an adulterous but otherwise innocent love; the idea of love as fate, with physical desire predominating; a woman narrator torn between a sense of guilt; and a passionate, even rebellious attraction on the part of the heroine, undeterred by a sense of conjugal duty.

21

JEANNE DE FLORE, Author of *Contes amoureux, touchant la punition que faict Vénus de ceux qui condamnent et mesprisent le vray amour* (Amorous Tales Regarding the Punishment by Venus of Those Who Condemn and Scorn True Love), 1541, addressed to "noble ladies in love," teaching them that physical love is nought but joy and that chastity brings nothing save the wrath of the gods. Paganism and crudity. A woman cannot read Jeanne Flore without here and there suspecting these writings of being the work of a man because of a certain "spiciness" that is quite unfeminine. Yet critics have identified her as being Jeanne Gaillarde, the "learned and polished" Jeanne Gaillarde or Gaillard whose praises Clément Marot sings and whose "light and delicate" pen won a prize for eloquence in its day, according to the scholar Verdun Saulnier.

22

MARGUERITE DE VALOIS, known as Queen Margot (1553–1613), daughter of Henry II and Catherine de Medecis, the unhappily married wife of Henry IV. She was the center of a little court where a worldly variety of Platonism reigned. She had many lovers, several of whom were hanged or murdered. Her *Mémoires* are written in a savory language, as is her *La Ruelle mal assortie* (The Ill-assorted Couple in the Bedchamber), which is so cruel to men who would dare be lovers and hence objects to a queen. Her verses and stanzas, on the other hand, are written in a beautiful though highly precious language, and bear noticeable traces of Platonism. Her love letters to Champvallon are full of an astonishing baroque beauty.

23

HENRIETTE DE BALZAC D'ENTRAIGUES, one of the great passions of Henry IV, though twenty-six years younger than he. He had promised her in writing to marry her, but instead married Marie de Medicis, for reasons of state which are readily imaginable. Henriette d'Entraigues took offense at this and reproached the king, who answered her coldly and in no uncertain terms, instructing her to send him back his written promise and the engagement ring he had given her.

24

MARIE DE BRABANT, daughter of Jean of Brabant, born around 1540. Becoming a Huguenot convert, she scolds women for their luxury in her *Épître aux Bombancières* (Epistle to Ostentatious Ladies), predicting that foolish virgins who are overfond of "variegated bodices and high platform shoes" will go to hell, but also writing praise of the nude female body in her paraphrase of the Song of Songs. See her *Annonce de l'esprit et de l'âme fidèle contenant Le Cantique des Cantiques de Salomon en langue française* (Annunciation of the Spirit and of the Faithful Soul Containing Solomon's Song of Songs in the French Language).

25

MADELEINE DE SCUDÉRY (1607–1701). An orphan at an early age, she and her brother Georges were educated with great care by her uncle. "One of the most witty and discriminating girls of France," she gave evidence both of her learning and of her dazzling gift for conversation, and was soon a celebrated guest at the Paris mansion of the Marquise de Rambouillet, in whose "blue chamber" the "Précieuses" movement was born. She was the author of interminable serial novels: *L'Illustre Vassa* (The Illustrious Vassa), *Le Grand Cyrus* (Cyrus The Great), and *Clélie* among them, certain of which run to ten to twelve volumes, depicting the manners and mores of nobles of her day under fictitious names. In 1652 she began to hold her "Saturdays," which made the "Précieuses," of whom she was the leader, famous (she was known by her guests as "Sapho"). She was celebrated during her lifetime, was the intimate of such famous writers as Madame de Sévigné, Madame de La Fayette, and La Rochefoucauld, and won a prize for eloquence. Her preciosity may be irritating to today's reader, but one must not forget that her invention of the "Map of the Tender Lover" was intended as a joke or a parlor game. What she contributed to letters was a lofty conception of gallantry and its "quintessence," comprised of respect, fidelity, and trust, and forswearing physical possession and marriage. In the end this gallantry became a sort of religion, aiming as it did at the absolute and based as it was on a complex casuistry which rendered a great service to the psychology of Madeleine de Scudéry's day.

26

MADAME DE LA SUZE, née Henriette de Coligny (1618–73), celebrated for her beauty, her love adventures, and her verses. Married twice, once to a Scottish lord and then to the Comte de la Suze, "A Huguenot, one-eyed, a drunk, and in debt." She was unfaithful to him on numerous occasions and finally became a convert to Catholicism in order to give herself an excuse for abandoning him. Known as "Doralise" in the *Dictionary of the Précieuses*, she wrote poems that often had a romantic air about them: her themes of the fatal nature of love, moral suffering, and solitude prefigure by two hundred years the famous nineteenth-century *mal du siècle*. She also frequently railed against the strait jacket of "modesty" and "honor" which made martyrs of the women of her day. Her works are collected in the *Recueil de pièces galantes en prose et en vers* (Anthology of Love Works in Prose and Verse), coauthored by Paul Pellisson (1664).

27

MADAME DE VILLEDIEU, née Marie Hortense Desjardins (1632–83). She made a point of not hiding the fact that she was in favor of "gallantry." Somewhat of an adventuress, she came from her native Alençon to Paris without a cent in order to seek her fortune. It is not known how this daughter of a chambermaid of Anne de Rohan's managed to receive an education. As predicted by the baroque poet Voiture, who saw her as a young child, she was a bright, witty woman, but something of a madcap. An unmarried mother at a very early age, she then became the protégée of the beautiful Duchesse de Montbazon, and frequented the elegant salons. She left Paris in order to follow one of her lovers to the provinces, where she went about capturing men, writing verses and novels, and provoking duels. A lively, sensuous woman, she was nonetheless, not a beauty. She met Molière and joined his theatrical troupe, and earned him great repute with her *Récit de la farce des Précieuses* (The Tale of the Farce Les Précieuses), a defense of his *Les Précieuses ridicules*. When she finally married a lover enamored of her, it was a most unusual match, for the wedding ceremony made a bigamist of her husband, Villedieu. When he died, she planned at first to become a nun, but in the end took to wandering and collecting lovers once more. She was greatly feted in Holland (*Recueil de quelques lettres ou relations galantes* [Collection of a Number of Letters or Tales of Love]). She then married a sexagenarian, the Marquis de Chaste, whom she also made a bigamist (though later she managed to have her first marriage annulled). By him she had a son for whom the Grande Mademoiselle, the first cousin of Louis XIV, stood as godmother and the Dauphin himself as godfather, giving us a good idea of the high standing of this adventuress at court. She then lost her husband and her son, one immediately after the other, retired to her mother's in Alençon, and eventually married the man who had made her pregnant many years before! She drank a great deal and ended her days in dire poverty. She writes of physical pleasure, and even celebrates happiness within marriage. This "grasshopper" wrote as she lived—with no hypocrisy whatsoever. She is the precise opposite, so to speak, of the prudish Madeleine de Scudéry.

28

MADAME DE LAUVERGNE, the "Lénodaride" of the *Dictionary of the Précieuses*, probably born about 1620; her maiden name was doubtless Leroix, since that is how she signed her *Recueil de poésies* (Collected Verse), published in 1680. This collection is composed of elegies and portraits that are *galant* and even a bit licentious. Her style is irritating, but it nonetheless is proof of the reign of "modesty" which made love a drama straight out of Pierre Corneille for many a woman of the seventeenth century.

29

MADAME DE LA FAYETTE (1634–93). It is a thankless task to try to present in a few lines the author of *La Princesse de Clèves* (The Princess of Cleves), the most mysterious, the purest, the most enigmatic of novels, and the first of the great French psychological novels. At the Hôtel de Nevers, the literary salon where everyone was given a nickname, she was known as *Brouillard* (Befuddled). Nonetheless, "divine reason" was her prime attribute, according to her great friend the Marquise de Sévigné. Born of parents who belonged to the ranks of the lesser nobility, Marie-Madeleine became a lady in waiting to the Queen. She married François de La Fayette, who brought her, if not a fortune, at least an honorable name. She lived only a short time with him in the country, then after the birth of her two sons came back to Paris, where she was a frequent guest at the Hôtel de Nevers. Well received at court (and by the King himself), she enjoyed the respect of everyone. Her advice was often sought by dignitaries of the court, and she became a "considerable personage" even when illness caused her to leave the court for the country. Discreet, clever, active, indefatigable, full of tact and worldly wisdom, the author of the *Princess of Cleves* spent her life attending to her affairs and proved to be an excellent businesswoman; she was also extremely interested in political matters. Without ever signing her works, and begging her friends to pretend they did not know who the author was, she published *La Princesse de Montpensier* in 1662, *Zaïre* in 1669, and *La Princesse de Clèves* in 1678. Her books made her famous in her lifetime. Her friendships with Madame de Sévigné and Gilles Ménage and her friendly relations with La Rochefoucauld ("Monsieur de la Rochefoucauld lives most honorably with Madame de La Fayette," Mademoiselle de Scudéry wrote enigmatically), became the most important things in her life. She constantly gives proof of a mistrust of love, though we do not know if it stemmed from her "reasonable" temperament or whether it concealed the fear of a passionate temperament: "love, that bothersome thing," she wrote at the early age of eighteen. She nonetheless penned a world-famous novel in which the heroine attains the absolute only by renouncing her desire.

30

MARIE-JEANNE L'HERITIER DE VILLANDON (1664–1734). Her father, a royal historiographer, was a learned man. She herself, though without a fortune, frequently received "fine minds" at her salon. She was a modest woman, brimming over with good humor. An intimate friend of Madeleine de Scudéry's, she was responsible for a work entitled *L'Apothéose de Mademoiselle de Scudéry* (The Apotheosis of Mademoiselle de Scudéry), and for translations of Ovid and collections of poetry (*Oeuvres Mêlés*), which give evidence both of facility and of a certain wit. She was the cousin of Charles Perrault, the collector of the *Mother Goose Tales*, and herself published a number of charming tales, among them "The Sincerity Gown," which foreshadows Andersen's "The Emperor's New Clothes," published some two hundred years later; "The Magic Spinning Wheel," long before the Grimm Brothers; and the plot of "The Fairies," before Perrault.

31

MARQUISE DE SÉVIGNÉ, née Marie de Rabutin-Chantal (1626–96). The most famous writer of letters in the French language. We shall merely point out that in the numerous volumes constituting her correspondence one must search long and hard to find any mention of love. Her own great love, full of enormous vitality, great passion, and great torment, was her life-long love for her daughter. More can be learned from the letters of this mother to her daughter than from reading the ardent correspondence of many a woman in love. But in no respect was Madame de Sévigné's an ordinary love.

32

COMTESSE DE MURAT, née Henriette Julie de Castelnau (1670–1716). The granddaughter of the Maréchal de Castelnau, she was born in Brest and married at the age of sixteen to the Comte de Murat. She was a sensation at court, for she appeared in a Breton costume and played at speaking Breton with the courtiers. She was celebrated by several poets and leading a full love-life when suddenly she was suspected of being one of the authors of a squib against Louis XIV. She was thereupon exiled to Loches, where she began to write a novel (*Mémoires*) in 1697, then a collection of fairy tales, the *Contes de Fées*, then a *Histoire galante des habitants de Loches* (Love

Tales of the Inhabitants of Loche), a *Histoire de la courtisane Rhodope* (Tales of the Courtesan Rhodope, 1708), and her best book, *Les Lutins du château de Kernossy* (The Elves of the Château de Kernossy). Her *Chansons et poésies fugitives* (Ephemeral Songs and Verses) is made up of poems on pleasure. Though her verses are extremely facile, her tales are marked by a great purity of taste and a good deal of personal discrimination. In one of her tales (unfortunately too long to be cited in this volume), she describes the punishment that a fairy chooses to visit on a pair of lovers: the two of them will be condemned to live together, alone in a superb château, and provided with the choicest viands, magically served. It is hell. And the comtesse ends this tale with the following moral: "The lovers, like the authors, came to grief with the epithalamium." Her exile came to an end with the death of Louis XIV in 1715, and she returned to Paris, dying the following year at the age of forty-six. Her fairy tales are marked by the style of her century, but her light irony and her "philosophy" make her part of the eighteenth century.

33

Ninon de Lenclos, Anne, known as Ninon (1620–1705). Yet another celebrated personality. Beautiful, extremely intelligent and cultivated, a dazzling conversationalist, Ninon was at once a model of the "libertine" freethinker of her day, espousing agnosticism in an age of faith (and was for a time shut up in a convent because of her daring remarks), and an extraordinary seducer of men who collected lovers all her life long and well into her seventies, earning their esteem as well as their affection. Her lovers (among whom figured both the husband and the son of Madame de Sévigné) used to say of her that she was both an ideal mistress and a "perfect gentleman." Among her many devoted women friends was Madeleine de Scudéry, who left a tender and delightful portrait of her, and Madame de Maintenon, despite the latter's having stolen one of her favorite lovers from her. Ninon published only one slight work, *La Coquette vengée* (The Coquette Avenged), and left few letters. But the quality of those that have survived makes us regret that there are so few of them. She was famous, however, for her witty sayings, which have come down to us through her friends (e.g., to one of her lovers: "I shall love you for three months. For me that will be an eternity"). She never married. Despite her madcap life, however, Ninon de Lenclos was never a courtesan. She had her own fortune and received the most brilliant men of her era, making no distinction whatsoever between the men who were her lovers and those who were not.

34

Antoinette Deshouliere (1638–94). The first woman to be elected to an academy (that at Arles). Beautiful and well schooled, she knew Latin, Spanish, and Italian, and was an excellent dancer. She lived as she pleased, and often received guests in her mansion on the Rue de l'Homme Armé. She was very famous for some time, then rapidly fell in the public's favor. She is definitely dated today, her greatest claim to fame being a sentimental verse about "little sheep" known to all French schoolchildren. She was also the author of a terrible poem making fun of Racine's *Phèdre*. Though criticized by Nicolas Boileau, the great arbiter of taste in her day, she was admired by a number of the best minds of her time, among them Ménage, Bayle, Vauban, and La Rochefoucauld, and took the side of the "moderns" in the famous Quarrel of the Ancients and Moderns. Her one published work was a volume of poetry (*Poésies*, 1688). Today a number of critics think that she deserved a better fate than the scant place reserved for her in manuals of literature, for her work contains some charming and graceful verses as well as poems full of spiritual anguish written during her long and painful last illness. Among these latter are several possessed of a genuine tragic beauty.

35

COMTESSE D'AUNEUIL, née Louise de Bossigny, the author of numerous fairy tales, among them "La Tyrannie des fées détruite" (The Fairies' Tyranny Put to an End, 1702), "L'Inconstance punie" (Fickleness Punished), and "Les Chevaliers errants et le génie familier" (The Wandering Chevaliers and the Familar Genius).

36

COMTESSE D'AULNOY, née Marie-Catherine Le Jumel de Barneville (1650?–1705). This woman who wrote of the terror and horror of young girls forced to marry "monsters" knew whereof she spoke for at the age of fifteen she was married against her will to a gambler, carouser, and woman-chaser. But it was she who became the real monster, for she mounted a plot to get her husband shut up in the Bastille. None of her biographers has anything good to say of her. Let us remember that she was only eighteen at the time, and that little is said about the many wives sent to prison for many long years by their husbands. But there is worse still. After having spent a short time shut up in a convent (her accomplices were beheaded, but she was from "a good family" and escaped with only a few years' confinement to the convent), she earned a brilliant reputation in society, but then found herself involved in another scandal, an attempted murder. But again she managed to get off easily. This woman is the author both of "moral tales" and of marvelous fairy tales; Charles Perrault, the author of the *Mother Goose Tales*, often merely copied the author of such tales as "The Blue Bird," that feminine myth par excellence, "The Girl with the Golden Hair," "The Green Serpent," "Garcieuse and Pertinet," and "The Doe in the Forest." It is hard to believe in her treacherous deeds unless one reads her original texts. These wonderful tales, among the most beautiful that have ever been written, are full of sadomasochistic references, symbols that are both angelic and demoniacal, and are witness to an extraordinary fascination for the riches, the jewels, the luxuries, of this world. They are tragic tales inasmuch as the lovers often lose their lives. The passages dealing with horrible events seem to have come from the pen of an author who is much closer to the "accursed" visionaries of the nineteenth century than she is to her contemporary Racine. She enjoyed enormous success in her day, and still does so today, despite the fact that many of the tales she invented are attributed to Perrault, who merely adapted them for his collections.

37

MADAME DE MAINTENON, Françoise d'Aubigné, marquise de Maintenon (1635–1719). Along with Joan of Arc, one of the most famous French-

women. But it is not because hundreds of schools bear her name or because
her portraits haunt history books that we French became acquainted with
her in our youth. Because of her, we learned a strange-sounding word: she
was described as the morganatic wife of Louis XIV, a word that sounded
straight out of a fairy tale about the Fairy Morgana. As we contemplated
her portrait, we wondered why Louis XIV, who had mistresses who were
much more striking, bothered to marry this severe person dressed all in
black—legitimately, legally, but clandestinely. Louis's reign was divided into
two periods, "before Madame de Maintenon" and "after Madame de Maintenon." But though we knew of her work as an educator, we were told nothing of her personal life. Françoise d'Aubigné was from a noble family which
had fallen on bad days. Her grandfather was the extraordinary poet who
wrote *Les Tragiques*, the Calvinist leader Agrippa d'Aubigné. Among his
children was a son, Constant, a fact that D'Aubigné dismissed as "a bothersome family detail." This man, who was Françoise's father, was a notorious
rake who was sent to prison for treason. His wife accompanied him to
prison, and it was there that there was born the little girl who was one day
to marry the most powerful monarch of the time. Françoise had a miserable
childhood. She was first sent off to the Antilles, and then after the death of
her father she was brought up by the austere Calvinist family of her aunt.
She was the poor relation, and at times was sent out to watch over the family flock of turkeys. After having been brought up in accordance with a forbidden religion, she was taken away from these "heretics" by a relative who
had managed to enlist the aid of Anne of Austria. She was sent to the Convent of the Ursulines in Paris, and after two years of bitter resistance was
finally converted to Catholicism. This twelve-year-old child had "wearied
the priests, Bible in hand," to prove them wrong. On leaving the convent,
she caused a sensation in Paris, being both extremely beautiful and extremely intelligent—though at the same time alone in the world and very
close to absolute poverty. Her neighbor, the satirical poet Paul Scarron,
offered either to marry her or to pay the sum necessary to provide her with
the dowry that would allow her to enter a convent. Scarron was old,
crippled, ill, not rich, and in bad repute at court. Françoise chose nonetheless to marry him, and at the age of seventeen she wedded this intelligent,
goodhearted buffoon known for his crude language and the notorious libertine company he kept. Françoise's ambition was to "enjoy a reputation
without reproach," and she managed to keep her head even in such "dissolute" company. Among her intimate friends, however, she numbered the no-
toriously "freethinking" Ninon de Lenclos. Left a widow at the age of
twenty-five, she retired to a convent but continued nonetheless to frequent
the world of high society, where people could not get over this young
woman "who allied so much virtue, the direst poverty, and charm." The
King's acknowledged official mistress, Madame de Montespan, "with whom
she had the most cordial relations due to her wit and the charms of conversation," asked her to raise the children of the King that she had had in secret. Françoise's answer was a measure of her personality: "If these are indeed the King's children, I am most willing. I would not take charge of
Madame de Montespan's without scruples. Hence it is necessary that this

charge come from the King. That is my last word on the subject." The King stepped in, and she then established herself on the rue de Vaugirard, where she raised and educated these little royal bastards with taste and devotion, amid the greatest secrecy. The King was prejudiced against her, considering her to be "a find mind that had need of sublime things," but on meeting her personally he came to esteem her more and more. In 1673 he recognized his bastard children and had them brought to court. Young Madame Scarron followed them and shared the apartments of the King's favorite. Louis XIV then gave her the estate of Maintenon and ordered her to adopt the title of Madame de Maintenon. There followed six years of veiled hostility on the part of the jealous favorite, Madame de Montespan, against this unfailingly gentle, angelic, and sensible governess of her numerous children. Faithful to her motto that "there is nothing more clever than irreproachable conduct," Françoise had the brilliant idea of pleading the cause of virtue and religion with the King—the best possible means of getting the better of the proud, pleasure-loving favorite. Despite the King's numerous affairs of the heart (among them La Fontanges), Madame de Maintenon enjoyed increasing influence at court, even after Madame de Montespan left it. Still playing the role of the virtuous woman, she then sought to reconcile the King and Queen, thus strengthening her position. When the Queen died in 1683, the King found he could not get along without this granddaughter of a famous heretic, widow of a poor crippled libertine poet, and former governess of his bastards, who through a campaign conducted with tact, wit, and a "strangely veiled" sensual attraction, had quite literally charmed him. She resisted living with him, however, until he offered her the "morganatic marriage" that conferred on her a position "more elevated than noble." And for twenty years she was the extremely powerful person to whom the Pope, kings, princes, and dukes addressed themselves most respectfully. She did not even attempt to be crowned Queen; Saint-Simon wrote that she resigned herself to being "a transparent enigma," ruling over the King and his conscience if not the kingdom. As every Frenchman knows, she then passionately devoted herself to her great love, pedagogy, establishing the famous Saint-Cyr school for young ladies ("that is what I have in mind, that is what my heart is set on"), which for centuries set the pattern for female education. It was for her and her charges that Racine wrote *Esther* and *Athalie*. But this woman who had been married at seventeen to an aged, infirm husband now found herself married to an elderly, dictatorial, difficult King. For twenty years her daily duty was to distract the King, care for him, and put up with him. . . . During his last illness she devoted herself to him, but in her weariness left him before the end, retiring to Saint-Cyr and "her girls" two days before his death, without returning to see him on his deathbed. She survived Louis by four years, spent at Saint-Cyr, precisely as she wished: "All I have need of now is God and my charges."

38

CATHERINE MEURDRAC, Madame de la Guette: We know her from her charming journal, discovered after her death: how she married a soldier who took her away from a recalcitrant father, etc. Neither Catherine Meurdrac nor her husband belonged to the nobility, and the tone in which she writes the story of her life is a refreshing change from the preciosity of her day and the tone that reigned among members of the nobility in general.

39

CATHERINE BERNARD (1662–1712). The niece of Pierre Corneille, this woman born a Protestant in Rouen converted to Catholicism on arriving in Paris to live. A witty and sensible person, her friendship was greatly appreciated by Madame de Sévigné and Madame de Coulanges, among others. The philosopher Bernard Le Bovier de Fontenelle was also a friend, and it is widely believed that her writings were written in collaboration with him. Catherine Bernard, who remains unknown today, was in fact one of the founders, with Madame de La Fayette, of the French psychological novel. She wrote tragedies in verse (*Brutus*, 1691, was written with Fontenelle), but is best known for two delightful, perceptive fairy tales inserted in her *Ines de Cordoue* (Ines of Córdoba, 1696). One of them is none other than the first version of her "Crested Cricket" (see p. 132), which is far better written than Perrault's version. The other is "The Rose Tree," a marvelous tale which deserves to be better known. Her *Relation de l'Isle de Bornéo* (A Description of the Island of Borneo) and her *Les Malheurs de l'amour* (The Misfortunes of Love) also give proof of great delicacy of touch and a curious pessimism. It is tears which restore the rose tree to the state of prince, not kisses, and both her tales have unhappy endings: The Rose Tree Prince is carried away by love of an adolescent and betrays his beautiful princess; Crested-Cricket and his wife are very unhappy together. In fact, Catherine Bernard, who never married, has nothing but ill to say of marriage. One of her tales ends with the words: "Marriage as usual put an end to all the pleasures of their lives."

40

MADAME DE SABLÉ (1599–1678). A "Précieuse," the very model of the sensible, lovable, distinguished woman of the first half of the seventeenth century. She was the model for the beautiful Parthénie of whom Madame de Scudéry says in *Cyrus* that she "effaced all other beauties" and was "loved by several and hated by many." Madame de La Fayette was her rival for the affections of La Rochefoucauld. With time she became less of a coquette and gradually came to be known as a sensible and discriminating woman. She is known for a volume of *Maximes*, published by the Abbé d'Ailly in 1678. While never brilliant, she was the model of probity and dignity.

41

MARIE DE SAINS, a nun of Lille who was tried for witchcraft.

42

MADAME GUYON, Jeanne-Marie de la Motte (1648–1717). Unhappily married, she was the mother of five children, three of whom died at an early age; after being badly scarred by smallpox, she took to religion. She is the cocreator, with her great admirer Fénelon, of the Quietist movement. She gave lectures to spread her principal ideas: detachment from the goods of this world; a mistrust of science, theology, and casuistry. Her religion is that of sublimely serene mystical happiness. She was the author of *Le Moyen Court* (The Short Way), a commentary on the Song of Songs, and *Les*

Torrents spirituels. The great Bishop Bossuet attacked her, and Fénelon defended her in a famous theological quarrel of the day. The remainder of her life was spent shut up in remote convents or the Bastille. She became known as "the mother of the Church within the Church." Her *poésies et cantiques spirituels* (Spiritual Poems and Hymns) were published in Germany. One finds in Madame Guyon the principal characteristic of most feminine mystics, an erotic lyricism, but her mystic masochism is surrounded by a strange aura of serenity.

43
PRINCESSE DE MODENA (Charlotte de Valois). She was a royal princess, and the Duc de Richelieu, an inveterate seducer of women, disguised himself in order to meet with her—once as a convict, and another time as a young girl. He also invented an ingenious system of pivoting panels hidden by a jam closet which allowed him access to her apartments. This dangerous liaison lasted for some time, however, and brought Richelieu imprisonment in the Bastille. To save the man she loved from execution, Charlotte de Valois agreed to renounce him publicly and announce her marriage to the Prince of Modena. This marriage nonetheless caused her great suffering, for during the ceremony Richelieu, who was one of the guests, kept staring at all the pretty girls present—more than was necessary, in Charlotte's view, to disguise his passion for her. Richelieu later joined her in Italy—disguised as a book peddler.

44
MARIE-JEANNE DE STAAL DE LAUNAY (1684–1750). Marie-Jeanne Cordier, known as Rose de Launay, was born in Paris. For mysterious reasons, her father fled to exile in England, and she was raised at the priory of Saint-Louis in Rouen: The superior found her to be a child prodigy and took her under his wing and educated her. She lives thus under her benefactor's protection, becoming highly educated and highly esteemed, until his death. She was then twenty-six years old, and was obliged to exchange this delightful protected life for what she called "the most total servitude." She became the chambermaid of the Duchesse de Maine: "My fate was precisely the contrary of the one we see in novels, where the heroine is raised as a simple shepherdess and finds herself one day an illustrious princess," she wrote. In a state of deep depression she attempted suicide, then wrote an anonymous letter to Fontenelle telling him of her sad state; this letter was so beautifully written that it made the rounds of all Paris, and once its writer became known she found herself a famous figure. Discovering her great intellectual capacities, her fearsome employer had her write plays for her theater at Sceaux. She also arranged a marriage of convenience for her with a foreign gentleman, Monsieur de Staal. Drawing a portrait of herself, she writes most perceptively: "Her character and her mind are like her person: there is nothing basically wrong with them, but they have no charm. Her folly has always been her wish to be reasonable; and as women whose corset is too tight imagine that they are plump, so she, made uncomfortable by her reason, believed that she possessed a great deal of it." When the Duchesse de Maine was shut up in the Bastille, she followed her to prison (1718–20). Her *Mémoires* are remarkably vivid, straightforward, and plain-

spoken, whereas her few verses are very precious. Her *Lettres* give a fine picture of Regency society.

45

JULIE TALMA, the abandoned wife of the great actor and roué François Talma. In 1798 when she was forty-two she met the writer Benjamin Constant and became deeply attached to him. Constant merely wished to be good friends with her, whereupon Julie's love grew all the greater, and she wrote him strange, vibrant letters. Little by little she became no more than his confidante, and it was at her home that Constant met Anna Lindsay, the great love of his life.

46

AÏSSÉ (1695–1733), a Circassian princess, bought at the age of four in a slave market at Constantinople by the French ambassador to the Ottoman Empire, Monsieur de Ferriol, for his own private pleasure. He sent her to his sister in Paris to be educated by her, and the beautiful, well-behaved little girl acquired the greatest refinement. But she remained the possession of her "aga," whom she rarely saw and greatly feared. The regent himself became fond of her, but she was able to resist his advances. But she encouraged another of her admirers, a knight of the Order of Malta, the Chevalier d'Aydie, who loved her deeply and sincerely. He was unable to marry her since it would mean the loss of his title and his fortune. A little girl was born to the couple, who raised it—very well—in secret at Sens, taking turns visiting her. One summer Aïssé met a Calvinist woman from Geneva who made her ashamed of her conduct and tried to convert her. Mademoiselle Aïssé thereupon underwent a religious crisis, and was so torn between her faith and her genuine love for Aydie, whom the Geneva prude accused of being "dissolute," that it shortened her life; she died of tuberculosis the year following her fortieth birthday, having done her best to the end to leave her beloved Chevalier. Her pure and ardent spirit, her elegantly simple style, the memory of her great exotic beauty, and her curious destiny as a slave, woman of the world, and frequenter of court circles brought her a great posthumous love: the famous critic Sainte-Beuve, who rediscovered her *Lettres*, published in 1787, wrote a touching article about them.

47

MADAME DU DEFFAND (1697–1780). Marie de Vichy-Chamrond, Marquise du Deffand. At twenty-five she married the Marquis du Deffand, but soon separated from him, for she did not love him. Having come to Paris to live, she held a salon and took a great number of lovers. Her salon was a highly fashionable one at first, remaining so as long as she was the mistress of Hénault, a royal magistrate. Then after 1730, when she met D'Alembert, she began to receive scholars and *philosophes*, among them Montesquieu, Fontenelle, Marmontel, La Harpe, Turgot, and Condorcet, as well as such writers as Marivaux and Sedaine. She was an extremely dissolute woman, but very sure of herself, managing to keep both her imagination and her love affairs in close rein. In 1753 she began to lose her eyesight and invited Julie de Lespinasse to come live with her, as her companion at first and later as cohostess of her salon. When she found out that Julie was holding a salon of her own in her apartments on the second floor of her Paris mansion, receiving all the Encyclopédistes, she dismissed Julie, in 1763. At the age of sixty-eight she fell in love with Horace Walpole, who was much younger than she. This blind old woman, once so cynical and wise in the ways of the world, fell in love with this Englishman whom she had never seen, in a manner mindful of an adolescent. She has a vigorous, incisive, picturesque style all her own, and analyzes extremely well the boredom and sadness of a life with no faith whatsoever, and burdened with a series of infirmities.

48

ADELAIDE-GILLETTE DUFRESNOY, née Billet (1765–1825). Daughter of a rich Parisian jeweler, she was only sixteen when she married a king's counselor, Monsieur Petit Dufresnoy, who had been as attracted by her grace and youth and intelligence as by the fortune of her parents. She wrote a number of nice poems, but it was events that gave her her vocation as a writer. The Revolution forced Dufresnoy to leave France; he installed himself in Italy and found a post as court clerk, then went blind. She began by keeping books and records for her husband, then tried to earn a little more money by writing texts and novels for "young people." She also published a number of elegies. She was finally able to return to France, and in 1815 she was crowned by the French Academy. The Romantic critic Sainte-Beuve appreciated her "simple expression of her tender sentiments." She portrays love "naked," as he put it—an idea that would have shocked her. Her portrayal is nonetheless a passionate one. (Her works: *Élégies*, 1807; *Oeuvre poétique*, Paris, 1827. See also Sainte-Beuve's *Portraits de femmes* and *Les Nouveaux Lundis*.)

49

MADAME ROLAND, Manon Philpon, Madame Roland de la Platière (1754–93). The sole surviving child (of seven) of an engraver on the Île de la Cité in Paris, she received a good education. She was by nature highly intelligent, and also became widely read: she not only learned English and Italian for her own pleasure but also read Plutarch, the authors of antiquity, and above all Jean-Jacques Rousseau, who became her god. Later she even dared to pay him a visit to express her admiration; she was received at the door by Thérèse Levasseur, his common-law wife, who did not even allow her to come in. A bright and independent young lady, Manon's talents were stifled at home by a father she did not love (she had lost her mother, whom she adored, at an early age), and her time was spent in a milieu of craft workers and shopkeepers. She soon came to scorn the nobility, and as early as eighteen or twenty became a true *philosophe* in the then current meaning of that word, that is to say a "natural philosopher," an agnostic, and a freethinker. She wanted a husband, nonetheless, and did not disdain hunting for one of noble blood. An intellectually honest and not very sensual young woman, she was in favor of marriage despite her scorn as a Deist for the Church and its superstitions, and alternately feared and hoped to marry, expecting marriage to be a profound union of mind and heart. After a number of apparently reasonably motivated postponements, in 1780 she finally married Roland de la Platière, an inspector of the royal manufactories twenty years older than she who ruled their household with an iron hand. She was happy with Roland, had a daughter by him, helped her husband write his technical books, and accompanied him to England in search of documentation. Settling first in Amiens, then later in Lyons, the Rolands eventually came to Paris to live in 1791. Manon soon opened her salon to all the revolutionary thinkers, from Brissot the Girondin to Robespierre the Montagnard. Her husband, Roland, became a radical Jacobin. Manon soon acquired a remarkable influence because of her social graces, her somewhat "classic" eloquence, the loftiness of her thought, and not least her fresh, calm, charming person. Robespierre did not like her, but she nonetheless became the principal patroness of the Girondins. Her husband was named Minister of the Interior in 1792, a post which she herself occupied in effect. Manon at the time was thirty-eight and Roland a melancholy, jaundiced fifty-eight. She was overcome with a profound passion for François Buzot, the Girondin leader, who was six years her junior. She did not deceive her husband; instead, like the Princess of Cleves, she confessed her passion for another to her husband, while assuring him at the same time of her loyal devotion. To her surprise, Roland took this badly, and not at all "in the Roman style," as she had hoped. She remained faithful to her lofty conception of life and her ideals, kept her marriage vows, but nonetheless continued to be in love with Buzot. The Rolands chose to share the fate of the Girondins. When her husband was accused of treason on May 31, 1793, Manon went to plead his cause at the Convention. The next day she was arrested, whereas her husband managed to make his escape. She was not executed until November 8, 1793. During these long months of waiting for her death, she remained stoical, drafting her memoirs, and never ceasing to reassure Buzot how much she appreciated this confinement that finally allowed her to think of him to the last without being physically unfaithful to her husband.

50

ELISABETH GUIBERT (1725–87). She was one of the very rare writers to receive a royal pension from Louis XV, who was scarcely a patron of belles-lettres. Very conformist, Elisabeth Guibert is very representative of a certain "reasonable" style of writing about love, made up of moderation, smiling equanimity, and resignation. She published poetry in the *Almanach des Muses* from 1766 to 1769. *La Coquette corrigée* (The Coquette Punished), a tragedy in verse, visits a dire punishment on the woman who would be independent, thus espousing the most reactionary morality possible in an age that in general was quite inclined to be indulgent.

51

MADAME DE VILLENEUVE, Gabrielle Suzanne Barbot, Madame Jean-Baptiste de Gaalon de Villeneuve (1695–1755). The author of numerous precious but charming fairy tales, in particular a first version of "Beauty and the Beast," which was much less sentimental than that of Madame Leprince de Beaumont. Madame de Villeneuve's version is much more surrealistic; magic statues and potions, enchanged mirrors, gold and diamonds, fluttering birds, and strange lights play a large role in making Beauty fall in love with the Beast. Gabrielle Barbot was the wife of Lieutenant Colonel de Villeneuve. She lived partly from her writings, publishing a good dozen volumes, among which were several dramas: *Les Belles solitaires* (The Solitary Beauties), *La Jardinière de Vincennes* (The Lady Gardener of Vincennes), and *Le Juge prévenu* (The Biased Judge).

52

LUCILE DESMOULINS Anne-Louise Duplessis, known as Lucie or Lucile (1771–94). The adorable, touching wife of the revolutionary journalist Camille Desmoulins, whom she married against her parents' will when she was nineteen, on December 29, 1790. They symbolized at the time the young revolutionary couple, handsome, talented, idealistic, and very much in love with each other as well as much taken by the great ideals of the Revolution. The witnesses at their marriage included such figures as Robespierre, Jean-Pierre Brisson, the leader of the Montagnards, and Jérôme Petion, the mayor of Paris. Camille Desmoulins had been Robespierre's schoolmate, and for a long time Robespierre's sentimental attachment to him allowed Desmoulins to make criticisms of him which he would not have tolerated from anyone else. But Desmoulins apparently went too far when he published his famous article on the rights of suspects in his journal, and Robespierre had him arrested on March 31, 1794, whereupon Lucile wrote him a vehement letter. She too was then arrested, and both of them were put to death. This young pair of martyrs long remained a model of grace and bravery in the popular imagination. Lucile left a "red notebook" in which she wrote little verses and copied out the poems of men friends.

53

JULIE DE LESPINASSE (1732–76). The illegitimate daughter of the Comtesse d'Albon and Monsieur de Vichy, the brother of Madame du Deffand, who later married another daughter of the latter's. At the age of eighteen she discovered that she was the governess of the children of her own sister and brother-in-law, who was also her father. In 1754 Madame du Deffand, going blind, asked her to come live with her as her companion. She soon occupied an important place in Madame du Deffand's salon, thanks to her charm, her youth, and above all her lively intelligence. D'Alembert fell in love with her and remained in love with her all his life. When Madame du Deffand became jealous of her (see biography 47) she went to live at d'Alembert's (though there was nothing between them save a great affection on the latter's part; his contemporaries suspected him of being impotent). Julie continued to receive the Encyclopédistes, and this poor and illegitimate girl saw all the noble ladies of society flock to her salon. At thirty-seven she fell in love with the son of the Spanish ambassador, the Marquis de Mora, twelve years her junior, who was madly in love with her. He proved to be tubercular, and Julie, who had kept a cool head up to this point, fell head over heels in love with Monsieur de Guibert, another young man twenty-five years old, to whom she gave herself one fine night. That same night, Monsieur de Mora had a fatal lung hemorrhage in Bordeaux. Julie accused herself of being the cause of his death by having given herself to another man, and was stricken with remorse. But the more she sought to fight her passion, the more overcome by it she was. Monsieur de Guibert, a brilliant young strategist, the author of books on military tactics, married a very rich young lady in 1775; in a fit of despair, Julie began to take large doses of opium and died soon thereafter. Her letters to Guibert date from several decades before the Romantic movement in literature, yet are among the first portrayals of fatal passion. They are probably the most beautiful love letters that exist in the French language, conjoining as they do the expression of great passion and a prodigious clear-sightedness: Julie analyzes herself with implacable precision. Her style, moreover, is truly admirable, for her language is a model of purity and simplicity; her letters remain proof that the most classic possible French can be a vehicle for the most delirious sentimental passion without ever becoming facile. "I love nothing that is halfway, imprecise, approximate," she once wrote. She died a few hours after composing one last letter to Guibert.

54

COMTESSE DE SABRAN, Françoise Éléonore de Jean de Manville (1750–1827). Éléonore's mother died at her birth, and she was raised by a stepmother whom she detested. Taken in by an elderly relative, Madame de Montigny, she received a consummate education at the Convent of the Conception. A dark-eyed blonde, she was both beautiful and charming, and at the age of sixteen she married the Count of Sabran, who was fifty years older than she. "I married an aged invalid whose nurse I should have been rather than a wife . . . but I took little notice of the possible consequences; everything seemed fine and equally good to me; I felt for my nice husband the same affection as for my father and my grandfather, a sweet sentiment that quite sufficed for me at the moment. Time has since opened my eyes," she wrote to her lover on the eve of the marriage of her daughter. She had two children, a son and a daughter, of whom she was extremely fond; she took care of all the details of their education herself, applying principles that have become recognized as valid only in our own day. The Comte de Sabran left her a widow at a very early age. Several years later, she met the Chevalier de Boufflers, of whom Grimm said that he had "a great deal of wit and talent and an infinity of foolish ideas." A libertine with great gifts, he was the son of the Marquise de Boufflers, the mistress of King Stanislas of Poland, who was his godfather. Seminary changed him scarcely at all. He exchanged brilliant letters with Voltaire, and waged valiant battle campaigns. He was thirty-nine years old when he met Éléonore, a widow of twenty-seven. There was genuine love between them, as well as profound friendship, mutual trust and devotion, charm and humor—traits which make their relationship seem almost a modern one. By marrying, the chevalier stood to lose his pensions and perquisites, and he was unwilling to live at his wife's expense. He therefore signed up in 1785 for a post in Senegal, hoping to earn the title and the pension that would allow him to leave holy orders and marry Éléonore. The two lovers wrote each other every day during each of the chevalier's two long stays in Senegal. They wrote in notebooks which were sent by ship via Lisbon. They told each other about the little happenings of their daily life for four years, during which their love and tenderness for each other never faltered. After waiting thirteen years, the chevalier at last became the Marquis de Boufflers and was able to marry Éléonore. But as nobles they were obliged to remain abroad after the Revolution. They finally were able to return to France in 1800, where the marquis found his chair at the French Academy waiting for him. He died in 1815. Éléonore, whose son lived with her for the rest of her life, survived him by twelve years. The correspondence between the Comtesse de Sabran and the Chevalier de Boufflers was published in 1875.

55

ADRIENNE LECOUVREUR (1692–1730), an actress; played at first in the provinces and then at the Comédie-Française. She excelled both in tragedy and comedy, and more or less revolutionized the style of acting of her day by her simplicity and naturalness, which earned her enormous fame. A witty and high-spirited young woman, she had numerous love adventures, but her great love was the Maréchal de Saxe, the great-grandfather of George Sand, a well-known seducer and ladies' man. In order to help him pay his debts, she had her gold table service and her jewels melted down. She was nonetheless abandoned by him, and suffered greatly. She was poisoned to death at the age of thirty-eight, doubtless by a rival. Being an actress, her body could not be given Christian burial. The notables of her day, among them Voltaire, were scandalized by this. Adrienne Lecouvreur, the greatest actress of her time, and the most tender and devoted mistress, was buried by night in a Paris garden.

56

MADAME LEPRINCE DE BEAUMONT, Marie (1711–80). Everyone knows the story of "Beauty and the Beast," which she borrowed from Madame de Villedieu. It is less well known that she was the grandmother of Prosper Mérimée. A sweet grandmother, who wrote a collection of "moral tales" (*Contes moraux*, 1774), and above all texts for schoolchildren, which she titled *Magasins*, the word at the time for the miscellaneous publications which eventually came to be known as magazines. In her hands the story of "Beauty and the Beast" loses many of its luxurious magic trimmings. There are fewer precious stones, pearls, sumptuous apartments, soft music, and mirrors repeating images to infinity; there is more sentiment (it is now the eighteenth century), and in particular a more total, almost exaggerated devotion of the young girl to the father who delivers her over to the Beast. The father-daughter couple remains one of the most mysterious and enigmatic elements in fairy stories written by women.

57

SOPHIE DE MONNIER, Marie-Thérèse, Richard de Ruffey, Marquise de Monnier (1754–89). Born in Franche-Comté; her father, a noble and a royal magistrate, wanted to marry her to the naturalist Buffon, who was forty-seven years older than she. Instead she married the Marquis de Monnier when she was eighteen and he sixty-three! When she was twenty-one she met the son of the famous Mirabeau, Gabriel Honoré, an ardent young man vastly in debt, separated from his wife, and hounded by his father. This mad genius thereupon abducted her, whereupon they had the many adventures which doubtless caused their liaison to become an enduring one; both at one time were sent to prison by order of their respective fathers. From their prison cells they wrote each other jealous, passionate letters including frankly erotic passages in code which would bring a blush to the cheeks of a latter-day Danish pornographer. But they were also able to live for some time together in Holland. Life together suited them, despite kidnapings, prison sentences, and a series of separations and passionate reunions. Moreover, once they finally began living together, Mirabeau took a new mistress and she a new lover. When this charming officer died, she committed suicide. She was thirty-five years old.

58
SOPHIE DE CONDORCET, Sophie de Grouchy, Marquise de Condorcet (1765–1822). She was the beloved wife of the most ardent feminist among the eighteenth-century *philosophes*: Antoine-Nicolas de Condorcet. She was twenty-two years younger than her husband, who loved her tenderly and protectively. She had a salon before and during the early days of the Revolution, where the writer Jean-François Marmontel, the Marquis de la Fayette, Caron de Beaumarchais, the Italian poet Vittorio Alfieri, Adam Smith, and others frequently gathered. When her husband was ordered arrested by the revolutionary authorities, she asked him for a divorce in order to save her daughter's (and her own) life. When she obtained the divorce, Condorcet was already dead, having poisoned himself when his hiding place was discovered, without Sophie's learning of it. For some time she lived in direst poverty, but under the Directory her life took a turn for the better and she rediscovered many friends. It was during this time that she fell madly in love with a handsome good-for-nothing, Maillia Garat, the brother of a famous opera singer who was himself a worthless journalist. Sophie was famous for her *bon mot* on hearing Bonaparte declare that women should not meddle in politics. "In a country where they get their heads cut off, women would like to know the reason why!" she retorted. But her love affairs scarcely proved her as daring as this witty reply. Maillia Garat deceived her; she found out, but nonetheless continued to live with him. When later he fell in love with her best friend, Aimée de Coigny (André Chénier's "Young Captive"), she even offered to live in a *ménage à trois*, but he refused. After being ingloriously abandoned Sophie was at first plunged into despair, but then later found peace and calm once again with a young scholar, Claude Fauriel, and again held a serious and brilliant salon.

59
BELLE DE CHARRIÈRE Elisabeth van Tuyll van Serooskerken van Zuylen. Madame de Charrière (1740–85). Born in Holland, she married a Swiss noble and settled in the canton of Neuchâtel, where her home became a center of culture. She was a fashionable novelist: *Lettres neuchâteloises* (Letters from Neuchâtel, 1784) *Caliste ou Lettres écrites de Lausanne* (Calixtus or Letters Written from Lausanne, 1788), for whom love was the main subject. Benjamin Constant, a young man at the time, became an intimate friend, despite the fact that she was twenty-seven years older than he. Like all Constant's women intimates, she was worldly-wise, brilliant, and sensitive—and beautiful as well, to judge from La Tour's well-known portrait of her.

60
MARQUISE DE LAMBERT, Anne Thérèse de Marguent de Courcelles (1647–1733). Married to the Marquis de Lambert in 1666, widowed in

1686, Madame de Lambert at first devoted her life to the education of her children, then opened a salon in 1690. This began a new life for her, entertaining her brilliant guests at her Hôtel de Nevers and writing treatises on manners and morals and education (*Avis d'une mère à son fils* [A Mother's Advice to her Son, 1726], *Avis d'une mère à sa fille* [A Mother's Advice to Her Daughter, 1728], *Traité de l'amitié* [Treatise on Friendship], *Réflexions sur la Vieillesse* [Reflections on Old Age], *Réflexions sur les femmes* [Reflections on Women], *Quelques Discours* [Miscellaneous Discourses], *Psyché*). A feminist, she was one of the first to deplore Molière's bourgeois antifeminism. "I was hurt that men should be so ignorant of their own interests as to condemn the women who occupied their minds. . . . I have examined whether a better use might not be made of them." The program that she outlines for the education of girls includes Greek and sciences, and neither the reading of novels nor attendance at the theater is forbidden them—a shocking suggestion in her day.

61

COMTESSE POTACKA, Hélène Massalska, later Princesse de Ligne, then Comtesse Potocka (1765–?). Having inherited vast estates in the Baltic at the age of seven, Hélène, an orphan, was taken to Paris to the Convent of the Abbaye au Bois by her uncle, the Prince-Bishop Massalski. She remained there eight years, keeping a young girl's diary, a marvelous document of exceptional interest for the history of the education of little girls of the nobility in the eighteenth century (see L. Perey, *La Princesse de Ligne*). It is in this diary that she tells of the marriages of her schoolmates at a tender age. She later married the son of the famous Prince de Ligne and had a daughter by him. Spoiled and feted at the witty and liberal-minded court held by her most likable father-in-law and adored by her young husband, Hélène nonetheless fell madly in love with Comte Potocki, a Pole who was married and the father of a family and who had already kidnaped one young woman and taken her to the wilds of the Ukraine. There then began a life of endless lawsuits (Potocki needed money and Hélène was unable to inherit the fortune left her after leaving her husband's domicile) and endless travel (France, Poland, the Ukraine). The woman whom Potocki had compromised eventually died, and he was able at last to marry Hélène, who had been left a widow when her husband was killed in battle. The Potockis settled down in Paris and remained happily in love for the rest of their days. Besides her remarkable schoolgirl's diary, Hélène Massalaka left splendid love letters to Comte Potocki.

62

GENEVIÈVE DE MALBOISSIÈRE, Geneviève Randon de Malboissière (1746–67). The daughter of a wealthy financier who lived in the Marais quarter of Paris. Raised at home by attentive and affectionate parents, Geneviève had a friend, Mademoiselle Méliand (the future Marquise de la Grange), who was her age and lived a few houses away. She wrote her little schoolgirlish notes several times a week, and continued this correspondence during the summer when she accompanied her parents to the country. All these letters were rediscovered in an attic by the Comte de Luppé, who had them published. They constitute very precious documentation on the education of a young girl in the eighteenth century. Geneviève learned Italian, English, and German, mastering all of them well enough to correspond with her friend and neighbor in them—especially Italian when she wished to speak of affairs of the heart and did not want her secrets discovered by the servants who carried her messages or by her "tutors." She also knew Latin and Greek; she studied natural history, philosophy, etc. But she tells not only how she occupies her very full day but also how she spends her vacations with her cousin Randon de Lucenay, and tells of her views on marriage and love, proving herself a most intelligent adolescent. Geneviève eventually became engaged, but died suddenly at the age of twenty before the marriage.

63
Anonymous, in the *Journal des Dames*, Octobre 1777.

64
MADAME DE PUISIEUX, née Madeleine d'Arsant. The wife of the Monsieur de Puisieux who wrote a little feminist manifesto entitled *La Femme n'est pas inférieure à l'homme* (The Woman Is Not Inferior to the Man, 1750). She herself was the author of *Conseils à une amie* (Advice to a Woman Friend, 1749); in it she discusses the education of young girls and deplores in particular the custom of giving them uneducated women as personal maids: "I am quite convinced that women of merit would be less rare if they spent their time in the company of persons in a position to cultivate the happy dispositions with which their charges were born." She is also the author of a short treatise, *Les Caractères* (Portraits, 1750); an allegorical tale, *Le Plaisir et la volupté* (Pleasure and Sensuality, 1752); and a novel: *Alzarac ou la nécessité d'être inconstant* (Alzarac or the Necessity of Being Fickle, 1762).

65
MADAME DE LA FAYETTE, Adrienne de Noailles, Marquise de La Fayette, (1759–1807). Adrienne was still a very young girl, almost a child, when she married the young Marquis de La Fayette. She had received a remarkable education by her mother, the Duchesse d'Ayen. She was graceful, but not beautiful, and her husband neglected her badly, preferring to devote himself to his dreams, his ambitions, his aid to the American revolutionaries, and his mistresses. From the first moment of her marriage, however, she proved an adoring wife, with a love for her husband that lasted all her life. It was a complex and profound love—a combination of passion and lucidity, of conjugal devotion pushed to the point of idolization, of unqualifed admiration for the hero her husband was, but also of gentle protection of him, for as events proved, Adrienne was no doubt stronger and more intelligent than her husband. The letters cited in this volume have been taken from André Maurois's biography of her, which merits reading. When La Fayette was imprisoned in a terrible dungeon of the fortress of Olmütz, Madame de La Fayette and her two daughters took difficult and dangerous steps in order to have the honor of sharing his captivity. For years she lived in this dungeon, with her adored husband all to herself at last. This extraordinary conjugal devotion impressed the French, and Adrienne de La Fayette enjoyed genuine celebrity as a saint of marriage—which in fact she was, for the legend of

her devotion was a true story. Madame de La Fayette continued her whole life long to express her love of her husband, piously rejoicing in the thought that it was God who had given her this husband she adored. Just after her death, La Fayette wrote an extraordinarily moving letter to tell of her last moments; by her affection and devotion she had become her husband's one and only love.

66

MADAME DU CHÂTELET, née Gabrielle Émilie Le Tonnelier de Breteuil (1706–49). Married to the Marquis de Châtelet-Lomont, she soon abandoned him, and with her companion Voltaire installed herself in her château at Cirey. Madame du Châtelet was a true bluestocking. She encouraged Voltaire to study chemistry and physics, coauthored a treatise on fire with him, and helped him with his biblical exegeses. She translated the classic authors and seriously studied the German philosophers. She published a *Treatise on Happiness* (Traité sur le bonheur) in which she expresses her ideal: a sense of proportion and the happy medium in all things. And yet this intelligent woman who since 1733 had shared the life and work of the greatest mind of her time, who dealt rationally with the world and preached rationality in all things, fell madly in love with a pale, mediocre poet, Saint-Lambert, who was ten years younger than she. She was prepared to sacrifice everything for him, and died giving birth to his child. Voltaire was extremely surprised to learn that she had been unfaithful to him.

67

DANIEL STERN, Marie de Flavigny, Comtesse d'Agoult (1805–97). Blond, beautiful, an aristocrat through and through, this incarnation of the fashionable Faubourg Saint-Germain in the time of Balzac and Stendhal had one of the most brilliant salons in Paris. It was thus that she met Franz Liszt, with whom she ran away. These two "slaves of love" were the very image of Romantic passion: the noble and refined woman who scorns the opinion of society and flees with a great artist of simple origins, but handsome and a genius. They had two daughters, one of whom became Richard Wagner's second wife; the other married Émile Ollivier. She separated from Liszt painfully and permanently, 1844, after having really lived her passion, though in the end her role had become a false and exhausting one. She was the model for Balzac's *Béatrix*, but she doubtless deserved a more flattering portrait than this acid one. She began to write under the pseudonym of Daniel Stern, published several novels, and more important, several very serious and interesting political studies, such as her *Histoire de la Révolution de 1848* (1851). Her life was a most dignified one, and her writings, which have been completely forgotten today, merit rediscovery, if only for their fine "sociological sense."

68

ANAÏS SÉGALAS, née Anne Caroline Ménard, married to Victor Ségalas (1814–93). A poetess who enjoyed great popularity from 1830 to the end of the Second Empire. She wrote a great deal: quantities of verse, novels, plays which were performed at the Comédie-Française. She was, in short, a celebrity. She was the extremely sentimental poet of tender maternal feeling, children, birds, Christian sentiments, and crystal-clear brooks. She often imitated others; her *Les Algériennes* was inspired by Victor Hugo's *Les Orientales*, etc. One of her poems even found its way into Paul Meurice's *La Dernière gerbe* (The Last Bouquet), a collection of the last works of Hugo!

69

CÉLESTE MOGADOR, Elisabeth Céleste Vénard, later Comtesse Lionel de Chabrillan, known as Céleste Mogador (1824–1909). The daughter of a hatmaker, born on the boulevard du Temple, she had a poverty-stricken childhood with her mother following the death of her father. She was dragged from pillar to post thanks to her mother's numerous love affairs, and at fourteen she was raped by one of her mother's lovers. She then became a dance-hostess at the Bal Mabille and a bareback rider at the Hippodrome; her celebrity dates from this period. She married one of her lovers, the Comte de Chabrillan, in 1854, and published her *Mémoires*, which were seized because of their scandalous content: the simple story of her life. Later she wrote novels: *Sapho* (1858), *Miss Pewel* (1859), *Les Voleurs d'or* (The Gold Thieves, 1864). Her momentary literary fame did not keep her from poverty, and she died in an asylum in 1909.

70

GEORGE SAND, Aurore Dupin, Baronne Dudevant (1804–76). We shall not attempt to retrace the well-known life of George Sand. We hope that the texts and above all the passages from letters published here will be proof of the striking modernity of her writing. They are "liberated" writings in the best sense: extremely personal, and based on no existing models. The reader will find here extracts from her novels *Indiana*, *Lélia*, and *Jacques*, and passages of letters addressed to Alfred de Musset and to Michel de Bourges, plus the famous letter, studded with question marks, which she wrote at Musset's bedside as she cared for him during an illness; how could the addressee of this letter, Musset's physician, Pagello, have helped falling madly in love after this shower of incandescent sparks, one wonders?

71

MARIE BASHKIRTSEFF (1860–84). She came to Paris from Russia at the age of ten. She died at twenty-four. She had tried to make herself a reputation as a painter (she signed her works Marie Konstantinovna Russ) and was just beginning to show her works when her illness—tuberculosis—interrupted her career and gradually killed her. In 1887 one of the most curious works in French literature was published: Marie's *Journal*, begun in 1877, broken off for a time, and then continued just before her death. In 1925 her equally striking private diaries (*Cahiers intimes*) were published. There has never been another intimate journal like hers. It can of course be pointed out that she was precocious, brilliant, rich, well traveled, and no stranger to Europe's cosmopolitan circles, which are interesting in and of themselves. But the most striking thing about these writings, which were never intended for publication, is the absolute candor with which she reveals her boundless narcissism. Marie loved herself, adored herself, and told herself so without mincing words. And then there was her ambition: loving herself as she did, she naturally could not conceive for herself any destiny save the summits of power, glory, and authority. Marie's journals reveal what could really take place in the head of a young girl in a day and age where young girls were supposed to be sweet and modest. Dominating, intelligent, ambitious, her life remained a short one and in the end a mediocre one.

72

MARIE DORVAL, Marie Delaunay, Madame Dorval (1798–1849). A famous actress of the Romantic era, Marie Dorval was brought up on the boards; the daughter of actors, she married at sixteen another actor, Allan, known as Dorval, during one of the family's tours. She was discovered one day by an actor from the Comédie-Française, and made her début in Paris in a melodrama when she was twenty. The famous Romantic actor Frédérick Lemaître often played opposite her, and her audiences were moved to floods of tears by her performances. Among her famous roles were Madame d'Hervey (alias Mélanie Waldor) in Alexandre Dumas's *Antony* ("She resisted me. I have murdered her!"); Hugo's Marion Delorme, a role she created; and the touchingly exquisite Kitty Bell of *Chatterton*, which Alfred de Vigny wrote for her. An unmarried mother, the good pal of a second husband, Merle, who was easy to get along with, as gay and vivacious offstage as she was delicate and pathetic onstage. Marie Dorval always had all the lovers she pleased, without the slightest twinge of remorse. Goodhearted, a touch vulgar, very sensual, and generous-spirited, Marie was for six years the great passion of the poet Alfred de Vigny, her polar opposite. She loved him too, as he wished to be loved—passionately; but that did not keep him from deceiving her with other women, or her from eternally complaining of his infidelities. Her great friend was George Sand; among her other intimates was Alexandre Dumas, Sr., who was occasionally her lover and always her good friend. This very incarnation of Romantic heroines was a gay, sensitive, and spontaneous woman, whose manners and language were very free. She died in near poverty.

73

MARCELINE DESBORDES-VALMORE (1785–1859). The most miraculous French love poet. A poor child, the daughter of a painter of coats of arms and religious objects for churches, born in Douai; one day she came across a book of poetry and was absolutely dazzled. On the outbreak of the Revolution, her father was left jobless, and the family left for Guadeloupe in order to survive; she arrived at the age of fourteen, in the middle of the rebellion of the blacks, and was unable to find the relative who was to help her. Her mother died and Marceline came back to France alone; she sang and acted in order to stay alive. She appeared on the stage all over the provinces, and dramatists began to write parts for her. "She was one of those figures whom one does not forget: a profile of a great purity, blue eyes, blonde hair . . . a charming voice; her language, the air about her, her manners give proof of a rare and constant distinction. She was frail and wan, and seemed ill," a contemporary writes. From her earliest years she seems always to have been passionately in love. Around 1805 she had an unknown lover, and around 1810 she met the poet Henri de Latouche, to whom she gave herself body and soul. She then wrote the elegies of which Baudelaire has said: "If the outcry, the natural signs of an élite soul, if the desperate ambition of the heart, if the sudden spontaneous faculties, if everything that is gratuitous and a gift of God suffice to make a great poet—Marceline Valmore is and will always be a great poet." He also adds: "She was a woman, always a woman, absolutely nothing but a woman; but to an extraordinary degree she was the poetic expression of all the natural beauties of woman." In 1817 she married an upright actor with little talent, François Lanchantin, called Valmore. She had two daughters by him, and adored them; both of them died before her. She was obliged to fight poverty and to work her whole life long. Her *Oeuvres complètes* were published in three volumes in 1886–87, after numerous editions that had won her the admiration of Sainte-Beuve and of Paul Verlaine, who adored "these reminiscences of the age of woman."

74
JULIE CHARLES, Julie Bouchaud des Hérettes, Madame Charles, called Elvire (1784–1817). In 1804 she married a famous physicist forty years her elder. An ardent, passionate, melancholy woman, she had several liaisons before galloping consumption caused her to take a rest cure in the mountains. She went to Aix-les-Bains, and on the lake one day, in the midst of a raging storm, she met the young Alphonse de Lamartine. He was twenty-six years old, and she thirty-two. It was a passionate love, brought to a sudden end by her illness—a year after their first meeting, Julie was dead. Only four letters of hers are extant, oddly punctuated and brimful of effusive love, in the style of the era. The religious sentiments are not due solely to Lamartine's influence.

75
JULIETTE DROUET, Juliette Gauvain, called Juliette Drouet (1806–83). She was surpassingly beautiful. After being raised in a convent, she became a model and something of a courtesan, had a daughter by the sculptor James Pradier, and become an actress thanks to the protection of her benefactor, Harel. She lived well, amid great luxury and heavy debts, which were paid by various generous gentlemen friends. She then became the mistress of Victor Hugo, on February 16, 1833. For the next fifty years, her life was lived solely for him. A voluntary recluse, Juliette agreed never to go out without him. She often spent her days without a fire, even in winter, or without provisions, rather than betray the nun's vows of love that she had taken. She wrote to him twice a day, and we have some ten thousand letters of hers. She did not wish to interfere with his family, political, or professional life. Long a total recluse, thanks to her passionate discretion she eventually became acquainted with his wife and children, who greatly esteemed her. In latter years Juliette followed Hugo wherever his destiny led him, including trips to Brussels and to Guernsey; a great deal of her time was spent copying his manuscripts. Above all she waited. Her absolutely devoted love survived every obstacle, including the nasty trick played on her by one of Hugo's other mistresses, who sent her back a beribboned packet of passionate letters she had written to him. She ended her life still in the same utter solitude, devoted to her veritable cult of Hugo. Her letters were published

in our century; hundreds of them are so beautiful that they make us think that there is a mysticism of the affections that reaches the loftiest of summits.

76

ELISA MERCOEUR (1809–35). An illegitimate child, the daughter of a Rouen lawyer who was unable to recognize her, Elisa took the name of the street on which she was born in Nantes. From the age of twelve, she gave English lessons to help her mother; she also knew Latin and Greek and studied Arabic. She published her first verses at sixteen; provincial academies awarded the volume a prize and published it, the Duchesse de Berri sent her money, and the Minister of Fine Arts awarded her a pension! Lamartine, Chateaubriand, the Prime Minister, de Martignac, everyone praised her, encouraged her, helped her financially. But this "muse of Britanny" found out that such success was short-lived; she was soon faced with the necessity of supporting herself and her mother. A tragedy of hers was refused at the Comédie-Française despite its having an influential protector, and her days were lived in what one of her biographers calls "that Romantic melancholy that is unforgiving." She died at the age of twenty-six, leaving a body of work that in the final analysis is mediocre, despite her obvious facility. One wonders precisely why her verses were crowned with such success, unless it was because she had the good fortune to be a poetess who was young and beautiful; in any event, a fine tomb was built for her after a national subscription, and her *Oeuvres complètes* were published in three volumes beginning in 1843.

77

MÉLANIE WALDOR, née Mélanie de Villenave (1796–1871). A long life, despite the melodramatic suicide she so romantically prepared to stage in order to bring back her lover Alexandre Dumas—an event that never went beyond the planning stage. In her maturity and old age she proved a steady and reliable friend, helping a number of people and becoming the trusted friend of her lover's son, the young Alexandre Dumas of *The Lady of the Camilias*. But before this she was a hyper-Romantic petty bourgeoise, married to an officer whom she deceived with great regularity, in particular with that genial giant Alexandre Dumas, Sr., who remained passionately in love with this pale and not very pretty creature for two years. His *Antony* is based partly on his experiences with Mélanie. She for her part wrote him a great many letters, in which there is frequent mention of a geranium, and sometimes of a broken-stemmed geranium—a delicate way of referring to her menstrual periods, her miscarriage, and her hopes of becoming a mother. She also wrote quantities of insipid verses. "Do not ask me for loftier verses: what harmony they have is owed to my heart, not to genius" she once wrote in due modesty. As Alphonse Séché concludes in his *Les Muse Françaises*: ". . . languor, mealancholy, passion, moonlight, a pale young man, a voice full of doom, the thought of death—the whole apparatus!" She must have had a certain charm to have had the friends she did, the most surprising of whom is Dumas, Sr. Perhaps we owe *Antony*, that masterpiece of Romantic theater, to the pale Romanticism preached to that hearty giant by this little versifier from Nantes.

78

LAURE DE BERNY (1777–1836). He called her his "Dilecta." Is there any reason why we should not be as delighted as Honoré de Balzac was with this adorable woman who seems the very incarnation of sincerity, tenderness, and dignity? Would there have been a *Lys dans la vallée* (The Lily in the Valley) if there had not been a Laure de Berny in Balzac's life? She was as innocent as its heroine, Madame de Mortsauf, though not as chaste. It is interesting to see how Balzac betrayed the truth in his portrait of his mistress, his initiatrix, his great love, for reality has been distorted in order to make her a more ideal figure. To begin with, she was in reality twenty-two years older than her lover; Balzac was sixteen and she thirty-eight. Then too Laure was the mother of nine children, not two as in the novel. (Balzac even thought at one point of marrying her daughter.) And finally, she was not at all reluctant to become his mistress; Laure was a vibrant, sensual woman, who at the age of fifty and more wrote him letters testifying to the passion she on her part felt for him in this most passionate of relationships, for she was not at all merely a "muse" for Balzac's literary production, as certain manuals would have us believe. It is quite true, on the other hand, that she was unfailingly good to this young genius whose budding talents she had encouraged; she helped him, became for him the tender mother that his own stern, severe mother had never been, educated him, and aided him financially. On the last afternoon of her life, she had herself rolled in her wheel chair over to the window to watch for him; he never came. He nonetheless long grieved for her. And it is comforting to know that in 1835, before her death, she had the best possible recompense: the publication of *Le Lys dans la vallée.* As a matter of fact, it was at her suggestion that he rewrote the novel to make his Madame de Mortsauf more chaste.

79

CONSTANCE DE SALM, Constance-Marie de Théis, later Madame Pipelet, and then after being widowed and remarrying, Princesse de Salm-Dyck (1767–1845). A child prodigy with an excellent education, she wrote verses from adolescence on. The wife later of a doctor named Pipelet (a name borrowed by Eugène Sue for a character in his *Mystères de Paris*), she had a salon in which she staged a tragedy of hers, *Sapho,* and then published the *Epîtres à Sophie,* a work that is feminist in inspiration in an era in which feminism was rare and not approved of. Later she was most happily married to the Prince de Salm-Dyck. One of her most curious works is a short novel that is not really a novel at all: *Vingt-quatre heures d'une femme sensible* (Twenty-four Hours in the Life of a Sensitive Woman). She is often depicted as a "reasonable" woman of letters, a cold intellectual. But in fact she was one of the first Romantics to rebel against her condition as a woman.

80

GERMAINE DE STAËL, Germaine Necker, Baronne de Staël-Holstein, and then after being widowed and remarrying, Madame de Rocca (1766–1817). Germaine de Staël is too well known to attempt to give a résumé of her very full life. We shall merely mention some of her ideas on marriage. She was so much in favor of divorce that her mother wrote her treatise against it in an attempt to dissuade her from ending her own marriage in that fashion. Marriage to her meant principally the occasion for opening a literary and philosophical salon. Her first husband, whom she had rarely seen, died in 1802, and Germaine then married a young Swiss twenty years younger than she. It is often forgotten that Germaine de Staël had five children: This intellectual, this fecond writer, this passionate woman, this indefatigable traveler, was what today would be called the mother of a large family. Her loves were always most enthusiastic ones, for she spent an extraordinary amount of energy charming the men in her life. Curiously enough this generous-hearted man-eater, this dominating woman who insisted on fulfilling her desires, expressed herself in the most chaste and sentimental manner possible to imagine, writing of the gift of self and of the poor-feeble-woman-who-has-only-her-love-to-give in such a way that the concepts became part of the Romantic movement's literary baggage. Her heroines are nonetheless geniuses, creators who are more gifted than their lovers, in short "superior women" (*Delphine*, 1802, *Corinne*, 1807). But they shed tears over their condition as women forced to "submit" to men, having only their love as a career, as a lady of the seventeenth century would never have had the idea of doing. There is a striking contrast between the language of her heroines or in her letters to Benjamin Constant, Narbonne, Roederer, and others—a language of the total gift of self, of the fear of not being loved, of exultant but submissive protestations of passion—and her own conduct, which is governed by one single passion, the will to be independent, intellectually, politically, and personally. Love for her was primarily a supplementary excitement which best set off her life and thought. And this woman who was herself passionately in love more than once writes that love destroys.

81

LOUISE COLET, née Louise Revoil (1810–76). A very pretty blonde, the daughter of rich Lyonnais wine merchants, who married a composer who was later a professor at the Paris Conservatory. The moment that the couple left the South of France and came to settle in Paris, the beautiful Louise set about making friends with men in positions of power. Wishing to become a writer, she soon became the mistress of Victor Cousin, a member of the French Academy. She had a daughter by him, and a protection that allowed her to obtain several prizes from the Academy for very mediocre works. Annoyed at the critic and humorist Alphonse Karr for gibing at Cousin in his *Les Guêpes* (The Wasps), she planted a knife between his shoulder blades. Karr disarmed her and published a drawing of a kitchen knife with the caption "A present from Madame Louise Colet—in the back." She had affairs with Alfred de Musset and with James Pradier, the sculptor, at whose home she met Flaubert. Her tragicomic loves with the latter are better known, thanks to the fact that their correspondence is extant. A selfish and vindictive woman, Louise Colet did not endear herself to the memory of her lovers, who grew tired of her interference in their affairs and her demands for money. She published a version of Musset's love affair with George Sand that was flattering to the latter. Flaubert tried to help her in her literary endeavors, doing his best to cure her of her two principal defects: what he called "philosophism, that muddiness that comes from Voltaire" and "vagueness, that female tendromania."

82

PAULINE GUIZOT, née Pauline de Meulan (1773–1827). Very well educated, Pauline de Meulan began to try to earn her living by writing at an early age, for her father had been ruined by the Revolution. So he published novels imitating English models (*La Chapelle d'Ayton* [The Chapel of Ayton], 1801) and worked as a journalist on Suard's *Publiciste*. Certain of her articles were published as a collection entitled *Histoire du théâtre français*. One time when she was ill, an unknown writer offered to fill in for her at the newspaper, and she discovered that it was François Guizot, soon to become a famous minister of state. He was only twenty at the time and she was close to thirty-five. They married nonetheless, and on becoming a mother she began to write many books for children, plus the *Journal d'une mère* and the *Lettre de famille sur l'education domestique*. Although she died in 1827, her books for children went through countless editions all through the nineteenth century. Born a Catholic, Pauline converted to her husband's Protestant religion, and her treatises on education are full of evangelical moralizing.

83

DELPHINE DE GIRARDIN, née Delphine Gay (1804–55). Daughter of the novelist Sophie Gay, she was called Delphine after Madame de Staël's heroine. She married the great journalist and newspaper publisher Émile de Girardin. She was known for her elegiac poetry, and Lamartine called her "the tenth muse" (*Madeleine, Ourika, La Vision de Jeanne d'Arc*). A friend of all the better-known poets, her work was praised by all of them. She was one of the first to appreciate Balzac. When her husband founded his mass-circulation paper *La Presse*, she published, under the pseudonym "Vicomte de Launay," a long series of witty chronicles, *Les Lettres parisiennes*, in it; it remains a gold mine of anecdotes concerning the July Monarchy. She had an excellent gift for observation. She published novels, tragedies (*Judith*), comedies (*L'École des journalistes, Lady Tartuffe*, etc). These are often drawing room comedies, but *L'École des journalistes* was the most daring work of her life, and its performance at the Comédie-Française was forbidden by the censor. She was a blonde with blue eyes, vivacious, energetic, and gay. "When she died one could almost feel the level of intelligence, sentiment, and glory of the century decline," Lamartine wrote.

84

CAROLINE WUIET (1766–1829). An astonishing journalist of the beginning of the nineteenth century, who founded several papers in succession: *Le Cercle* (The Circle), *Le Papillon, journal des arts et des plaisirs dedié aux muses at aux grâces* (The Butterfly, Journal of Arts and Pleasures Dedicated to the Muses and Graces), which later became *Le Phénix* and then *La Mouche* (The Fly). She later became a journalist with the *Journal des dames*. Born in Vienna, a child prodigy, and a protégée of Marie-Antoinette, she was turned over to Gretry for musical training because of her gifts, to Beaumarchais who taught her letters, and to the painter Greuze for art lessons. After a tour through Germany as a pianist, she came back to France, was arrested and condemned to exile during the Revolution, left for England and Holland, then came back to France during the Terror. She founded a Women's Club that was forbidden. She enjoyed a certain celebrity during the Directory and was able to live comfortably, thanks to the romances she wrote. She put out her periodicals all by herself, taking care of everything from the political articles to the printing and distributing. She was most famous for her lively attacks on the parvenus of the Directory. She dressed as a man, since she had calculated that this cost her less. She even went so far as to fight a duel with another woman. She then married a colonel of the Empire who was killed during Napoleon's retreat from Russia, and she died of cholera in a shack, alone and poverty-stricken.

85

DONATINE THIERY, a journalist with *L'Observateur des dames et des modes*, from 1818 to 1823.

86

FLORA TRISTAN, Flore Tristan-Morcoso (1803–44). The illegitimate daughter of a Peruvian father and a French mother, in 1821 she married André Chazal, a talented engraver, and became the mother of two children by him. She did not love her husband, and the two of them separated. He tried to kill her, and a lamentable lawsuit followed, at the end of which Chazal was sentenced to twenty years in prison. She had previously traveled to Peru to try to recover the inheritance due from her father. She was struck by the miserable lot of Peruvian women, and the tale of her voyage, entitled *Pérégrinations d'une paria*, is extraordinary. Flora then took up with the Saint-Simonians and the Socialists. She went to England to make a survey of working conditions and published her admirable *Promenades dans Londres* in 1840. Persuaded that the only solution for the proletariat was unity, Flora made herself the propagandist for a Workers' Union, and made a long and arduous tour of French workers. At the same time she remained an ardent feminist, and never ceased espousing the rights of women, whom she considered underprivileged. She was unable to finish her long tour of France, and died of an illness in Bordeaux, where grateful workers erected a monument to her. Intelligent and extraordinarily sensitive, Flora Tristan devoted her entire lonely life to the unity of the proletariat and the emancipation of women. According to Jules Simon, she was "better than beautiful —pretty"; a brunette with blue eyes and a most musical voice. She was the grandmother of Paul Gauguin.

87

CAMILLE PERT, Louise Hortense Gille. A prolific novelist of the end of the nineteenth century. Wrote only on love: *Armantes* (1895), *L'Amour vainqueur, L'Amour vengeur, La Loi de l'amour*, etc. Possessed of no great talent, she is nonetheless extremely representative of her era.

88

MADAME NECKER, née Suzanne Churchod (1739–94). The wife of the financier Necker, and mother of Germaine de Staël. She was the daughter of a Swiss pastor. She had a salon frequented by Buffon, Marmontel,

Diderot, Grimm, Suard, Saint-Lambert, La Harpe, etc. She became interested in social work and particularly in hospitals; she founded the Necker hospital in Paris and published a *Mémoire sur l'établissement des hospices* (Memorandum on the Founding of Hospitals) in 1786. Very happily married herself, she was most upset by the irregularity of her daughter's life. When the latter was thinking of divorcing the Baron de Staël, her mother published her *Réflexions sur le divorce* (1794).

89

CLARA FRANCIA-MOLLARD (1804–43) Daughter of the hairdresser of the Théâtre des Célestins in Lyons, she began her acting career by playing successfully in light minor roles. She then abandoned the theater for poetry. Her model was Victor Hugo and she always attempted the "grandiose" effect. On submitting some of her verses to Hugo, he indulgently wrote her in a friendly letter: "There is in your verse the profound and serious reverie of womankind."

90

PAULINE DE FLAUGERGUES, Marie Anne Françoise Flaugergues (1799–1878). Like Marceline Desbordes-Valmore, she was madly, profoundly in love with the poet Hyacinthe (called Henri) de Latouche. Pauline tried to support her whole family when her father, who was violently opposed to Bonaparte, lost first his post and then his entire fortune. She went off to Portugal to be reader to the young Queen, Dona Maria, in her château at Belem. She published translations from English and poems based on English models. She met Hyacinthe de Latouche when he was already advanced in age, living in his small house in the Vallée-aux-Loups. Despite this elderly seducer's irritability and bitterness due to a long illness, she never once left him. Upon his death she buried the poet's heart beneath a larch tree, put portraits of the dead man everywhere, left his bedroom precisely as it was, dressed only in black, and thus awaited her death. During the Franco-Prussian War she was forced out of the house, and on her return found the sanctuary of her love totally sacked. Certain charitable souls who knew that she was dying of hunger tried to place her in an asylum; she clung to Latouche's chair, refusing to leave, and then clung to the trees outside. George Sand was fond of her and appreciated her poetry: *Au bord du Tage* (On the Banks of the Tagus), *Les Bruyerèts* (Heather).

91

ADINE RIOM, née Adine Broband (1818–99). She lived in Nantes, where she had a well-attended salon. She wrote a great deal under various pseudonyms: Louise d'Isole or the Comte de Saint-Jean. Influenced by Lamartine and Marceline Desbordes-Valmore, she is without talent but representative of her era.

92

MADAME LAFARGE, (née Marie Capelle (1813–53). Married at twenty-six to the ironmaster Lafarge. The following year he died under suspicious circumstances. Certain experts, among them the noted Orfila, found an abnormal proportion of arsenic in his remains. Others, among them the famous Raspail, maintained that he appeared to have died a normal death. All

France followed this trial with bated breath. Madame Lafarge was con-demned to prison at hard labor by a jury that had been most unfavorably impressed by the fact that jewelry stolen from a woman friend had been found in her home. She was pardoned by Louis-Napoleon Bonaparte, who had never believed that she was guilty. But she died the year after being let out of prison. She left two works: *Mémoires* (1841) and *Heures de prison* (1845).

93

CLAIRE DEMAR. A revolutionary young Saint-Simonian who wrote in *La Femme libre*, which later became *La Tribune des femmes* (1832–34). She considered marriage to be "legal prostitution." She lived with her lover, Per-ret-Dessessart, a Saint-Simonian, in which she explained that she was "dying of doubt," Claire and her very young lover committed double suicide by throwing themselves in the Isère River. She also left a note stating that she had been "too daring," and a short tract entitled *Ma loi d'avenir* (My Law for the Future), which her comrades on the *Tribune des femmes* reverently published in 1833, the year of her death at twenty-five.

94

SUZANNE VOILQUIN, a girl from the lowest class, she became first an embroiderer, and then studied to become a midwife. An ardent Saint-Simonian, she accompanied her husband on the expedition to Egypt under-taken by Prosper Enfantin and his faithful. The plague began to rage, and several members of the Saint-Simonian "family" were taken ill. Enfantin took a boat for France; Suzanne stayed behind to care for those who were sick. Once back in France, she worked on the *Tribune des femmes* and had the singular audacity to announce in an article several pages long that since her relations with her husband were "not at all ardent," and since he seemed to be interested in another woman, she considered that the two of them were divorced, even though divorce had been done away with. Her husband had a letter of thanks to her published, and announced that he was giving her back her freedom—a bizarre letter in which he refers to her as "a theoretical woman with an enigmatic heart," a not altogether stupid opin-ion of her. Suzanne wrote of herself in a lively autobiography: *Mémoires d'une fille du people* (Memoirs of a Daughter of the People), as well as in a still unpublished manuscript in which she tells of her seven-year stay in Rus-sia; having left to work in Russia as a midwife and further feminism, she was the first to introduce homeopathy into that country.

95

JULIETTE ADAM, née Juliette Lamber (1836–1936). The adversary of Pierre-Joseph Proudhon, the socialist theoretician; published in 1858 a clever refutation of the latter's *Idées proudhonniennes sur l'amour, la femme et le mariage*. Very much influenced by George Sand, she too wrote socially uplifting rural tales. Her second marriage was to Edmond Adam, named prefect of police in 1870, and a senator; she thereupon opened a salon frequented by the leading Republicans, among them Gambetta. Her husband died in 1877, leaving her a fortune. She thereupon founded *La Nouvelle Revue* and began a long second career (she was one hundred years old when she died) passionately devoted to the Nationalist and Republican cause. She is the author of *Paienne* (The Pagan Woman, 1883) and also of *Chrétienne* (The Christian Woman, 1913): a return to Catholicism by one of the leading women of the bourgeoisie during the Third Republic.

96
HORTENSE ALLART, Hortense Allart de Méritens (1801–79). A charming, independent person, Hortense Allart chose not to marry even though she was pregnant—an extraordinary decision in that day and age. Despite her illegitimate child, her love affairs, and her advanced ideas, she was always received in society. She wished to testify to the right to passion—and by that she meant both carnal and sentimental love, as well as a certain mystical feeling that is close to being religious. She wrote a most curious book, entitled *Les Enchantements de prudence*, which is surely largely autobiographical. She had a long affair with the writer François-René de Chateaubriand, who worshiped her.

97
Article signed "La Vieille Dame," in *Le Journal des femmes*, Février, 1833.

98
MARIE NIZET (1859–1922). A daughter of the curator of the Royal Library of Belgium, she became an impassioned supporter of the cause of Romania in its struggle for independence from Russia. She wrote verses in celebration of this country that she had never seen (*Romania*, 1878). Married, a mother, and finally divorced, she died in 1922 without anyone's suspecting that among her papers there would later be found a collection of ardently erotic verse, entitled *Pour Axel* (For Axel), written about 1885. Alex Veneglia, with whom she was in love, disappeared in the course of a long ocean voyage. In her poems, which are well in advance of their time, Marie Nizet disdains lawful unions and security and "prefers waiting, uncertainty, forbidden embraces and taboo places, those mindful of Baudelaire" (Jeanine Moulin). These poems were published posthumously in Belgium in 1923. "We who knew neither prejudice nor fear/Who find today guaranteed by yesterday/And leave behind with no constraint/Our free, proud love."

99
LÉOCADIE PENQUER, née Léocadie Hersent (1817–?). A Breton girl raised in admiration of Chateaubriand and the Romantics, she published several collections of poems that bear witness to a pantheism very much like that of women in the twentieth century; other poems (*Chants du foyer*) [Songs of the Hearth], *Révélations poétiques*) of a tenderness that hears the mark of Lamartine; and a sort of epic of Britanny, *Velléda* (1868).

100
CÉCILE FOURNEL. Wife of the engineer Henri Fournel, a fervent Saint-Simonian. A graduate of Polytechnique, he was director of the Creusot foundry when he dropped everything to follow Prosper Enfantin in the 1830s. Obeying this husband whom she adored. Cécile was obliged to separate from him so that he could go live in the Saint-Simonian community in Ménilmontant, leaving her alone with her little daughter. Moreover, at her husband's request she gave her entire fortune to the Saint-Simonians. She worked for the "freeing of woman" without personal conviction, in the

hope of not losing her husband. She collaborated on the journal that these "prophets" had asked their wives to edit, entitled *The Acts of the Apostles*, no less. She left this journal to follow her husband on the extravagant expedition to Egypt, which an outbreak of cholera cut short.

101

ADÈLE MORLANE (née Adélaide Riffé). A devoted Saint-Simonian; a widow with a grown daughter, directress of the post office at Meudon, she met Prosper Enfantin in 1826 and became more or less his slave. At times sought out by him, and at other times rejected, she nonetheless remained attached to him. It is to her that Enfantin wrote: "I wish to be adored." He fathered a child by her, Arthur, whom he never recognized and never had the slightest concern for. He likewise refused to marry her. Adèle's letters are in the Arsenal Library, Paris.

102

AGLAE SAINT-HILAIRE, one of the grandes dames of Saint-Simonian, an intimate friend of Pauline Rolland, the great feminist militant and revolutionary.

103

CLORINDE ROGÉ. The prettiest of the female followers of Saint-Simon, she was the wife of the musician Rogé. Profoundly in love with her husband, she followed the Saint-Simonians to Turkey (where they were seeking the "Mother of the Human Race"!), to Egypt, to Russia, and to the United States, where she went to preach the Saint-Simonian gospel. Later she rebelled against this misspent life and even went so far as to attack Father Enfantin; the letter here cited is dated June 20, 1845.

104
VALENTINE DE SAINT-POINT.

105
HÉLÈNE PICARD.

106
JANE CATULLE-MENDÈS.

107
ANNA DE NOAILLES.

108
RAÏSSA MARITAIN.

109
CÉLINE ARNAULD.

110
SABINE SICAUD.

111
HÉLÈNE VACARESCO.

112
LUCIE DELARUE-MARDRUS.

113
MARIE DE SORMIOU.

114
RENÉE VIVIEN.

115
CÉCILE SAUVAGE.

116
HENRIETTE CHARASSON.

117
MARGUERITE BURNAT-PROVINS.

118
RACHILDE.

119
COLETTE.

120
ANNE SYLVESTRE.

121
ANDRÉE SODENKAMP.

122
MARIE DAUGUET.

123
CLAUDE DE BURINE.

124
THÉRÈSE AUBRAY.

125
MIREILLE SORGUE.

Grateful acknowledgment is made to the following:

ALBIN MICHEL
Colette: *La vagabonde*
L'ARBALETE
Lena Leclercq: *Poèmes insoumis*
GUY AUTHIER
Catherine Breillat: *Le Soupirail*
BUCHET-CHASTEL
Janette Deletang-Tardif: *Confidences des Iles*
CALMANN-LÉVY
Anna de Noailles: *Les Éblouissements*
PIERRE CAILLER
Marie Laurencin: *Le Carnet des Nuits*
CAHIERS DU SUD
Laurence Algan: *Les Tours du silence*
CIVILISATIONS NOUVELLES
Catherine Breillat:
Le silence Après . . .
F. *Winille* dans *Littérature Érotique Féminine* par Denise Miège
GUY CHAMBELLAND
Claudine Chonez: *La Mise au monde*
DEBRESSE
André Vernay: *Dernière terre*
DELPEUCH
Hélène Picard: *Pour un mauvais garçon*
DESCLÉE DE BROUWER
Raïssa Maritain:
Lettre de Nuit - La vie donnée
ÉMILE-PAL FRÈRES
Nathalie Clifford-Barney:
Poèmes et Poèmes
Pensées d'une Amazone
Henriette Charasson: *Attente 1914–1917*

FASQUELLE
Jane Catulle-Mendès: *Les Charmes*
Lucie Delarue-Mardrus: *Occident. Horizons*
FAYARD
Colette: *Chéri*
Anna de Noailles:
Les Innocentes ou la sagesse des femmes
Les Forces éternelles
FLAMMARION
Colette: *L'Entrave*
L'Envers du Music-Hall
La naissance du jour
GALLIMARD
Suzanne Allen: *L'Ile du dedans*
Simone de Beauvoir: *Le Deuxième Sexe*
Lucienne Desnoues: *La Fraîche*
Catherine Pozzi
Dans N.R.F. N° 195 du 1/2/1929
GRASSET-FASQUELLE
Lucie Delarue-Mardrus: *Occident*
Annie Leclercq: *Parole de Femme*
HACHETTE (M. GOUDEKET)
Colette: *Ces Plaisirs*
Les vrilles de la vigne
JULLIARD
Françoise Mallet-Jorris:
Le Rempart des Béguines
Anne Philipe:
Le Temps d'un Soupir
LEMERRE
Renée Vivien: *La Vénus des Avengles*
A l'ehure des Mains Jointes
Hélène de Zuylen de Nyevelt:
Effeuillements

GUY LÉVIS MANO
Céline Arnault: *Les Réseaux du Réveil*
Thérèse Aubray: *Battements III*
V. Penrose: *Herbe à la Lune*
LIBRAIRIE SAINT-GERMAIN-DES-PRÉS
Jeanine Moulin: *Les Mains nues*
MERCURE DE FRANCE
Janine Aeply: *Une fille à Marier*
Vita Hessel: *La désaccoutumance*
Rachilde: *La Tour d'Amour*
Cécile Sauvage: *Le Vallon*
ÉDITIONS DE MINUIT
Monique Wittig: *Les Guerillères*
MESSEIN
Marie Dauguet:
Ce n'est rien, c'est la vie
Valentine de Saint-Point:
Poèmes de la mer et du soleil
ROBERT MOREL
Mireille Sorgue: *L'Amant*
INTERSONG TUTTI
Barbara: *Bref*
Anne Sylvestre: *Eléonore*
J. J. PAUVERT
Joyce Manson: *Les Gisants satisfaits*
Pauline Réage: *Histoire d'O*
PLON
Marie de Sormiou: *Chants du Soleil*
Hélène Vacaresco: *Le Jardin Passionné*

DE RACHE
Andrée Södenkamp: *Femmes des longs matins*
RICHELIEU
Rina Lasnier: *Féerie Indienne*
ROUGERIE
Claude de Burine: *Lettres à l'Enfance*
SANSOT
Marguerite Burnat-Provins:
Poèmes troubles. Le livre pour toi
Claudine Funck-Brentano: *Les Appels*
Hélène Picard:
En attendant la vie. L'instant éternel
SEGHERS
Catherine Faulne: *Poèmes inédits*
Catherine Faulne, in Jeanine Moulin:
La Poésie féminine, Époque moderne
Amélie Murat, in Jeanine Moulin:
La Poésie féminine, Époque moderne
Amélie Murat, in Jeanine Moulin:
La Poésie féminine, Époque moderne
Marie Dominique: *La Muie*
SEUIL
Anne Hébert: *Je suis la terre et l'eau*
STOCK
Matie Noël:
Les Chansons et les Heures
Chants d'arrière saison
Sabine Sicaud: *Poèmes*